D1562715

FEMINISM AND DEMOCRACY

FEMINISM AND DEMOCRACY

WOMEN'S SUFFRAGE AND REFORM POLITICS IN BRITAIN 1900–1918

SANDRA STANLEY HOLTON

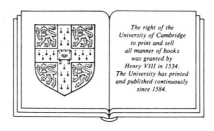

The right of the
University of Cambridge
to print and sell
all manner of books
was granted by
Henry VIII in 1534.
The University has printed
and published continuously
since 1584.

CAMBRIDGE UNIVERSITY PRESS

Cambridge

London   New York   New Rochelle
Melbourne   Sydney

Published by the Press Syndicate of the University of Cambridge
The Pitt Building, Trumpington Street, Cambridge CB2 1RP
32 East 57th Street, New York, NY 10022, USA
10 Stamford Road, Oakleigh, Melbourne 3166, Australia

First published 1986

Printed in the United States of America

Library of Congress Cataloging-in-Publication Data
Holton, Sandra Stanley
Feminism and democracy.
Bibliography: p.
Includes index.
1. Women – Suffrage – Great Britain – History – 20th
century.   2. Great Britain – Politics and government –
1901–1936.   I. Title.
JN979.H65   1986   324.6'23'0941   86–4160
ISBN 0 521 32855 1

British Library Cataloging-in-Publication applied for

For my parents
Ida and Reginald Stanley

CONTENTS

ACKNOWLEDGEMENTS

This book has been a number of years in the writing and I have incurred many debts during that time. I must thank, first of all, the University of Stirling and the Social Science Research Council for supporting the original research for a doctoral thesis out of which this study has grown, and my supervisors, Professor Roy Campbell and Dr. Iain Hutchinson, for their help and encouragement. The originally anonymous readers for Cambridge University Press, Martha Vicinus and Ellen DuBois, gave invaluable advice on how to develop the ideas and better present for publication the material embodied in the thesis. Carole Adams, Robert Dare, and Hugh Stretton all generously read the penultimate draft, and their comments helped me still further in clarifying aspects of the argument and presenting it in more readable prose.

Many libraries and archives aided me in my research, and I thank them all, but I would like especially to express my gratitude to the Fawcett Library, and to David Doughan and Katherine Ireland for their unfailingly enthusiastic and courteous assistance. It is always the greatest pleasure to spend a day at work in this storehouse of feminist history. I thank, too, Ms. Evamaria Brailsford, for permission to quote from the letters of H. N. Brailsford; Mr. C. Blair, executor of J. L. Nevinson's estate, for permission to quote from the diaries of H. W. Nevinson; Mrs. Helen Blackstone for permission to quote from the papers of Maude Royden; Sir Richard Acland for permission to quote from the letters of Eleanor Acland; Dr. Richard Pankhurst for permission to quote from letters of Sylvia Pankhurst; Mr. G. T. Marshall for permission to quote from the Catherine Marshall Papers; the Keeper of Manuscripts, the British Library, for permission to quote from the memoranda of C. P. Scott; the executrix of the late Malcolm MacDonald for permission to quote from the letters of James Ramsay MacDonald in the Public Record Office; and the Fawcett Society for permission to quote from the records of the London Society for Women's Suffrage. Bev Arnold and her staff in the History Office at the University of Adelaide, together with Chris Gradolf and Ina Cooper, struggled with my handwriting and revisions with continuing patience.

My friends among the feminist scholars in Adelaide, Carole Adams, Margaret Allen, Anne Aungles, Carol Bacchi, Carole Johnstone, Joy Parham, Kay Shafer, and Anna Yeatman have provided good company and enjoyable talk, perhaps the best kind of support and reward for this kind of labour. Bob Holton has lived with this project for more years than he or I sometimes care to remember. His encouragement and example ensured that I kept at it through those strains and stresses which seem to be an unavoidable part of transferring ideas to paper. My children, George and Flora, though sometimes a drain on my stationery supplies, have continued to hearten me with their own creativity and love of learning.

I, of course, bear all responsibility for any errors, inadequacies, or infelicities that may remain in what follows.

S.S.H.

Glenelg

ABBREVIATIONS

EFF	Election Fighting Fund
ELFS	East London Federation of Suffragettes
ILP	Independent Labour Party
LCTOWRC	Lancashire and Cheshire Textile and Other Workers Representation Committee
LRC	Labour Representation Committee
LWSU	Liberal Women's Suffrage Union
NUSEC	National Union of Societies for Equal Citizenship
NUWSS	National Union of Women's Suffrage Societies
PSF	People's Suffrage Federation
SDF	Social Democratic Federation
UDC	Union for Democratic Control
WCG	Women's Cooperative Guild
WCTU	Women's Christian Temperance Union
WFL	Women's Freedom League
WILPF	Women's International League for Peace and Freedom
WLF	Women's Liberal Federation
WLL	Women's Labour League
WSPU	Women's Social and Political Union

Millicent Fawcett, *c.* 1915. (Photograph by J. Russell & Sons. By permission of the Fawcett Library, the City of London Polytechnic.)

Houghton-le-Spring by-election. 'Some of our workers' (from left to right): Mrs. Aldersley, Miss G. M. Gordon, Mrs. Oldham, Mrs. Rothwell, Miss Entwistle, Miss Dring. (Photograph, Newcastle Illustrated Chronicle. From *The Common Cause,* 14 March 1913. By permission of the Fawcett Library, the City of London Polytechnic.)

K. D. Courtney, honourable secretary, NUWSS. (From *The Common Cause*, 27 April 1911. By permission of the Fawcett Library, the City of London Polytechnic.)

Selina Cooper, suffragette and socialist, *c.* 1910–1912. Taken from a postcard, 'Make no more Grants Oh Lord/ But elevate the Race at once'. (Photograph by E. Buck, Clitheroe. By permission of the Fawcett Library, the City of London Polytechnic.)

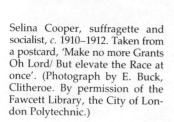

Margaret Robertson, chief organiser to the Election Fighting Fund Committee. (From *The Common Cause*, 26 September 1913. By permission of the Fawcett Library, the City of London Polytechnic.)

F. T. Swanick, member of Executive Committee, NUWSS, and editor, *The Common Cause*. (Photograph by Elliot & Fry. From *The Common Cause*, 8 February 1912. By permission of the Fawcett Library, the City of London Polytechnic.)

First suffrage caravan tour through Leicestershire and Northamptonshire, 1909. Helga Gill (second from left), organiser, NUWSS. (By permission of the Fawcett Library, the City of London Polytechnic.)

Suffragette rally, Hyde Park, 1913. 'Millicent Fawcett addresses a meeting'. (By permission of the Fawcett Library, the City of London Polytechnic.)

INTRODUCTION

It has become a truism to say that, in conventional scholarship, women have been 'hidden from history'[1] and are only now 'becoming visible'.[2] It might be argued that the British women's suffragists are the exception which proves this rule. The activities of some of the movement's leading figures, notably the Pankhurst family, were well publicized at the time, and have since assumed an almost mythical standing. Their campaigning has been recorded in numerous memoirs,[3] together with more scholarly studies[4] and biographies,[5] and in a television series. Feminist scholarship itself exhibits a certain ambivalence in regard to the history of the suffrage movement. It has been argued that suffragists have received a disproportionate share of historians' attention, to the neglect of other more pressing issues in women's history.[6] Special urgency has been attached to the task of researching 'the social history of the ordinary, everyday lives of women'[7] and 'the existential experience of being female'.[8] Behind such arguments lie assumptions concerning the remoteness of 'politics' from 'everyday life' and the atypicality of politically active women. By their visibility and articulateness suffragists are taken to be exceptional and extraordinary beings among their sex. There is the contention, too, that the very enterprise of suffrage history mistakenly assumes the causal centrality of politics to processes of social change affecting women.[9]

From such standpoints this study might appear doubly misconceived. To begin with, it provides an account of the suffrage movement in Britain between 1900 and 1918, formal participation in which was, indeed, not a typical pursuit among women. Further, it concentrates on two aspects of the political dimensions of that movement: first, in its analysis of the internal debates and struggles concerning the strategies and tactics to be developed in the campaign for votes for women; and secondly in its focus on the relations between labour-movement women and middle-class, Liberal feminists, between rank-and-file provincial suffrage societies and the national leadership in London, and between feminist and party politics, especially labour politics, between 1900 and 1918. For whereas middle-class feminists had dominated women's suffrage

1

organisations in the late nineteenth century, working-class women, and especially those organised within the labour movement, were becoming an increasingly significant presence among rank-and-file suffragists by the early years of this century. As a consequence, this study will argue, issues of class as well as sex equality become central to the politics of the movement.

To undertake such a study as this does not imply a rejection of the value of what has been termed the 'new women's history'.[10] Recent explorations of 'female worlds' and 'women's culture', with their emphasis on gender roles, the female life cycle, and female sexuality, have undoubtedly increased our understanding of nineteenth-century women's lives,[11] and in ways which provide insights, too, into the history of women's political activity in this period.[12] But it does assert the equal validity of what has been characterised by one self-professed 'new women's historian' as 'traditional women's history', with its emphasis on organisations and social movements.[13] In so doing, it necessarily disputes the tenability of some of the reservations concerning 'traditional women's history' raised on behalf of the 'new women's history'. The concept of 'the average woman' lies behind much of this present unease, for it gives rise to the question: If suffragists were not 'average' or 'typical' women, how useful is it to study their activities? Such a concern is based on the assumption that there is a generality to women's experience from which some women depart and that the 'quintessential female experiences' are ones quite divorced from the world of politics.[14]

The difficulty with such a proposition – at least as a critique of suffrage history – is the impossibility of defining such a typicality or generality for British women at the turn of this century in such a way that suffragists are necessarily excluded by virtue of being suffragists. Though such women were exceptional in their political activism, this is not sufficient ground to assume that they thereby differed absolutely from 'the average woman', or that their political life was something quite divorced from and unrelated to the rest of their existence. Whereas the majority of women had no formal association with the suffrage movement, neither were the majority of suffragists members of some elite caste that had abdicated 'women's estate' for membership of something quite other. Though individuals may be atypical in any number of ways, their lives may nonetheless provide the historian with insights into some more generalised experience. This has been most amply demonstrated in the first thoroughgoing study of provincial, working-class suffragism, Jill Liddington and Jill Norris's *One Hand Tied behind Us*, and in Doris Nield Chew's collection of her mother Ada's writings, and an account of her life as a working-class organiser for the suffrage movement, *The Life and Writings of a Working Woman*.[15] Such studies offer a new perspective on the suffrage movement at the same time as they rescue the rank-and-file suffragist from what E. P. Thompson once termed 'the enormous condescension of posterity'.[16] They also suggest how research on the suffrage movement may be combined with attempts to recover the everyday experience of ordinary women.

Nor need the undertaking of political history, of itself, imply assumptions on the part of the historian concerning the causal centrality of politics to processes of social change. To write suffrage history is to assert only that political activity may form as significant a part of 'the existential reality' of women as, say, sexual relations or mothering. It is also to recognise the cultural, symbolic significance of the vote in our society, a significance which requires the historian to look beyond its potential, or otherwise, for effecting change. Campaigning for women's enfranchisement, I will argue, involved suffragists in an active attempt to redefine not only female roles but political life. It was the well-reasoned response of a wide variety of women to the connections they perceived between the problems and concerns of their everyday lives and the broader social and political issues of their society. Further, as Joan Wallach Scott has argued recently:

To ignore politics in the recovery of the female subject is to accept the reality of public/private distinctions and the separate or distinctive qualities of women's character and experience. It misses the chance not only to challenge the accuracy of binary distinctions between men and women in the past and present, but to expose the very political nature of a history written in those terms.[17]

In all these respects much of the critical assessment of 'traditional women's history' is founded on significantly impoverished understandings of the historical meaning of the campaigns for women's enfranchisement.[18] It also seriously underestimates the potential of the history of women's political activity for revising existing understandings of particular periods or issues. The votes-for-women campaigns well illustrate this last point, for they played a notable part in the realignment of British party politics which was occurring in the period preceding the First World War. The examination of the politics of the women's suffrage movement that follows aims to bring this aspect of the campaigns more clearly into focus, and to demonstrate once more how historians' blindness to women may render their accounts inadequate. For, ironically, the relation between the women's suffrage campaigns and the party-political struggles of the period has previously received little attention.[19] P. F. Clarke's work *Lancashire and the New Liberalism* has suggested the importance of the women's-suffrage issue for the fate of British Liberalism.[20] David Morgan's study *Suffragists and Liberals* supports this contention, and traces the twists and turns of parliamentary and Liberal government consideration of the question.[21] But the women's suffragists themselves make only brief appearances in Morgan's work, and are almost invisible in Clarke's. Women's suffrage was also a repeatedly discussed issue at early Labour Party conferences, and women's suffragists were a presence in local labour-movement politics in the first decades of the twentieth century. But again they remain unseen in Ross McKibbin's *The Evolution of the Labour Party*.[22] Jill Liddington and Jill Norris's study of working-class suffragists reveals aspects of the interrelation of feminist and labour politics but necessarily only in one locality. The implications of such an alliance for feminist politics, for party politics, and for the eventual success of the votes-for-women campaigns have not previously been explored.

That project, undertaken here, requires a modification of the existing historical convention which emphasises a division of the British suffrage movement into two distinct wings, the 'militants', whose best-known organisation was the Women's Social and Political Union, and the lesser-known 'constitutionalists', most of whom were organised within the National Union of Women's Suffrage Societies.[23] These organisations' differences are generally taken to centre on the question of the use of violence in demonstrations. That is to say, a mode of campaigning, a style of agitation, is held to be the critical issue among British suffragists. Yet if 'militancy' involved simply a preparedness to resort to extreme forms of violence, few 'militants' were 'militant' and then only from 1912 onwards. The following analysis will argue that an equally fundamental question for early-twentieth-century feminists was the issue of political strategy. Once this dimension to the constitutional/militant division is acknowledged the analytical imprecision of the two terms becomes even more evident. If, as will be argued, militancy connoted among suffragists a willingness to take the issue onto the streets, or if it sometimes indicated labour and socialist affiliations, then, it will be shown, many 'constitutionalists' were also 'militant'. The most consistent sense in which the two terms might be used would be to indicate membership of particular organisations. But even this usage is complicated by the fact that many belonged to both militant and constitutionalist societies simultaneously, suggesting that, for a certain period at least, many suffragists did not themselves view the two approaches to campaigning as either mutually exclusive or at odds with one another. The present historiographic tradition rests largely on an uncritical application of this terminology, and offers in consequence an interpretation of the British suffrage movement that does not mirror adequately its full complexity. The distinction militant/constitutional is not only difficult to apply in any consistent way, but it also tends to obscure those currents within the suffrage movement which cut across it.

The term 'radical' carries similar problems when applied to women's suffragists. Sometimes it is used to characterise the militant wing and reinforce its distinctiveness from the older societies.[24] More recently it has been used to identify the movement among working-class women in the textile towns of Lancashire.[25] In either case the nature of the radicalism remains ill defined and where it is defined appears to hinge on labour-movement affiliations. In this sense it cannot be restricted either to militant or working-class suffragists if it is to be used at all consistently. There are, too, other very different candidates for the appellation 'radical suffragists'. The separatists among the militants, for instance, and the sexual libertarians around *The Freewoman* offered more fundamental challenges to the existing order of male–female relations, and Sylvia Pankhurst and other dissident militants became involved in organising far more radical challenges to the political order of the day. In sum, the complexity and variety of the cross-currents within the suffrage movement are not given recognition within our current frameworks, nor can they be adequately represented simply in terms of membership of one or other wing or organisation.

This study will argue that a significant aspect of these cross-currents was the conflicts of loyalty experienced by women's suffragists campaigning for sexual equality in the very period when working-class movements began to organise for the independent representation of their interests in parliament. Most suffragists brought to their campaigning pre-existing class and party loyalties and, in the party-political context of the day, the progressives among them found these frequently cutting across their loyalty to the cause of their sex. The Liberal Party, while embarking on an extensive programme of social reform, was seriously divided on the issue of votes for women, and was led from 1908 by one of its most emphatic antisuffragists, Herbert Asquith. The Labour Party was engaged in building for the first time a united and effective presence in the House of Commons and thus in a challenge to the Liberal Party as the party of reform or the representative of working-class interests. Its attitude to women's enfranchisement between 1905 and 1912 was at best ambiguous, and many within its ranks were openly hostile to equal votes for women under the existing franchise laws. Many of the tensions, conflicts, and drives among women's suffragists can only be understood against this parliamentary party-political background to their campaigning.

One particular issue was to be a recurrent source of discord and debate within all sections of the suffrage movement. This was the question of whether, and if so how, to relate the demand for *equal votes for women* to that for a fully independent Labour Party in the House of Commons and the associated call for *adult suffrage*.[26] Both militants and constitutionalists were to be found, at various times, working for an alliance between the two demands. Margaret Llewelyn Davies, a leader of the working-class organisation the Women's Cooperative Guild, coined the term 'democratic suffragist' to designate and rally this body of opinion.[27] Identifying such a democratic-suffragist current within the different factions and organisations of the movement, and its varying fortunes within them, is one of the principal objects of this study. The aim is not only to recover aspects of suffrage history that have been lost to view or largely ignored but also to suggest a new perspective on some of its better-known aspects.

Democratic suffragists covered a broad spectrum of political affiliation from 'progressive' liberalism[28] to revolutionary and 'rebel' socialism.[29] Largely as a consequence of this they did not form an organised, united faction within the movement until the First World War. Even then they worked through a number of organisations, and their unity was transitory. No doubt this is part of the reason why they have been so difficult to 'see', for their one shared characteristic was a desire to secure women's suffrage as part of a more general democratisation of British society. A feminist–labour alliance seemed to the majority of democratic suffragists the best strategy by which to achieve such a goal. They became an increasingly influential presence in both wings of the movement despite their lack of organisational cohesiveness or even of mutual acknowledgement, and the politics of the suffrage movement may only fully be understood once their presence is recognised.

The work of democratic suffragists within the National Union of Women's Suffrage Societies was to prove especially fruitful and provides the core of the research presented here. A large part of this study will draw extensively on a previously little-used collection of papers left by the democratic suffragist Catherine Marshall.[30] Catherine Marshall was at the centre of suffrage politics from 1911, when she began to act as parliamentary secretary for the National Union of Women's Suffrage Societies. In the following year she was one of those who negotiated with the Labour Party leadership on the implementation of her organisation's new electoral policy. This resulted in the establishment of an Election Fighting Fund for the support of Labour parliamentary candidates. As Election Fighting Fund secretary, Catherine Marshall was to manage the day-to-day activities of constitutional suffragists on behalf of the Labour Party. She was, as a consequence, in frequent correspondence with numerous suffrage-movement organisers in the provinces. Through letters left among her papers, the voice of many rank-and-file suffragists, both middle-class and working-class, may be heard again. The collection offers one of the clearest windows on suffrage-movement politics at present available to the historian.

It was the successful realisation of democratic-suffragist strategy in feminist–labour alliances such as this which ensured the eventual granting of the vote to women, not militancy as the leaders of the Women's Social and Political Union were afterwards to claim. Recognition for their part in this achievement belongs to democratic suffragists in every section of the movement, not to militants or constitutionalists as such. Neither dogged parliamentary lobbying nor violent demonstration in itself secured success. Political vision and political acumen were needed, and both were provided in large part by the democratic suffragists. Their goal was to ally their cause with more generalised movements for radical social change, and to give expression to their conviction that women's subordination was enmeshed with other structures of social inequality. It was in this way that they were able to forge an alliance with the new force in radical politics in this period, the Labour Party. The demand for votes for women was transformed into a mass social movement, and for the first time working-class women were involved in suffrage activity in significant numbers. Democratic suffragism was able to speak to their discontents both as women and as members of the working class.

Such a conception of suffrage campaigning both drew upon, and helped to maintain to a significant degree, the considerable sense of sexual solidarity among women from all classes which characterised the ethos of the suffrage movement in Britain. The first chapter in this study will explore the ideological roots of this ethos and its articulation through suffragist polemic. The ideas of British suffragists have only recently begun to receive any detailed attention.[31] It will be argued here that there was a marked degree of ideological homogeneity among suffrage supporters with otherwise varying class and party-political outlooks. This lay in a common understanding of women as a quite distinct subspecies to men and one with skills, attributes, and forms of knowledge particularly relevant to the pursuit of social reform. From such a perspective, votes for women could be viewed as an integral, indeed essential, part of progressive politics. It was in this sense that suffragists claimed theirs as 'the common cause'. Such a conviction in turn served to sustain day-to-day relationships between militant and constitutionalist, between middle-class and working-class, and between Liberal and Labour suffragists.[32]

Suffragist analysis of women's subjection further fostered a sense of sexual solidarity in suggesting that all women were joined in membership of a sex class: Whatever their economic position, all women were the victims of the existing exploitative organisation of sexuality in favour of male interests. But the idea of a sex class carried within it an implicit analogy with socialist understandings of inequality that focused on concepts of class derived from economic relationships. Paradoxically, then, this aspect of suffragist ideology served also to highlight the issue which was to be the most divisive for British suffragists – whether or not to recognise class as well as sexual inequality in the campaign for votes for women. The significance of the democratic-suffragist current lay in its unification of these potentially divisive concerns. This was achieved by arguing for a commitment from both the suffrage and labour movements to a conception of political democracy that took account of each form of inequality. It asked Labour supporters to acknowledge that the disenfranchisement of middle-class women by virtue of their sex was as unjust as that of working-class men by virtue of their lack of property. It asked middle-class Liberal women to acknowledge that social justice required the independent representation of working-class interests in

parliament as much as sexual equality in the franchise laws. The ethos
of the suffrage movement helped make the democratic-suffragist strategy an effective possibility. But it also rendered it the most compelling
necessity. For out of this ethos also grew the sex-war outlook adopted
by some among the leadership of the Women's Social and Political Union
during the later stages of the campaigns, an outlook which threatened
the whole suffrage cause with the disintegration and marginalisation
that were eventually to befall that organisation.

The second chapter looks more closely at the nature of the constitutional–militant division and argues that this did not represent rigid or
static characteristics. The content of both militancy and constitutionalism changed in significant ways over time, and only gradually did the
two wings come to be at complete odds with each other. The third chapter looks at the emergence of the democratic-suffragist current in the
first few years of the twentieth century, and at some early efforts by
democratic suffragists to secure a greater degree of cooperation between
the feminist and labour movements. These first three chapters, then, are
largely discursive and aim to provide a context for the narrative which
follows in the final four. The latter are concerned with the establishment
of an electoral alliance between the Labour Party and the National Union
of Women's Suffrage Societies under the guidance of democratic suffragists in the two years or so before the outbreak of war, and with the
impact of war upon both the suffrage movement and the final enfranchisement of women in 1918.

CHAPTER 1

'FEMINISING DEMOCRACY': THE ETHOS OF THE WOMEN'S-SUFFRAGE MOVEMENT

In America the ideological complexion of the suffrage movement there has been the subject of sustained research and debate over the past two decades. Though some have argued the innately conservative nature of the ideas of American suffragists, other more recent work has stressed the radicalism of women's movements there in the latter half of the nineteenth century.[1] In contrast the ideas of the suffrage movement in Britain have received little detailed attention.[2] This chapter can offer only a preliminary analysis. It is based on material drawn from the large body of suffragist literature still extant, a resource so far little used by historians of the movement in Britain, and suggests the need for some modification of our existing understanding in this area.[3]

Most present accounts assert that the ideas of the suffrage movement in Britain descended directly from Enlightenment political philosophy and nineteenth-century liberal theory, notably through Mary Wollstonecraft's *Vindication of the Rights of Woman* and John Stuart Mill's *The Subjection of Women*.[4] These two early feminist theorists expounded what might be termed a 'humanist' case for feminism. Although they drew on quite different schools of social and political theory, they shared one fundamental theoretical premise, the common human attributes of men and women and the consequent social injustice involved in their unequal treatment. The Jacobin Mary Wollstonecraft identified these universal human characteristics as the faculties of reason and conscience. At present, she argued, these faculties were being warped and suppressed in women because of the inferior content of their education, and because of their economic subservience to men. These two factors prevented women from acting as the fully rational, fully moral beings they had the potential to be. Humanist feminism explained existing differences in the characteristics of the two sexes in terms of environmental influences. It denied or remained agnostic concerning the existence of innate sexual characters specific to men and women. Mary Wollstonecraft insisted: 'I here throw down my gauntlet, and deny the existence of sexual virtues, not excepting modesty. For man and woman, truth, if I understand the meaning of the word, must be the same.'[5] More cautiously, the philosophical radical John Stuart Mill argued that the existence or otherwise of distinct male and female natures could only be determined when both sexes shared equal opportunities to develop their full potential. The principles of utility and expediency also required that every human being be afforded such opportunity. Each individual had interests which only he or she could represent, and on these grounds Mill justified votes for women.[6]

Like Wollstonecraft and Mill, the utopian socialist William Thompson believed women's emancipation could be secured by social engineering.[7] But his introduction of a new factor into the discussion of women's subjection has generally been ignored. In his *Appeal on Behalf of One Half the Human Race* Thompson suggested a biological base to women's oppression in their role in reproduction. It was because they had to mother that women were subject to men. Mill and Wollstonecraft also assumed that the responsibilities of motherhood must be a central facet of women's existence. Indeed Mary Wollstonecraft's case for women's emancipation was largely built upon the importance of women's role as the moral guides of children. She argued that artificial restrictions on the development of women had serious consequences for the creation of a moral citizenry: 'The virtue of man will be worm-eaten by the insect whom he keeps under his feet . . . womanish follies will stick to the character throughout life. The weakness of the mother will be visited upon the children.'[8] But Mary Wollstonecraft's account of women's emancipation paid no attention to the consequences of motherhood for women's capacity to avail themselves of equal opportunities with men. Similarly, Mill appeared unaware of the contradiction between his call for equal opportunities and his expectation that most women would retire into domesticity after marriage.[9]

For all three writers motherhood was a natural given which defined women's existence. But Thompson, like other socialists of his time, argued that its consequences for women's social standing were undesirable. Such analyses led many socialists to propose very radical changes in the organisation of sexuality and of family life. Thompson advocated marriage reform, and also believed it was necessary to compensate women for the time and energy they gave up to motherhood.[10] His *Appeal* was one of the first attempts to make a case for what we today recognise as 'positive discrimination' in pursuit of substantive, as opposed to purely formal, equality. That is to say, he believed social reconstruction could compensate for the biological handicap of being female, even though it could not obviate sexual difference. As a consequence of these differences Thompson believed that men and women would always have sex-particular social roles. For Thompson, women's biological function was related to the contrasting and distinct talents he perceived in the two sexes. He believed that women's greater involvement in domestic relationships to some extent undermined their capacity for larger social responsibilities.[11] Many other socialist feminists, like Thompson's mentor

Anna Wheeler, sought to turn this perceived moral differentiation in the sexes to women's advantage. Barbara Taylor has recently suggested that Anna Wheeler evidenced 'an unresolved tension between the desire to minimize sexual difference and the need to re-assert it in women's favour'.[12] Like other socialist feminists, she argued that women possessed a unique moral mission consequent on the very nature of womanhood. Among such early socialist feminists, then, what might be termed an essentialist case for feminism was beginning to be formulated.[13]

Olive Banks's account of British feminism does not address this major departure by socialists from the humanist case for feminism.[14] However, her analysis of what she terms 'the evangelical face' of nineteenth-century feminism suggests that such essentialist arguments may also have been informing ideas outside utopian-socialist circles. Middle-class women philanthropists and social reformers were also to justify much of their work in terms of women's particular social mission, one that reflected their sex-specific natures.[15] Like William Thompson, they argued that it was the motherhood of women, either actual or potential, which produced characteristics particular to them. Frances Power Cobbe, for example, in her essay for Josephine Butler's collection *Woman's Work and Woman's Culture*, saw mothering as something given in women's make-up, an inherited 'set' of mind transmitted from generation to generation: 'Not only, therefore, does the woman of the present day suffer deflection from intellectual pursuits through her proper motherly instincts, but inherited proclivities act upon her mind, like a multiplying galvanometer, to augment indefinitely the force of deflection. *Tendency* is immanent even in spinsters to warp them from intellect to baby-love.'[16] Women's suffragists, too, were frequently to argue that because women mothered they were more caring and more nurturant. As a consequence of their reproductive role women were held to have a higher regard for the sanctity of human life, and to be more religious, more altruistic, more moral than men. Such feminists believed that with women's enfranchisement political life would become purer and more elevated. It was also claimed that women, because they nurtured and men did not, could offer skills and understanding of particular relevance to some of the newer concerns of the state – the education of children, public health, and the management and care of the poor.

It has been suggested that such claims were more characteristic of American feminism,[17] but a reading of British suffragist literature indicates that this was not the case. It is possible, though, that such essentialist claims met more deliberate resistance in Britain. John Stuart Mill's wife, Harriet Taylor, had detected a similar change of emphasis within American feminism as early as 1851. Reviewing a recent women's-rights convention, she condemned

those who would meekly attempt to combine nominal equality between men and women, with enforced distinctions in their privileges and functions. What is wanted for women is equal rights, equal admission to all social privileges; not a position apart, a sort of sentimental priesthood. . . . The strength of the cause lies in the support of those who are influenced by reason and principle; and to attempt to recommend it by sentimentalities, absurd in reason, and inconsistent with the principle on which the movement is founded, is to place a good cause on a level with a bad one.[18]

Yet by the early 1870s Helen Taylor, Harriet's daughter and Mill's step-daughter, was to be found arguing for votes for women on the grounds of women's sex-particular natures:

It was just because there was so much difference between men and women that it was essential the feminine side of things should be allowed full and free expression. In these times when we had learnt that brute strength was not the source of righteous law, they would rejoice to take among law-givers that half of the human race which represented its most pitiful and sympathetic instincts.[19]

Similarly, Millicent Garrett Fawcett, the suffragist leader and one of the earliest women public speakers in Britain, insisted:

We do not want women to be bad imitations of men; we neither deny nor min-imize the differences between men and women. The claim of women to repre-sentation depends to a large extent on these differences. Women bring some-thing to the service of the state different to that which can be brought by men.[20]

The particular and specific contribution women might make to political life was to become a commonplace in suffragist tracts, pamphlets, and journals in the fifty years between 1870 and 1920. An early-twentieth-century suffragist argued:

We desire the right of voting not that we may cease to be women, but because we are women, and because Parliament, chosen at present by men alone, is making laws that must influence very closely our work, the training of children and the conduct of home life. It is our very womanhood, with its inborn instinct to childward care, not merely the human nature which we share with men, that makes many of us eager to be politically enfranchised.[21]

Such an essentialist case for women's enfranchisement was being expounded by middle-class feminists from the earliest years of the or-ganised demand for votes for women, the late 1860s. Mill's *Subjection of Women* appeared in the same year, 1869, as Josephine Butler's collection of essays *Woman's Work and Woman's Culture* (though it had, of course, been written some years earlier). The title of Butler's collection itself ex-pressed a conviction of the distinctiveness of the female, and many of its contributions provide further evidence of a feminist belief in the ex-istence of fundamentally different male and female natures.[22] Such a viewpoint represented a radical departure from the humanist case out-lined in the works of Mary Wollstonecraft and John Stuart Mill. Earlier assumptions of the overriding influence on the British women's-suffrage movement of ideas derived from the Enlightenment and liberal political theory therefore require considerable modification.

The essentialist case for women's political emancipation was built upon an analysis of what it is to be female that conflated sex and gender. The biological capacity to give birth was held to be the determining factor in femininity. Femaleness *was* femininity and vice versa. In such a line of argument there was no acknowledgement of the social factors that construct the characteristics of masculinity and femininity. Each was an immutable given, rather than a historically and culturally determined phenomenon. Sexual difference was entirely biologically determined. Men were men and women were women, and as such each was a quite distinct subspecies of the category 'human'. Men could not possibly provide the skills, attributes, and understanding particular to women, characteristics which were also morally superior to men's. Hence female enfranchisement could be argued to be essential to the creation of a more caring state through the furtherance of social reforms informed by feminine understanding and experience.

To accept gender differentiation as naturally given was not, however, necessarily to accede to the hierarchical ordering of the sexes on the basis of that differentiation. Nor did it necessarily involve acceptance of totally segregated spheres of action consequent on that differentiation. This second issue was to be at the heart of antisuffragism. In contrast to women's suffragists there were some reformers during the later nineteenth century who sought to improve their sex's position by insisting upon, and elaborating, the notion of separate spheres. They believed that the nature of women left them unfit for the competition and struggle of the male world. Women had a sphere of their own, and efforts to improve their social position should be concentrated on elevating the status of that sphere, and securing women's autonomy and authority within it. Such reformers opposed women's-rights campaigns as seeking entry into inappropriate areas like politics. One such was the popular novelist Mary Humphry Ward, a leading figure in the Anti-Suffrage League.[23] In a manifesto published by women antisuffragists, including Mary Humphry Ward, it was argued that the state could be no business of women because it rested, finally, upon the exercise of physical force. Women could never provide the stern hand needed for the government of empire. Mrs. Humphry Ward's position on local government was quite different, for she regarded this simply as a matter of housekeeping on a grand scale. As such it was eminently the work of women, and Mary Humphry Ward was herself active in local government bodies.[24]

The suffragists countered such arguments by presenting very different conceptions of the state and of the home, conceptions that challenged the very notion of the separateness of public and domestic spheres. This may be seen in contrasting John Ruskin's vision of the home provided in his essay 'Of Queen's Gardens'[25] with that of Josephine Butler in her Introduction to *Woman's Work and Woman's Culture*. Ruskin's essay represents one of the clearest formulations of separate-spheres ideology. He wrote:

This is the true nature of home – it is the place of Peace; the shelter, not only from all injury, but from all terror, doubt and division. In so far as it is not this, it is not home: so far as the anxieties of the outer life penetrate into it, and the inconsistently-minded, unknown, unloved, or hostile society of the outer world is allowed by either husband or wife to cross the threshold it ceases to be home; it is then only a part of that outer world which you have roofed over, and lighted fire in.[26]

Josephine Butler claimed a similar appreciation of the value of the home, but rejected 'the too often selfish comforts and exclusive enjoyments' which many homes represented.[27] She offered this alternative vision:

I think I see that a great enlargement of hearts, and a free opening out and giving forth of the influences of homes, as reservoirs of blessing for the common good, would ultimately result in the restored security of all the best elements in our present ideal of Home. . . . Fair and happy homes would gather again, in larger groups, and their happiness would be placed on a surer foundation than that of the home-lovers of today.[28]

Among such feminists the home was conceived of as a social agency rather than a private haven, a potential community resource rather than a domestic retreat. As such Josephine Butler argued for 'the extension beyond our homes of the home influence . . . nothing whatever will avail but the infusion of Home elements into Workhouses, Hospitals, Schools, Orphanages, Lunatic Asylums, Reformatories, and even Prison'.[29] This dynamic, outward-looking conception of the home allowed British feminists, like their American counterparts, to use women's domestic specialisation as grounds for their entry into the public world of politics. Suffragists were, by such arguments, able to stress the vote as an essential instrument for the fulfilment of women's domestic duties. Mrs. Pankhurst summed up this aspect of their case:

I assure you that not one woman who enters this agitation need feel that she has got to give up a single one of women's duties in the home. She learns to feel that she is attaching a larger meaning to those duties which have been women's duties since the race began, and will be till the race has ceased to be. After all, home is a very, very big thing indeed . . . home is the home of everybody in the nation.[30]

As a corollary to this broadened vision of women's domestic duties, suffragists elaborated a conception of the state alternative to that of the antisuffragists. Rather than the controlling, regulatory aspect of the state, suffragists stressed its functions of nurturance, functions which they insisted could only be adequately fulfilled with women's assistance. Attacking the separate-spheres concept head on, Millicent Garrett Fawcett argued: 'Some said the sphere of woman was her home; that was quite true, but it was also one reason why women should take a part in political affairs. They wanted the home-side represented in politics . . . woman at her best stood for mercy, pity, peace, purity and love.'[31] Suffragists suggested that women's innate mothering capacities were fundamental to the creation of a nurturant state:

A mother's instinct is held to be unerring; her sympathies are supposed to be wider and more humanised; her altruism proverbial. . . . It cannot be too much insisted upon that motherhood is the strongest force in existence that makes for altruism, and altruism is the most essential factor in the wide and beneficial ordering of the State.[32]

Accordingly Millicent Garrett Fawcett urged suffragists, 'Do not give up one jot or tittle of your womanliness, your love of children, your care for the sick, your gentleness, your self-control, your obedience to conscience and duty, for all these things are terribly wanted in politics.'[33] While in earlier decades women's social mission had involved them in widespread philanthropic enterprises, feminists such as Josephine Butler now claimed that the conditions of modern society required that such activity become the concern of the state. Hence, to fulfil their mission women now needed

freedom and power to reach and deal with great social evils in their beginnings, and not only to a limited degree in their dire effects. . . . It has been well said that philanthropy and politics, now flowing apart, will unite in one stream when philanthropists become conscious of power to reach the sources of crimes and misery, and when statesmen understand that their functions are assigned to them for none but a philanthropic end.[34]

In sum, British feminists insisted on both the necessity of increasing state intervention in areas that had previously been part of women's domestic preserve and the concomitant need for women's participation in the work of the state. In asserting both, they challenged the notion that domestic and public matters could be kept apart as the separate concerns of women and men respectively.[35]

It was on the basis of such essentialist understandings that a relationship between feminism and the cause of social reform was frequently argued. This claim was often formulated in phrases like the need for 'the mother element' in politics,[36] in calls for 'the feminisation of democracy',[37] and in assertions that women were 'the sex most intimately connected with social reform'.[38] From such a viewpoint, votes for women took on added significance as a central force in progressive politics. One convinced observer, the radical journalist Brougham Villiers, wrote of the early-twentieth-century campaigns for votes for women in these terms:

The issue raised is the greatest of modern times. On its decision depends nothing less than the character of the whole progressive movement in England. Under our eyes, the young democracy is taking shape; it is stating its peculiar problems and formulating its answers to them. Questions of education, temperance, unemployment, housing, land, poverty and finance, little regarded by the last generation, form the subject matter of politics in the present, and will do so still more in the immediate future. Yet . . . so long as women remain without direct influence in the life of the nation those things can only come to life in a vitiated atmosphere.[39]

For it was above all in questions of social reform that suffragists were able to locate an area where men's and women's spheres could be argued to overlap. The concerns of the home and of the state respectively could be extended to converge on issues of community well-being. It was in no small part because suffragists conceived women's public duties in terms of their innate nurturant capacities that they were able to build an alliance between their own movement and the forces of progressive politics.

Nor was this alliance restricted to one with Liberal progressivism. Earlier socialist feminism, with its stress on sexual radicalism and critiques of the traditional family, would have been incompatible with much in the ethos of the later women's-suffrage movement. As yet we know little about the ideas of British socialists concerning 'the woman question' during the late nineteenth and early twentieth centuries. But Olive Banks has detected increasing ambiguities in socialist thought on women after the decline of utopian and communitarian socialism.[40] Sheila Rowbotham and Jeffrey Weeks have gone further and have suggested an increasing conservatism by the 1890s in British socialist ideas concerning women. They find that critiques of conventional monogamy were being replaced by an increasing emphasis on the importance of the family, and that once again a belief in the distinct natures of male and female was evident in many socialists' thought.[41] Sheila Rowbotham argues that Edward Carpenter, for example, himself a sexual radical closely associated with the Independent Labour Party, 'followed other contemporary socialist writers like Engels in assuming that the sexual division of labour was natural because of the biological differences between men and women and he accepted "masculine" and "feminine" as fixed characteristics'.[42] Carpenter tended to idealise the working-class women he knew as symbols of motherliness and nurturance. In Sheila Rowbotham's words, 'universal "woman" replaces real women . . . he reduces her to the biological role of reproducer'.[43] Similarly, Angus McLaren's work suggests that the leading members of the marxist Social Democratic Federation 'revealed a pronounced social conservatism when dealing with any issue relating to women'. They believed women should 'remain primarily as wives and mothers'.[44] In this, British marxism was not altogether out of step with German Social Democracy. By the early 1900s some leading party theorists in Germany were propounding a programme for women's emancipation that argued from an essentialist conception of innate female domesticity. They looked forward to a time when women could be released from participation in the workforce to realise their true natures in the home.[45]

So, although British socialism still contained sexual radicals with whom many suffragists did not wish to be associated, figures like Edward Carpenter were increasingly rare. Moreover, even his thought revealed parallels between suffragist and socialist conceptions of women's nature and women's potential role in political life. In this respect, the ideology of the socialist movement by the turn of the twentieth century was compatible with that of the suffrage movement. Many socialists shared bourgeois feminists' conviction of the fundamental need for women's presence in politics if extensive social reform were to be both rightly conceived and achieved. Middle-class or working-class, liberal or socialist, supporters of women's suffrage could unite in both a pragmatic sense of its expediency if social reform were to advance, and an ideological conviction of its rightness. The latter derived not simply from shared general principles but also, like the former, from a common ontology of womankind. On such a base suffragists were able to construct an ethos of sexual solidarity which served to ease the association between the largely middle-class suffrage organisations and sections of the labour and socialist movements in the last years of the campaign.

The humanist–essentialist distinction so far pursued in this discussion, like the distinctions in the American literature between 'radical feminism' and 'social feminism' or 'justice' arguments and 'expediency' arguments, inevitably oversimplifies the historical reality. Late-nineteenth- and early-twentieth-century suffragists in Britain never completely abandoned a humanist perspective. Rather they added, and gave ever-increasing prominence to, an essentialist case for women's political emancipation with little apparent awareness of some of the contradictions involved in so doing. Hence suffragism was never the monolithic ideology such a categorisation might suggest. It exhibited a range of varying emphases and convictions.[46] Some suffragists, like *The Common Cause*'s founding editor, Helena Swanwick, even felt uncomfortable with the term 'feminist', wishing rather that suffragists could have appropriated the label 'humanist' to signify a concern for the liberation of all human beings. Hence the title of her journal.[47] Others, like Christabel Pankhurst, founder of the Women's Social and Political Union, and Cicely Hamilton, a prominent member of the Women's Freedom League, expressed an increasing conviction that relations between the sexes could only ever be destructive of women.[48] In consequence they advocated celibacy and promoted a more separatist perspective on feminist campaigning. The distinction between humanist and essentialist forms of feminist ideology is useful not because the movement can be neatly divided into distinct phases or groupings but because such a formulation pinpoints clearly the theoretical alternatives embodied in two main lines of argument followed by feminists over the course of the nineteenth century. A feminism that presumes a distinct female nature and the biological determination of women's social functions would appear to be fundamentally conservative. It supposes as fixed for all time certain socially determined aspects of what it is to be a woman. However, the history of nineteenth-century British suffragism demonstrates how it might also inform quite radical challenges to restrictive ideologies concerning women.

As DuBois has argued in relation to American feminism, the demand for the vote was inherently radical in itself, for it challenged the concept of separate spheres and the exclusivity of male involvement in the domain of politics.[49] But the suffragist literature from Britain discussed above suggests that by the late nineteenth century, at least, feminists here had extended the radical nature of their demand even further. Possession of the vote was no longer seen simply as the symbol for middle-class women's accession to the political status accorded their male counterparts. Rather suffragism emphasised women's right to vote in terms of their specific social mission arising from their innate and distinct natures. Its adherents identified not with men, but with the generality of women. The vote, then, became a tool with which women of all classes were to reconstruct society in accordance with female values and needs, to create a reformed and 'feminised' democracy. That is to say, suffragists did not seek merely an entry to a male-defined sphere, but the opportunity to redefine that sphere. They rejected the characterisation of political life in terms of masculine qualities, and sought to redefine the state by asserting for it a nurturant role. British suffragists aimed to reform their society by domesticating public life. The most striking aspect of British suffragism, then, is that it did not present feminist goals in terms of equivalence with men but in terms of an autonomously created system of values derived from women's particular experience.[50]

Another historian of American feminism, Gerda Lerner, has argued that there are two orders of feminist consciousness, 'woman's rights feminism' and 'woman's emancipation feminism'.[51] According to Lerner's definition, 'Woman's rights advocates ask for equality with men, emancipationists seek women-defined goals and process.' Woman's righters 'want into the system in male-defined terms' while emancipationists want 'the transformation of patriarchy into a different system'.[52] As such, in Gerda Lerner's view, woman's emancipationists exhibit a higher order of feminist consciousness than woman's righters, namely 'a woman-centerd consciousness', in contrast to the androcentric consciousness of woman's righters.[53] Lerner has categorised American suffragists as being largely androcentric in outlook, but the evidence above would suggest that such an assessment could not be maintained in relation to the British material. Here votes for women was transformed far beyond an equal-rights demand, to an assertion of the need for the cultural and political transformation of society according to a female value system. To this extent British suffragism could be argued to be an emancipationist form of feminism, inasmuch as it exhibited a clearly 'woman-centred consciousness'.

Some possible preconditions for the formation of such a feminist consciousness are suggested by Carroll Smith Rosenberg's recent account of the 'female world'. This is her preferred formulation of another concept current in women's history, the concept of 'women's culture'.[54] It rests upon the identification of women's cultural and structural segregation in the nineteenth century, and posits the creation of distinct forms of consciousness when women inhabit such worlds. Carroll Smith Rosenberg's analysis of female networks, their relationship to women's consciousness, and the emergence of feminism contains three hypotheses: first, that the separation of domestic from economic life resulted in the establishment of female communities with a pattern of existence quite distinct from men's; secondly, that these female communities created distinct outlooks, mentalities, or in her words 'Weltanschauungen' based upon symbolic and cosmological systems particular to a world of 'women-identified women'; and finally, that such Weltanschauungen, combined with experience of women's organisations, may be basic preconditions for the founding of a feminist movement, inasmuch as they create within women a sense of themselves as a distinct group, alongside an experience of sexual solidarity.[55]

Temma Kaplan has recently built upon a similar understanding in her concept of 'female consciousness' to explain the nature of women's strikes in Barcelona in the early twentieth century.[56] Kaplan argues that out of women's experience in segregated female communities there arises what she terms 'female consciousness', a consciousness informed by women's experiences as the sustainers of human life. Because of their roles as mothers, nurturers, foragers, and providers of the means of existence, women's consciousness in working-class communities in early-twentieth-century Barcelona was dominated by the goal of preserving human life and dignity, and their actions directed to maintaining the conditions under which women might pursue this goal. Kaplan insists that though 'female consciousness' may frequently involve women in reactionary political stances, it has a fundamentally revolutionary potential in asserting a value system that sets the maintenance of human life above all other considerations.[57]

Smith Rosenberg's work concerns nineteenth-century middle-class women in America, and Kaplan's, working-class Spanish women in the early years of the twentieth century. Yet there are interesting parallels with the history of women in Britain over a similar time span. We have, as yet, no study of the creation of a 'women's sphere' in Britain comparable with Nancy Cott's work on New England between 1780 and 1835.[58] However, Eric Richards has traced a similar decline in women's participation rates in the economy, and Sally Alexander's analysis of women's work in London suggests the rigidification of pre-existing sexual divisions of labour. Those women who did remain in the workforce were increasingly segregated into separate industries, processes, and workplaces.[59] Recent British scholarship on aspects of gender definitions of women in Victorian Britain also indicates significant parallels with American research especially in regard to an intensifying sense of the distinctiveness of the female in this period.[60] Similarly, biographical material like Jo Manton's lives of Elizabeth Garrett Anderson and Mary Carpenter, together with Prochaska's study of women and philanthropy in the nineteenth century, suggests the existence of middle-class women's networks,[61] while Liddington and Norris's study of working-class suffragists in Lancashire indicates the importance of similar women's networks in working-class communities for mobilisation and agitation around women's issues.[62]

In general, then, it would appear that British women, too, experienced an increasing degree of segregation from men, as production was more and more separated from the household, and that female communities and networks formed a significant aspect of many women's lives in the nineteenth century. It is clear that such networks were important in the creation of a women's suffrage movement, in providing a base on which suffragists could build their organisations.[63] But it is also conceivable that the greater significance given essentialist arguments for feminist reforms at this time reflected this generation of women's intensified experience of their own distinctiveness as a sex. To this extent the concepts 'female worlds' and 'female consciousness' may prove helpful in advancing our understanding of the ethos of British suffragism. For though suffragists were critical of much that contemporary convention required of women, they did not devalue everything that was sex-specific in their own experience. They built a social movement upon existing women's networks, and the ethos of that movement was founded upon a belief in a specifically female value system derived from women's particular experience in female worlds. It could not be argued for Britain, as DuBois does for America, that 'the suffrage movement grew out of a critique of what we are calling women's culture',[64] if that is to be understood in terms of the concepts 'female world' and 'female consciousness'. Rather it seems likely that it derived much of its strength and potency from these. If the radicalism of British suffragism lay in its abandonment of male models of emancipation in favour of women-defined conceptions of political life, a female consciousness might be argued to have been fundamental to this. Paradoxically, it appears British suffragism was radical precisely because it moved away from a humanist feminist understanding of the significance of the vote.

It cannot be denied, however, that British suffragism failed to promote 'emancipation' in Gerda Lerner's fullest exposition of the term. This, she argues, would require resistance to all oppressive restrictions imposed either by social or by biological sexual differentiation.[65] As we have seen, British suffragists frequently upheld the notion of sexually specific natures in men and women, and accepted much in existing gender stereotyping. While their ideology implied a radical challenge to both Victorian conceptions of women's social position and definitions of political life derived from masculine stereotypes, it could never have been adequate to the task of liberation, if that is understood in terms of the destruction of restrictive gender definitions. In the end, the historical significance of suffragism as an ideology lies rather in the potential it offered for building up a sense of sexual solidarity among women from very different social backgrounds. It served also to further the alliance between feminist and progressive politics in the early years of the twentieth century by asserting that the possibility of social reform lay only within a feminised polity. The demand for equal votes could, in consequence, be given far greater significance than the simple single-issue campaign among middle-class women it had started out as in the late 1860s.

As well as a resort to an essentialist case for feminism, one other aspect of the ideas of British women's suffragists also helped to promote an ethos of sexual solidarity within the movement. In much of the pamphlet and periodical literature from about the turn of the century there is developed a sex-class analysis of women's oppression which further served to moderate some of the tensions between feminists from very different social and political backgrounds. Suffragist conceptions of a sex class generally focused on the sexual relations between men and women as the main mechanism of women's oppression. Marriage and prostitution formed the nexus of women's sexual and economic exploitation. In relation to these institutions, it was argued, all women shared interests in conflict with those of all men. On this issue *The Common Cause* declared:

It is impossible to show the depth and moral passion of the women's liberation movement without showing the root at once of woman's weakness and woman's strength. Mere sex is the ground of her disability. How can one deal effectively with the one unless one speaks truly and candidly of the other? . . . all the questions of women's economic, legal, and political subjection, the future of the race, the hope of humanity, are involved in the question whether the rival trades of marriage and prostitution are those alone which shall be open to women.[66]

According to such a viewpoint, all women experienced subjection in consequence of the dominance of male interests in the organisation of human sexuality. Interconnected with this sexual exploitation was women's economic subordination. Helena Swanwick, the editor of *The Common Cause*, argued:

No discussion of the economic position of women would be honest which did not take into account the undoubted fact that women can make more money by the sale of their bodies than in any other way . . . every poor sweated girl knows she can in one night double her week's wages if she chooses. This is a fact. If we do not fearlessly face it, we may as well give up talking about the women's movement, for it will only be play.[67]

There were several disparate strands of thinking within the suffrage movement on questions of sexuality. Some rejected the notion of female sexuality altogether; others thought it to be no more than the desire for motherhood. Left to themselves, women would seek sexual expression only in consequence of the desire to procreate.[68] There were others who held the sexual urge to be as strong in women as in men,[69] but only a very few preached sexual emancipation and the end to institutionalised monogamy. The majority of suffragists remained defensive about women's sexuality. Even many with more progressive views on sexual relations, like Helena Swanwick, saw sexuality as the main source of women's vulnerability to exploitation. Although they were critical of the existing organisation of marriage, they felt it still secured women from being the general sexual right of any man. Suffragist suspicions of the birth-control movement and sexual liberation sprang from the conviction that they would serve only to render women available for greater sexual exploitation by men.[70] Voluntary motherhood by sexual abstinence within marriage was the most generally promoted policy among feminists at this time.[71] The curbing of male sexuality by the enforcement of a single repressive standard of sexual morality was the suffragists' goal.

Such attitudes found fullest expression in suffragist campaigns against commercialised vice and for the control of venereal disease. These aspects of suffragist activity have been viewed with considerable distaste by many writers on the movement.[72] They are frequently presented as the warped concerns of a few pathologically deranged extremists.[73] Others have suggested that the social-purity movement represented the attempts of middle-class women to control the sexuality of young working-class women.[74] But it is clear from the literature of the suffrage movement that some sense of sexual solidarity also informed the contemporaneous social-purity crusade.[75] The evidence that accumulated as a result of investigations prompted by the suffrage and social-purity movements indicated that feminists had significant grounds for concern. Testimony before the Royal Commission on Venereal Disease, for example, indicated that many women were kept in ignorance of their own venereal infection, out of medical practitioners' belief that they should not interfere in the marriage relationship; a large part of the work of a major London women's hospital concerned the gonorrheal infection of respectably married women, while a significant proportion of the still-births were adjudged the result of syphilitic infection.[76] For many women the publicity surrounding these campaigns was in itself a revelation, for the conventions of the time ensured that many had been kept in total ignorance of the nature of venereal diseases and their implications for women, particularly in their role as mothers. While gonorrheal infection might render a woman barren, syphilis often destroyed the life of her unborn child, or handicapped surviving offspring. As such, the spread of these diseases represented a fundamental threat to women whose identity was centred upon procreation and nurturance.[77]

Turning to suffragist analysis of women's economic subordination, there is apparent a dual focus, first on the plight of the woman industrial worker, and secondly on the economic dependency involved in marriage. Both were related back to women's sexual vulnerability. The pressing economic needs created by unemployment, underemployment, and low pay, it was argued, left many open to sexual exploitation in commercialised vice, or forced women into economic dependency in marriage. Suffragists were particularly concerned about a number of attempts in the early years of the century to limit women's work opportunities, notably legislation aimed at ending women's employment as barmaids, at the pit-brow, and as printers. A suggestion from cabinet minister John Burns, that there should be legislation to prevent married women's work as a possible solution to the unemployment problem, provoked particular anger. Mrs. Pankhurst referred to the proposal as 'an act of tyranny'. Whereas the legislation was presented as an attempt to free married women of additional burdens, it proposed no compensation for loss of earning nor gave any rights to the wife over some part of her husband's earnings. Mrs. Pankhurst insisted: 'Infantile mortality and physical degeneration are not found in the homes of well-paid factory operatives but in the slums and among the families of casual workers.'[78] On this issue Cicely Hamilton protested that society was 'drifting towards an era of repressive legislation – of class legislation – whose aim and object will be the exclusion of women from the paid labour market and the confinement of the larger half of the community to some form of (chiefly unpaid) work as it pleases the male portion of the nation to assign to them'.[79]

Feminist views on the question of protective labour legislation for women were generally more complex. An equal-rights perspective had frequently led feminists to oppose such legislation.[80] But by the turn of the century many suffragists, like Clementina Black of the National Union of Women's Suffrage Societies, had acquired extensive experience in trying to improve the lot of women workers over the previous two decades or so. As a consequence they had now become firm advocates of the extension of protective legislation for women.[81] Such feminists explained women's low wages and unemployment not as a result of discriminatory legislation, but because of the lack of training facilities for women and their transience in the workforce. The development of sweating, particularly in those trades which employed large numbers of women, was the critical factor in this change of emphasis among feminists. Organisation among such workers was notoriously difficult and no longer seemed adequate to ending this aspect of women's exploitation. Consequently Clementina Black, and those who thought like her, also became active in organisations like the Anti-Sweating League, and began to work for minimum-wage legislation and similar protective measures.[82] The early years of the century had seen numerous Sweated Industries Exhibitions, but as Mrs. Pankhurst noted in 1908: 'Nothing has come of it all . . . look at the Government. What do you get in the forefront of their programme? You get an eight hour day for miners. But you get nothing for the sweated women.' Miners had the vote, women did not. She concluded:

I think that women, realising the horrible degradation of these workers, the degradation not only to themselves but to all of us, caused by the evil of sweating, ought to be eager to get political freedom, in order that something may be done to get for the sweated woman labourer, some kind of pay that would enable her to live at least a moral and a decent life.[83]

Beyond the specific industrial and professional problems of women, suffragists also explored the issue of women's economic independence. Although they believed that the achievement of independence by single women would be straightforward once they were armed with the vote, the situation of married women gave rise to another set of tensions within suffragist ideas. Mrs. Pankhurst referred to the experience of the married textile workers:

These women say a shilling that they have earned themselves is worth two shillings of their husband's money, for it is their own. They know far better than their husbands how much money is needed for food, how much is needed to be spent on the home. . . . I do not think there is a woman in Lancashire who does not realise that it is better to earn an income of her own than to depend on her husband.

The well-to-do commonly provided nurses for their children, and, she asked, why should not the working-class woman? 'We should like to say this to Mr. John Burns [the cabinet minister who suggested restricting married women's work], that when women get the vote, they will take very much better care of babies than men have been able to do.'[84] Nevertheless, many suffragists subscribed to the belief in the specifically domestic nature of women and its centrality to the well-being of the home, the family, and the state. Their views on married women working, then, were frequently ambivalent. On the one hand they recognised the importance of establishing some degree of economic independence for all women, including the married, but on the other they believed that working mothers often meant ill-kept homes and ill-nurtured children. Thus, while admiring the independence of the married textile workers, Mrs. Pankhurst could also speak of 'the gross injustice of making economic independence impossible to the woman who is giving her time, care and labour to that which is, or should be, most precious to the community – the life and well-being of the children'.[85]

Nonetheless suffragists generally fought the ideas of those reformers associated with women's trade unionism who sought the exclusion of child-bearing women from industry. One such, Emilia Dilke, attacked the feminist position. She insisted that to argue that the Factory Acts

should under no circumstances take account of the differences of sex is to fight against indisputable facts which must, in the end, prove too strong for us. There is no danger to society in the recognising of equal human rights for both sexes, if we are also ready to recognise the divergence of their capabilities, for the relations of men and women to each other, their functions in the family and the state, must ultimately be determined – however ill it may please the most ardent female reformer – by the operation of natural law.

She concluded: 'This principle lies at the bottom of all reasoned Trade Unionism, which, insofar as it is concerned with the organisation of women's work, has for its ultimate object the restoration of as many as possible to their post of honour as queens of the hearth.' Consequently she argued that women's employment should be forbidden where the occupation endangered their child-bearing capacity, and that there should be limitations on work after childbirth.[86] Caroline Osler, a Birmingham suffragist, rejected the idea that the needs of the race required such protection for mothers, adding:

It is noteworthy, however, that the conception of legislative protection never goes beyond restrictions: no one proposes to supplement 'thou shalt not labour' by adding also, 'thou shalt be maintained'. Neither has it yet been proposed to hold an investigation into the habits of life of fathers, with a view to State interference with any outdoor pursuits of theirs which may tend toward physical danger to the race.

In support of working mothers Caroline Osler quoted the report of the Birmingham city medical officer for 1908 which showed that the infant mortality rate was 190 per 1,000 where the mother was working, but 207 per 1,000 where she was not.[87] Suffragists generally interpreted high infant mortality rates as evidence of female poverty rather than inadequate mothering.

In her testimony to the Royal Commission on Divorce in 1912 Helena Swanwick, too, spoke out against the suggestion that married women should be excluded from work outside the home: 'I think the whole difficulty is that we are trying to keep women in the home and making the home intolerable. If you want to keep women in the home you must give them independence.' She thought the existing Factory Act limitations on return to work following childbirth both unfair and unworkable: 'It simply prevents them from working and does not give them any provision. I should like to see some system of maternal insurance. I agree with women being protected most emphatically, but I do not regard the law as protecting them adequately, because it does not give that maintenance.' At present, she argued, women had to evade the law as a

matter of necessity. With a system of maternity insurance it would then
be possible to extend the limitation on the return to work after childbirth. Helena Swanwick insisted that under the existing system 'the very
fact of marriage' made women economically weak, and consequently
she understood why working-class women held on to their jobs when-
ever possible. Asked if she thought it better they should work than remain in the home, she replied: 'I speak as I should feel myself. If I were
a woman of that class I should want to have my own money.'[88] It was
as a consequence of this concern for the economic dependency of married women that suffragists took up the issue of the endowment of
motherhood. There were a number of variations on this scheme, but all
involved some state interference to ensure a minimum financial contribution to married women, either from the husband's pay packet or from
government funds. Mrs. Fawcett made this argument in support of some
such scheme to the Royal Commission on Divorce: 'The position of the
wife in the family would be improved if the economic value of her work
in her household were recognized by giving her a claim, either to a definite sum as wages, or a proportion of her husband's wages during his
life. . . . Their work is essential to the wellbeing of the family and the
State, but it is unrecognized.'[89]

The conditions of motherhood was another issue. Here suffragists attacked on a number of fronts. First, they promoted the concept of voluntary motherhood and women's right to choose the number and tim-
ing of the births of their children. One suffragist, writing in *The Common
Cause*, argued: 'Women are placed in such sex slavery when they marry
that the mistress is safer than the housewife. The wife may be forced to
bear children at the will of another. Could there be a more inconceivable
desecration of all that is divine in us than reluctant motherhood?'[90] The
Royal Commission on Divorce provided eloquent testimony of the distress and anguish suffered by many women through the too-frequent
bearing of children on insufficient financial means.[91] Beyond this, suffragists argued for the rationalisation and mechanisation of housework
in order to release women from some of the worst drudgery of domestic
labour. They explored schemes like cooperative housework. They sought
housing and sanitary reform to protect infant life, improve the environ-
ment of the housewife, and ease her daily work with provisions like
municipal laundries.[92] In such campaigns suffragists challenged the
rhetoric of the separate-spheres ideology by counterposing their own
conception of dignified motherhood against what they saw as the prevailing reality in a male-governed society:

To hear many of the 'Antis' [anti-suffragists] talk, one would imagine that all
the women of this country were sheltered inmates of happy homes, and that if
they were not, it was somehow their own fault. . . . What kind of homes are the
noisome, foul dens in which our sweated women workers drag out a miserable
existence? Homes in which baby faces are white with hunger, baby feet blue

with cold, baby hands set to hard and unfitting toil because the few miserable pence they can earn are necessary for the family exchequer.[93]

Through its focus on such issues the suffrage movement broke away from the viewpoint of earlier feminist campaigns, largely focused as they had been on the discontents of middle-class women. To this extent suffragism represented a democratisation in the concerns of feminists which was also to be reflected in the debates concerning political strategy to be explored in later chapters. All women were affected by matters concerning female sexuality, general economic subordination, and the conditions of motherhood. Any woman was the potential victim of an intemperate or venereally diseased husband. The economic survival of nearly all women depended upon the goodwill of some man. Possible sexual exploitation was the price any woman paid for this goodwill. On the basis of such a shared consciousness of women's wrongs, suffragists were able to build a sense of sexual solidarity among women from varying classes. One of the earliest working-class suffragist organisers, Jessie Craigen, appealed to both a sense of women's shared wrongs and a belief in women's shared natures in her attempt to cross class divisions:

> The great fact that has impressed itself on me tonight is that of the unity of womanhood, in which our claim is made. We are separated by many barriers of caste, creed and education. How vast is the interval which divides the rich lady from the poor mill worker; but these divisions though they are very real, are not deep or high . . . they do not separate the hearts of womanhood that beat in unity. . . . In the name of this common womanhood we are gathered here tonight, rich and poor, educated and untaught, to raise our voices altogether to ask for justice. Our sufferings have much in common. Gentlemen can be bad husbands as well as poor men. The money that should sustain a household can be melted in champagne as well as in beer or whisky. . . . The mother's love also is one. The richest woman here tonight that is the mother of children loves them dearly; the poorest . . . no less. And the laws which wrong the mother's love are an outrage on the common womanhood by the bond of which we have all been drawn together here.[94]

In promoting an analysis of women's social position as that of a sex class, suffragists sought to strengthen such claims of cross-social class identity among women and to make feminism pertinent to women from varying backgrounds. They argued that women as a sex shared a set of interests distinct from men's, that all women stood in a similar relationship to all men. Through the issues they chose to promote, notably those concerned with women's economic subordination and sexual exploitation, suffragists located the basis for a sense of sexual solidarity among women which could help militate against class tensions within the movement. One contemporary commentator noted how, in the course of the suffrage campaigns, women

> acquired a conception of their sex as an aggregate . . . acquired a new sense of solidarity and of power to help themselves . . . were inevitably impressed with

the idea of their community of interests. . . . It meant the realisation by each woman of the fact that she was an individual apart from each man, and it meant also the realisation by all women of the fact that they were a class apart from all men, with common interests different from, and often opposed to, those of the other sex.[95]

By and large the suffrage movement was ideologically homogeneous. A few suffragists like Helena Swanwick, editor of *The Common Cause*, held to a more deliberately rationalistic, humanistic conception of feminism.[96] While upholding the suffragists' analysis of women as a sex class, based as it was upon social-structural factors, such suffragists implicitly rejected much in the essentialist case for women's emancipation. Most, however, appeared unconscious of the potential contradictions between these two forms of feminist argument, and might happily deploy both within a single speech or article. A few suffragists chose to emphasise a single particular source of women's subjection, for example the institution of monogamous marriage. They argued for sexual emancipation and economic independence to create a vanguard of 'free-women'.[97] Yet others argued for female celibacy.[98] There is also discernible from about 1912 a growing antimale stance among some suffragists. The publication of Christabel Pankhurst's account of the extent of venereal disease among men, 'The Great Scourge',[99] was the most explicit statement of this position, and it appears such sentiments were widespread, particularly among the older generation of suffragists in all sections of the movement.[100] Such views promoted a quite clearly separatist inclination among some at least in the leadership of the militant wing of the movement. But issues of ideology were not at the root of the major conflicts and tensions between suffragists. In general, the ideology of suffragism served to counter division among feminists in its creation of a powerful sense of sexual identity and solidarity among women. Those internal dissensions which did arise reflected differences among suffragists concerning questions of organisation, modes of campaigning, political strategy, and the importance of economic class differences in the construction of social inequality.[101] A significant expression of some of these differences was the division of the movement into two wings, the 'constitutionalists' and the 'militants'.

CHAPTER 2

MILITANTS AND
CONSTITUTIONALISTS

Political strategy necessarily became an increasingly pressing issue among suffragists from 1906 onwards as the party-political and parliamentary situation which formed the context of their campaigns grew especially complex. There was now in power a Liberal government, elected on a 'landslide', with a very considerable majority within the House of Commons, and on a programme of extensive reform policies. In the next eight years, among this government's major concerns were to be the introduction of the National Insurance Bill, a protracted and eventually successful struggle with the House of Lords over its veto of Lloyd George's 'People's Budget', and an attempt to introduce Irish home rule. Outside parliament there was a situation of growing labour unrest and, eventually, serious industrial dislocation. As a consequence, the advent of a strong, reforming Liberal government was not to prove the benefit to the cause of votes for women that many had initially expected. Instead the women's-suffrage issue was repeatedly overshadowed by the government's other more pressing concerns, as David Morgan has shown so convincingly.[1]

For suffragists the problem of formulating an effective political strategy was further complicated by the fact that the two major parties in the House of Commons were split among themselves on the issue. Although in general the Liberal Party rank and file was sympathetic to the cause of women's enfranchisement, the party's leadership was seriously divided and contained a number of committed antisuffragists like the future prime minister, Herbert Asquith. Moreover, even among those within the party and the cabinet who supported the principle of sexual equality, there were many, like Lloyd George, who feared *equal* votes for women. This body of Liberal opinion believed such a measure would, in the main, enfranchise the wealthier woman and thus damage their party's interests, for the existing franchise was based on property qualifications. The Conservative Party was similarly split between opponents and supporters. Moreover, those in its ranks who were women's suffragists in general favoured a more limited measure of women's enfranchisement than most Liberal suffragists would have cared to see en-

29

acted.[2] In such ways party loyalties served to divide pro-women's-suffrage opinion within parliament.

Women's suffragists confronted two tasks in relation to the political context outlined here. First, they had to demonstrate the feasibility of getting a measure of women's enfranchisement through the houses of parliament, or at least through the House of Commons. A House of Lords veto could be expected for any but the most limited measure of women's suffrage, but even to get a bill through the lower house would represent a considerable achievement. Because of the splits on the issue within parties it was not possible to organise the necessary majority for a women's-suffrage bill simply on party lines. Cross-party support had to be organised and orchestrated. Then, for such a measure to get beyond its second reading, government support would ultimately be required, and this pointed up the second task confronting women's suffragists. They had not only to convince the Liberal government that the enactment of votes for women was possible, but also that it was as pressing an issue and commanded as extensive support as other questions before the cabinet.

The organisation of the suffrage movement into two wings after 1903 and the formation of a new suffrage body, the Women's Social and Political Union (WSPU), reflected differing responses to these tasks, and to a considerable degree entailed a division of labour in regard to them. The 'militant' activities of the WSPU in general were to be directed at demonstrating the urgency of the votes-for-women demand to the government. Initially, militant organisation centred on exhibitions of popular support. When these failed to make any apparent impact on the Liberal leadership, militant campaigning increasingly focused on threats to public order. In general militant strategy rested upon an aggressive stance in relation to the government of the day (for almost all this period a Liberal government), particularly in the organisation of popular and extraparliamentary pressure. The older body of the National Union of Women's Suffrage Societies (henceforth referred to as the National Union), was dubbed, in contrast, the 'constitutionalist' wing. Its efforts centred rather on developing and demonstrating the strength of pro-suffrage opinion within the House of Commons so as to convince the government of the feasibility of enfranchising women. Nominally, at least, it was neutral towards the governing party, and all other parties, in the House of Commons.

This division of labour was not absolute, of course, for militants also participated in parliamentary lobbying, while constitutionalists played a significant part in the organisation of major demonstrations, processions, and so on intended to illustrate the popularity of their cause. The centrality of parliamentary lobbying and pressure-group tactics was to remain a constant in women's-suffrage agitation, from its commencement in the late 1860s to its successful conclusion in 1918. What was new about the revival in suffrage campaigning which got under way in the 1900s was its growing involvement in popular politics and its increasingly successful attempts to create a mass movement behind the demand. Though this aspect was central to early militant strategy, a concern with the organisation of mass popular support was not limited to this wing of the movement. It was evident within all the major women's-suffrage organisations in the early twentieth century, and their efforts in this regard were arguably the most successful aspect of the campaigns between 1903 and 1912. Initially, constitutionalism and militancy worked harmoniously to achieve both a notable growth of the suffrage organisations themselves and a much broader extension of public interest in the issue. Existing understandings often present the creation of these two wings as indicative of a fundamental split within the suffrage movement from 1903 on, but this is an overly simple view of the relationship between the two bodies of suffragists, at least prior to the end of 1911.

The first purpose of this chapter is to show how, in the initial period after the formation of the WSPU, the two wings were in symbiosis. The efforts of each tended to the strengthening and consolidation of the work of the other. This aspect of their relationship has been lost to view largely because of conventional characterisations of 'militancy' solely in terms of a preparedness to resort to violent direct action. This aspect of WSPU campaigning was indeed to become a major source of discord within the movement from 1909 onwards, and was to make cooperation between the two wings virtually impossible from 1912. But early militancy involved, at most, civil disobedience only. The decision to form the WSPU needs to be understood as much in terms of a challenge to the existing parliamentary tactics pursued by suffragists as in terms of a mode of campaigning. It reflected a desire to pursue a new strategy to secure a hearing for the women's-suffrage demand in the House of Commons, and more especially within the Liberal government. It was these differences in regard to how best to intervene in party politics that to a large extent dictated the WSPU's different style of campaigning. The second purpose of this chapter, then, is to argue the importance of this dimension for understanding the militant–constitutionalist distinction among suffragists.

The long-established societies which formed the constitutional wing of the movement had joined together in 1897 to create the National Union.[3] It was headed by a veteran of the earliest suffrage campaign, Millicent Garrett Fawcett, widow of a former Liberal cabinet minister, Henry Fawcett. Millicent Garrett Fawcett had been closely associated with the women's movement since childhood. Her eldest sister, Elizabeth Garrett Anderson, became the first woman doctor to qualify and practise in England, while a close family friend, Emily Davies, became a pioneer of higher education for women. In 1865, at the age of eighteen, Millicent

Garrett, as she then was, had attended one of John Stuart Mill's election meetings, and she later recorded how it had 'kindled tenfold my enthusiasm for women's suffrage'.[4] In 1868 she became one of the first women to make a public speech on the issue, and thereafter regularly appeared on platforms at suffrage meetings around the country. In the late 1880s, after the death of her husband, she added social-purity campaigning to her public activities, working with the Vigilance Society. Patience, good sense, and a well-developed sense of humour were the characteristics most frequently noted in her by her friends. The significant degree of unity that was maintained within the suffrage movement despite the militant–constitutional controversy was due in large part to her considerable political skills and her open recognition of the militants' achievements on behalf of the suffrage cause. Under her leadership an irreconcilable split between constitutionalists and militants was avoided until 1912, even though the National Union followed a quite different political strategy from that pursued by the WSPU.

The National Union was dominated by women Liberals who put great faith in their party's reforming traditions and who in no way wished to embarrass a Liberal government.[5] They were prepared to play a waiting game, and continued to favour a strategy of political pressure through parliamentary lobbying. Their method was to organise pro-suffrage opinion from all parties in the House of Commons behind the introduction of a private-member women's-suffrage bill. They believed that the demonstration of this kind of support for the principle of votes for women would eventually ensure the introduction of a government measure, or the provision of full facilities by the government for a private member's bill. Hence the National Union gave primacy to securing the election of the maximum number possible of MPs committed to women's suffrage, and to the organisation of pro–women's-suffrage opinion in the House of Commons. Though the WSPU also participated in agitation in support of a succession of private members' bills in the next few years, its leadership had already lost faith in their usefulness as a means of pressuring the government.[6]

National Union election campaigns began with a canvass of all the candidates, and an attempt to extract written commitments to the introduction of women's suffrage. During by-elections, support was offered to the candidate who had demonstrated himself to be 'the best friend' to the cause. The National Union claimed to be non-party, but its policy was most frequently interpreted in favour of the Liberal Party. Though it did on occasion offer electoral support of Conservative and Labour candidates, its election campaigning between 1906 and 1912 more generally favoured the return of the Liberal government's candidates. Constitutional electioneering was still generally restricted to letters to the local press, the occasional public meeting, and possibly some canvassing. If no candidate, or more than one candidate, was found favourable, propaganda work only was undertaken, in the form of publicising the issue in the constituency concerned.

But not all constitutionalists were committed Liberals. Among the founding societies of the National Union there was one body which had given consideration, from the late 1890s, to an alternative party-political tactic, one that was later to inform early WSPU campaigning. The North of England Society, led by Esther Roper, and like the future WSPU based in Manchester, believed that the emergence of the movement for independent labour representation might also be harnessed to the cause of women's suffrage. Esther Roper and her friend and companion Eva Gore Booth were in close touch with women trade unionists in the Manchester area. The women textile workers, especially, were among the most highly organised of working-class women anywhere in the country. As strong unionists they had a clear interest in advancing independent labour representation. As women they had an equally clear interest in ensuring that such representation take cognisance of their needs, as well as their menfolks'. Securing their own enfranchisement would further both ends.

When Esther Roper and Eva Gore Booth began campaigning among these women they revolutionised the nature of suffrage activity in the area. For almost a decade the drawing-room meeting and the garden party were superseded by open-air campaigning, factory-gate meetings, and street-corner speaking. The textile workers collected large petitions which were taken to London and presented to the House of Commons amid considerable publicity. They successfully pressured a local Labour MP, David Shackleton, to take up their cause. Suffragists around the country were impressed with these achievements. Some sent funds to support the textile workers' campaigns; others sought to emulate the success among working women in other areas of the country.[7] Christabel Pankhurst, who was to become the militants' political strategist, first became actively involved in the suffrage movement during these campaigns. Early WSPU activities were to imitate their pattern. Meetings took place outdoors or among the Independent Labour Party (ILP) and trade union branches of the textile towns, and at the fairs which accompanied Wakes Week when the factories closed down.[8] For reasons that are not clear, the textile workers split away from the National Union in 1903 to form a new organisation, the Lancashire and Cheshire Textile and Other Workers Representation Committee (LCTOWRC).[9] It may be that, with a general election in view, they sought a closer alliance with the labour and socialist movements than National Union policy at the time allowed. Despite the formation of their own separate organisation, the textile workers still continued to work closely with the National Union.[10] Though early WSPU political strategy was to have close affinities with their own, the respectable working-class women who made up the LCTOWRC were, in general, hostile to its more sensational mode of campaigning.[11]

The first militant organisation, the WSPU, was founded in 1903 in Manchester by another veteran suffragist, Emmeline Pankhurst, and her daughter Christabel. Emmeline Pankhurst had been active in suffrage campaigns since the beginning of the 1880s. In 1889 she had helped found the Women's Franchise League, a body opposed to the coverture clause in the demand as formulated by the existing suffrage societies (which served to exclude married women from their claim). Together with her lawyer husband, Richard Pankhurst, himself a pioneer of the women's-suffrage cause, she also became active in the ILP in the early 1890s. In 1894 she won a place on the Chorlton Board of Guardians as an ILP candidate. On the death of her husband in 1897 she took up a post as a registrar of births, marriages, and deaths in Manchester. Experience in this work and as a Poor Law guardian reinforced her commitment to social-reform issues and socialist politics. She was to become one of the most forceful and compelling speakers for the suffrage cause.[12] In the earliest years of the twentieth century her eldest daughter, Christabel, was encouraged to take up law studies by Esther Roper, secretary of the North of England Society for Women's Suffrage. Under her influence, too, Christabel became active in the suffrage campaigning among the textile workers of the North-West.[13] Her charismatic style of speaking and leadership was to rival her mother's, and she was to become known throughout the movement simply as 'Christabel'.

The early 1900s also saw the formation of the Labour Party in an alliance of the ILP, trade unions, and the marxist Social Democratic Federation.[14] Its purpose was to secure the independent representation of labour-movement interests in parliament. Emmeline Pankhurst's decision to form the WSPU was prompted by her disquiet with the infant Labour Party's often equivocal attitude to the votes-for-women demand. She originally conceived of the new organization as a ginger group within the socialist and labour movements. At first she intended to call the new body the Women's Representation Committee, to reinforce the analogy its originators wished to make between their cause and that of the Labour Representation Committee (the name by which the future Labour Party was known at this time). On learning from Christabel that the textile workers planned a similar title for the organisation they were forming, it was decided instead that the new body be known as the Women's Social and Political Union.[15]

'Militancy' as a political policy was first put into operation in the WSPU campaigning that preceded the 1906 general election. It comprised an aggressive stance in relation to the Liberal Party, and aimed to secure a commitment to women's suffrage from the leaders of the expected Liberal government. Part of this aggression was realised through the public heckling and harassment of Liberal speakers at major election meetings. It was such an action which led to the first arrest of militants, when millworker Annie Kenney and Christabel Pankhurst were ejected from a Liberal meeting in the Free Trade Hall, Manchester, in October 1905. Their action also secured much-sought-after press coverage for the suffragists' demand.[16] This was the most contentious aspect of WSPU activity at this time, and has since dominated historical accounts of this period in its campaigning. It has variously been taken to represent a new radicalism among British suffragists[17] and the pathological condition of Edwardian society.[18] In such interpretations militancy is viewed above all as a mode of campaigning, and as a frame of mind; its significance in terms of political strategy tends to be disregarded.

Early-twentieth-century suffragists had to respond to two new factors in the party-political scene – the likelihood in the near future of the return of the Liberal Party to office after a long period of Conservative government, and the emergence of an independent Labour Party in the House of Commons.[19] From this time suffragist political strategy necessarily centred on how best to bring the Liberal Party to a commitment to women's suffrage. Suffragists had also to consider whether the Labour Party, which was expected generally to provide parliamentary support for the Liberal government, might also be brought to play an active role in furthering the cause of votes for women. The WSPU drew its initial strength from its ILP affiliations. Its founding members were active in socialist politics as well as in women's-suffrage campaigning. These origins determined in a number of ways the nature of the early militant campaigns. At this time the WSPU concentrated its activities on promoting support for votes for women within socialist and trade union branches in the Manchester area. At this time, too, Emmeline Pankhurst, from her position on the National Administrative Council of the ILP, worked to promote pro-suffrage sentiment more broadly within the socialist and labour movements.[20] In 1906 militants campaigned on behalf of ILP candidates like Keir Hardie during the general election which first saw the Labour Party offer a significant challenge to the Liberal Party's electoral base among working-class voters in industrial constituencies. Initially, then, the militant strategy of attacking the Liberal Party was pursued through the WSPU's affiliations with the labour and socialist movements.

These coloured many constitutionalists' first reactions to militancy. Indeed, militancy was sometimes viewed as a specifically working-class initiative. One of Mrs. Fawcett's correspondents wrote of her fears of militancy as in 'danger of making disunion in our party, and of setting the "ladies" in opposition to the working women'.[21] There was, too, considerable hostility among National Union societies to Christabel Pankhurst's and Annie Kenney's attack on the Liberal leader, Sir Edward Grey, at the Manchester Free Trade Hall meeting in 1905. The London Society decided to move a resolution criticising them at a forthcoming suffragist convention.[22] This society also felt it necessary to suspend one of its local committees from membership when it found the secretary, Dora Montefiore, very sympathetic to militancy.[23] She was also a member of the Social Democratic Federation, and her adherence to militancy could only reinforce the opinion among some suffragists that it represented a distinctly working-class and socialist interest in franchise reform.[24]

Neither militant nor constitutionalist political policies, however, were static, and such issues remained the most constant source of debate and discord within, as well as between, the two wings of the movement. It was to take another six years to secure any radical reformulation of National Union policy, for this required widespread disaffection among Liberal women. The circumstances of this change of constitutionalist policy will be explored in later chapters. In contrast the WSPU's leadership soon became dissatisfied with the Labour Party and retreated from its earlier socialist and labour-movement associations. The consequent modifications of WSPU tactics became evident within only a few months of the Liberal election victory in 1906. This period also saw the shift of WSPU headquarters from Manchester to London.[25] Initial WSPU campaigning after the general election has been concentrated on opposition to the government's candidates in the spate of by-elections that always followed the appointment of a new cabinet at this time. It continued to give support to some ILP candidates in a few of these. But at the end of 1906 this policy was abandoned.[26] Christabel Pankhurst increasingly sought to disassociate the WSPU from Labour politics, and was soon to begin canvassing possible support among Conservative Party leaders.[27] There is some evidence, however, that provincial branches of the WSPU often continued to work closely with their local ILP despite this policy change.[28]

It is not clear what considerations informed Christabel's decision to leave behind the WSPU's early labour and socialist affiliations. In her autobiography, she recorded:

Surveying the London work as I found it, I considered that in one sense it was too exclusively dependent for its demonstrations upon the women of the East End. . . . critical murmurs of 'stage army' were being quite unjustly made by Members of Parliament about the East End contingents, and it was evident that the House of Commons, and even its Labour members, were more impressed by the demonstrations of the feminine bourgeoisie than of the feminine proletariat.[29]

She further argued that political independence had become essential if the WSPU's feminist goals were not to become obscured and the organisation itself seen simply as an appendage of one of the existing parties.[30] Sylvia Pankhurst's account of this time suggests that the Labour Party's increasing commitment to franchise reform only in the form of adult suffrage was also a factor in Christabel's decision.[31] Almost certainly disappointment with the limited strength of the Labour Party in the 1906 parliament, and with the Labour Party's failure to make women's suffrage part of its parliamentary programme, were major considerations in this change of direction in militant policy. But equally important, it would seem that many among the WSPU's more recently acquired supporters from the social elite of London were unsympathetic to labour politics. Their influence was claimed to have secured the exclusion of sellers of *The Woman Worker* from a WSPU meeting in 1908. The women's columnist of *The Labour Leader*, Katharine Bruce Glasier, commented: 'There is growing reason to fear that "the Society Woman's Political Union" would be the honester interpretation of the WS and PU capitals.'[32] Disillusion with the WSPU among working-class suffragists was increasingly evident by this time. Nellie Best of Middlesbrough wrote to *The Woman Worker* that she had heard some WSPU meetings took place in evening dress. She asked: 'Is it intended to debar servants, laundresses, etc?'[33] A Women's Labour League organiser noted the WSPU's ability to raise an increasingly large campaign fund and suggested: 'It is certainly not from or *for* the class the WLL is working for.'[34]

The relations between the women's-suffrage movement and its sympathisers in the socialist and labour movements will be examined further in Chapter 3. It may be that the WSPU's abandonment of its early socialist associations dissipated some of the hostility to militancy already noted among a number of constitutionalists. Whatever was the case, Mrs. Fawcett showed her determination to halt any public dissension among suffragists. In a number of letters to newspapers and journals she offered advice of this kind: 'Let me counsel all friends of women's suffrage not to denounce the flag-waving women who ask questions about women's suffrage at meetings, even at the risk of rough-handling and jeers.'[35] She argued that such demonstrations were proving that women were now in earnest in their demand for the vote, and she was supported in this stand by other prominent members of the National Union. The journalist W. T. Stead wrote: 'I think you are entirely and absolutely right and we should back up our fighting forwards all we can. Already they have done more to compel the insolent average male to recognize that the question is serious and that the women mean business than all we have been able to do hitherto.'[36] Such views were clearly shared by many among the rank-and-file membership of the National Union, for joint membership of the two organisations was commonplace in the early years of militancy. In at least one locality the two wings appear to have become almost indistinguishable in organisational terms. The WSPU's journal *Votes for Women* reported the annual meeting of the National Union's Edinburgh Society thus: 'As most of our members still belong to the National, we thought it best to help them in their meetings in every way we could – advertising, stewarding, etc., etc.'[37]

There were a number of aspects to the symbiotic relationship between

the two wings of the movement during the early years after the formation of the WSPU. Militancy served to awaken public interest in the suffrage issue and rouse passive supporters to more active campaigning.
The constitutionalists readily conceded that their own enormous increase in membership and financial resources after 1906 directly reflected the impact of militancy. Mrs. Fawcett reported to the editor of
Jus Suffragii (the journal of the International Women's Suffrage Alliance)
that following the arrest of WSPU demonstrators in October 1906 'The
newspapers were most extraordinarily violent and abusive, but since
that time there has been a "boom" in women's suffrage. New members
are pouring into the societies, demands for literature come by every post
and cheques and banknotes flow into the treasury.'[38] One of the demonstrators, Annie Cobden Sanderson, daughter of Richard Cobden, was
an old friend of Mrs. Fawcett, and the National Union organised a Savoy
banquet to greet her and the other militants on their release from prison.[39]
But the constitutionalists' long-established skills in educational work on
the one hand, and in parliamentary lobbying on the other, were equally
important in consolidating the advance in public awareness that militancy had secured. In a letter to Mrs. Fawcett, the actress and writer
Elizabeth Robins argued that whereas militancy was required to rouse
public opinion, militants like herself recognised that 'they would stand
a poor chance indeed but for the past influence and present champion-
ship of yourself and others like you.'[40]

Though their political strategy differed and their election policies frequently conflicted, there were numerous instances of cooperation between the two wings of the movement during the early years of militancy. The period 1907–8, for example, saw a number of joint militant-
constitutionalist demonstrations and meetings in provincial centres like
Edinburgh, Manchester, and Leicester.[41] In October 1907 the constitutional and militant leaderships joined with the Women's Cooperative
Guild in efforts to pressure the Labour Party into introducing a wom-
en's-suffrage amendment to the King's Speech.[42] On another occasion
the National Union consulted with the WSPU in the preparation of a
leaflet that explained their differing election policies.[43] Even in by-elections
where militants and constitutionalists were pursuing conflicting policies, friendly relations appear to have been maintained. Isabella Ford, a
socialist suffragist active in the National Union, sent Mrs. Fawcett a report of the South Leeds by-election in February 1908 which indicated the
considerable sympathy many constitutionalists felt for militant policies:

The WSPU behaved splendidly – and there were no rows. I see more and more
their policy is far more workable than ours: but we never clashed. We only did
propaganda work – I longed to 'go for' the Liberal and had to hold myself down.
A man in his party (many Liberal men and women helped the WSPU) told me
Middlebrook had not put us in his address . . . till at the very last moment a
wire from London headquarters came saying 'put the women in your address'.

. . . The Liberal women in some parts of Leeds wouldn't work for their member – because of Asquith's speech – a few canvassed. . . . Mrs. Pankhurst's procession was fine and we cheered and waved as they passed our rooms – and they did too.

On the Liberal victory she added: 'We are so low – he will betray us.'[44]

As this letter indicates, though a few constitutionalists had resented early WSPU attacks on the Liberal Party and disliked its socialist affiliations, others felt frustrated by the unaggressive tenor of much National Union campaigning in relation to the government. Some also would undoubtedly have welcomed an opportunity to combine socialist and suffrage agitation as many militants were able to do. Again, although there were constitutionalists who found distasteful the 'unladylike' behaviour required by much militant activity, others admired the courage and freedom from conventional restraints it represented. The increasingly single-minded dedication to the suffrage cause among militants also appealed to constitutionalists frustrated by what sometimes appeared the divided loyalties of constitutionalist leaders committed also to Liberal Party concerns. It has been suggested that particular to militants were millenarian and sex-war attitudes appealing only to the fiercest of feminists.[45] But these aspects of militancy were not to emerge clearly until the last years of the pre–First World War campaigns and even then were not unknown among constitutionalists. In the early years of WSPU campaigning the militant stance had an appeal which extended far into the ranks of the constitutionalists. It is likely that for many the question of whether to join a militant or constitutionalist society was determined as much by friendship networks and by pre-existing class and party-political affiliations as by degree of feminist commitment or attitudes to unconventional modes of campaigning. The history of the National Union's Glasgow Society would also suggest that many found nothing contradictory about working within both wings of the movement simultaneously, or working within one but offering full moral and material support to the other. Among its leading members Margaret Irwin, Janie Allen, Grace Paterson, Marion Gilchrist, and Mrs. David Grieg were all in complete sympathy with militancy. They frequently appeared at meetings of the WSPU and its breakaway, the Women's Freedom League, and pressed for closer ties between the two wings.[46]

Glasgow suffragists were not unusual in this, and by the summer of 1908 there were hopes that the two wings of the movement might amalgamate. At this time Mrs. Fawcett's niece, Dr. Louisa Garrett Anderson, was working with the WSPU and pressing her aunt on the need for union.[47] Another leading militant, the writer Beatrice Harraden, pointed to the extensive overlap in the membership and insisted it was possible: 'Whether we are so-called suffragists or so-called suffragettes, what does it matter? Hundreds of us are both.'[48] Mrs. Fawcett took such representations for a militant–constitutionalist merger very seriously, but ulti-

Union

mately she felt them to be unrealistic. On one occasion she indicated that the differing election policies of the two organisations would make it impossible. In her autobiographical account of these years, however, she chose to emphasise as the main stumbling block the WSPU's lack of internal democracy, together with the increasing violence of its demonstrations.[49] No doubt all three factors were an element in Mrs. Fawcett's decision not to pursue further a unification of the two wings.

The differing political strategies of the two bodies in some senses determined their contrasting patterns of internal organisation and methods of campaigning, so that militancy and constitutionalism also involved differences in the government and day-to-day administration of the two major suffrage bodies. The National Union had begun as a loose federation of pre-existing societies which retained a significant degree of autonomy.[50] Its central Executive Committee was composed of delegates from the member societies. Initially Executive Committee functions were limited to the coordination of suffragist activity around the country, particularly during election campaigns, and the organisation of suffrage forces in the House of Commons. The Executive Committee's first major role in suffragist agitation was during the preparations for the 1906 general election. As new societies formed, and membership and funds rose rapidly, the role of the executive also grew in importance. Its powers were increasingly extended to cover such activities as the publication of campaign literature and the training and deployment of organisers. The growing level of suffragist activity in the House of Commons from 1906 also increased the scale and intensity of its parliamentary work. As such central organising functions became more complex and extensive, the power of the executive vis-à-vis the local societies expanded.

Policy was debated and democratically determined at twice-yearly council meetings composed of delegates from the societies. Following changes to the constitution these delegates also elected the executive. Nonetheless the growing resources available to the executive put it in an increasingly powerful position with regard to recommending policies and overseeing their operation. This situation was to give rise to recurrent tension between London headquarters and local societies out of sympathy with such policies. By 1910 the number of National Union societies had grown to such an extent – from 31 in 1906 to 207 – that plans were drawn up to federate them on a regional basis. It was hoped this would further improve the coordination of branch activities. But this initiative also clearly represented an attempt by the more influential provincial societies to wrest back some authority from the central executive.[51] The resultant federations were soon invested with the power to run election campaigns in their areas, although along lines laid down by National Union policy.[52] Some also began to train and employ their own organisers. The leadership of these federations was soon to provide the

National Union with a new generation of its central leadership in the critical years between 1912 and 1914.[53] Moreover, it was these provincial constitutionalists who were to lead the campaign for a revision of National Union political policy in favour of the Labour Party. Delegates from the federations met twice yearly at the provincial councils of the National Union in order to keep the executive fully informed of rank-and-file opinion around the country. Though the provincial councils had no power to alter policy, they provided a forum where new ideas were tested out by those societies dissatisfied with existing policy or with its operation by the executive.[54] There were, then, four regularly spaced occasions during the year, at general councils and at provincial councils, when the National Union leadership was brought into direct contact with rank-and-file opinion, and where constitutional policy and practice were examined and analysed.

In contrast, the WSPU had no formal constitution, and its lack of internal democracy was to be a recurring source of dissension in its ranks. The issue came to prominence in 1907 when Teresa Billington Greig, one of the WSPU's earliest organisers, drew up a constitution to be ratified at the WSPU's Annual Meeting. It is not clear what lay behind this initiative, but one contemporary commentator suggested that is was linked to rank-and-file disquiet at the leadership's new policy of seeking to disassociate the WSPU from socialist politics.[55] Previously Teresa Billington Greig had been an organiser for the Independent Labour Party, and her early campaigns in Scotland indicated the close association she felt between her suffragist and her socialist politics. The organisation of WSPU branches in Scotland was largely the result of her efforts, and it is possible that she hoped to use these as a base from which to challenge the now-London-based leadership. Emmeline and Christabel Pankhurst, however, felt that a democratic organisation was entirely inappropriate for the WSPU's kind of campaigning, which, in their view, required military discipline. They were committed instead to a charismatic style of leadership. Emmeline Pankhurst summoned the inner circle of loyal personal supporters who then composed the WSPU executive, cancelled the Annual Meeting, and dismissed the proposed constitution.[56] Dissidents gathered around Teresa Billington Greig and another socialist suffragist, Charlotte Despard. A meeting was organised and the constitution ratified. When this was ignored by the WSPU leadership the dissidents split away to form a new body, the Women's Freedom League (WFL). A significant number of WSPU branches in the provinces affiliated to the new organisation. Though claiming to share the WSPU's disillusion with Labour politicians, the WFL continued to work very closely with local socialist and labour organisations, and was to be found organising on behalf of Labour Party candidates in a number of by-elections which occurred immediately after the split.[57]

Though the WSPU might have been without a democratic constitu-

A Number of Splits

Dissension

tion, its branches must have enjoyed considerable autonomy in the day-to-day organisation of local suffrage activity. Only this would explain how some at least of its major societies retained close links with the local labour movement.[58] The main function required of provincial branches by London headquarters was the provision of large audiences for the succession of barnstorming campaigns around the country regularly undertaken by the London leadership. They were also expected to contribute numbers to the major demonstrations staged by the WSPU, and to raise funds for their own and headquarters' expenses. Activities surrounding events of national significance, like by-elections or the visits of leading Liberals, were directed from London. Organisers were appointed from London but were always responsible for quite large areas, and would move back and forth between various branches in a locality. So in their day-to-day activity local societies generally were self-directed. In contrast, the National Union leadership had to give far greater attention to details of local organisation, for its parliamentary work was dependent on an ability to arouse continuous and persistent pressure from the constituencies. Its recurrent intervention in such matters was not always appreciated by the local societies, and the arrival of an organiser sent by London frequently signalled a period of tension between the local society and headquarters, particularly when the local society was out of sympathy with National Union policy.[59]

Many of the National Union's routine activities centred on pre-existing networks of women's voluntary and political associations. The annual reports of the Nation Union societies, and later the lists of meetings in its journal, *The Common Cause,* record a continual round of meetings organised in cooperation with bodies like the Women's Liberal Associations, the Women's Cooperative Guilds, the British Women's Temperance Associations, adult schools, literary societies, and mothers' meetings. The National Union had firm roots in the more general women's movement and retained them throughout the campaigns. The WSPU failed to develop such links, for they were not relevant to its mode of campaigning. Educational work was the linchpin of constitutional strategy, and the routine activity of the local societies was organised around it. Reading circles were a characteristic of branch life, and by 1913 programmes for them were being drawn up by head office in accordance with decisions at the annual council.[60] The National Union also ran summer schools so that its members might pursue such studies further while receiving training in techniques like public speaking.[61]

A novel departure in campaigning was introduced when a leading figure in the Lake District suffrage societies, Catherine Marshall, instituted 'suffrage stalls' in the local markets to publicise the cause and sell propaganda and educational material. Catherine Marshall came of a well-to-do Cumberland family. She and her mother had been politically active in the Women's Liberal Federation from 1904. Her father was a Harrow housemaster and educationalist, and Catherine herself had taught music and singing as a volunteer in local schools. Throughout a long career in political campaigning she was to show considerable organisational skills. These were put to the full-time service of the suffrage movement when she became acting parliamentary secretary of the National Union in 1911.[62] One of her first achievements was to put the press work of the National Union on an effective basis. Branch societies sent reports concerning their local newspapers which were collated by a newly established Press Department and the results published regularly in *The Common Cause*. Within a year 566 national and provincial papers were being monitored, 70 papers had printed the National Union's 'Review of the Year', and 30 were providing a regular column for National Union reports and other articles.[63] The publication and distribution of campaign literature became such a significant part of constitutional activity that it, too, required the establishment of a separate department in 1912. Meanwhile in some provincial centres other constitutional suffragists imitated Catherine Marshall in organising suffrage stalls at the local markets through which to sell campaign literature and otherwise publicise their demand.[64] Such educational activities played only a minor part in WSPU campaigning.

The contrast in style of the two wings of the movement is further evidenced in the content of their respective journals. Emmeline and Frederick Pethick-Lawrence founded *Votes for Women* in 1907, having recently joined the WSPU leadership. Its content was largely concerned with the doings of this leadership, the arguments for militancy, and attacks on the Liberal government. When a new militant journal, the WFL's *The Vote*, began to appear in 1909 it was similarly very inward-looking. Both papers were essentially campaign bulletins. This was not the case with the National Union's journal, *The Common Cause*, originally established as an independent journal by a group of constitutional suffragists in Manchester in 1909.[65] Its founding editor, Helena Swanwick, came from an artistic and literary family. Her brothers were the successful painters Oswald and Walter Sickert. As a girl she had argued for educational opportunities equal to theirs and had studied political economy and sociology at Cambridge. She had had to go to Dublin to take her degree, for Oxford and Cambridge still refused to grant such academic recognition to women. After her marriage to a Manchester University lecturer she became active in local social work among working-class women. At the same time she was a free-lance journalist, contributing to one of the leading Liberal newspapers of the day, the *Manchester Guardian*. Its editor, C. P. Scott, was a close friend of hers and became her adviser in the management of *The Common Cause*.[66] Helena Swanwick believed the suffrage movement needed 'a paper of wider and more advanced political thinking'[67] and her editorship of *The Common Cause* was to reflect this commitment. Such an orientation was maintained even after its ownership passed to the National Union. Though it carried full reports of National Union activities throughout the country, it remained overwhelmingly educational in intent, and continued to fix the suffrage issue firmly within the wider context of reform politics.

But constitutional agitation was not restricted to these more sedate modes of campaigning for votes for women. The textile workers' campaigns had illustrated to the National Union leadership the value of demonstrations of popular support. It was, in fact, the National Union which held the first major suffrage procession in London, the so-called Mud March in 1907, and similar events were staged in other major cities over the next few years. The National Union's most impressive success in this form of demonstration was undoubtedly the Pilgrimage of 1913, when groups of suffragists set out from the furthest corners of the country, gathering others as they proceeded to march to London for a major rally. The Pilgrimage appears to have made a considerable impression upon both politicians and the national press.[68] Like the militants, the constitutionalists learned from socialist methods of agitation. They began to introduce caravan and cycle tours, so that activists might take the issue to the more outlying areas during their annual holidays. In the cities, street chalking, corner meetings, and street paper selling were all part of constitutionalist activity. Ray Strachey recalled how constitutionalist suffragists

> advocated the cause as they went about their ordinary lives. They lived as they had always lived, among people who knew and laughed at them, and they braved all the conventions by standing up at street corners and in the public parks to address passers-by. They chalked the pavements and sold their newspapers in the streets, they walked in the gutters with sandwich boards, and toiled from house to house canvassing for members, collecting money and advertising meetings.[69]

Helena Swanwick testified to the resolution needed for much of this work, but added: 'Perhaps my most fervent detestation was for the diabolical device which sent us to the polling booths, there to stand all day and collect the signatures of the voters for our Voters Petition.' She recalled how she had not found the work so bad in country and working-class districts, but at one polling station in the business centre of Manchester some male voters had adopted the practice of treating the suffragists as prostitutes touting for business. Being an active member of the National Union could require as much physical heroism, too, as membership of the WSPU. Frequently speakers were mobbed and bombarded with rubbish, often in mistake for militants. Helena Swanwick suffered such a fate in Macclesfield, where, with two other National Union speakers, she was chased from the town by a crowd stirred up by the local Liberals.[70]

Another National Union organiser, Maude Royden, has left a typescript autobiography which provides further evidence of the courage needed to be an active suffragist at this time.[71] The daughter of Sir Thomas Royden, Maude had been educated at Cheltenham Ladies' College and Lady Margaret Hall, Oxford, where she took a degree in modern history. After leaving university she became involved in settlement work in Liverpool, and then in adult education as an Oxford extension lecturer in history and literature.[72] She gave up this post to work full-time for the National Union and became one of its most popular speakers. From 1912 she also took over the editorship of *The Common Cause*, where she continued Helena Swanwick's editorial policy of placing women's suffrage within the wider context of progressive politics. Her settlement work had already caused her to become interested in socialism and to begin the move away from an earlier commitment to Liberal politics. Of her life as a National Union organiser she recalled:

For years I spoke to meetings every day in the week, often including Sunday, and sometimes twice in one day . . . . We all worked at this pitch and were all ready to help each other. . . .
It is a grim business starting an open-air speech when there is no one present but your colleague and a dog. Of course the colleague takes her stand in front of you and assumes an air of passionate interest, but even that does not help greatly.

Full-timers not only spoke but sold newspapers, gave out handbills, and not infrequently had to advertise their own meetings: 'Carrying a sandwich board is a really vile job.'[73] Maude Royden also experienced rough handling from rowdies who attempted to break up some of her meetings during the National Union's Pilgrimage in 1913.

One facet of campaigning in which the WSPU undoubtedly excelled the National Union was in attracting financial support. Emmeline Pethick-Lawrence had introduced a highly successful mode of fund raising by organising large rallies of supporters in London's major halls. Wealthy sympathisers were primed to make particularly generous donations during the rally, and the audience rapidly did its best to follow their example. The National Union was slow to adopt this method, but once it did so it was with equally impressive results. A meeting at the Albert Hall on 23 February 1912 raised £7,000; another in November of that year raised £5,700. Largely as a result of such methods National Union income rose from £21,000 in 1911 to £35,000 in 1912.[74]

In general, then, the two wings of the movement were distinguished by their internal organisation as well as by their differing political policies and styles of campaigning. But as we have seen, such differences did not result in any significant degree of conflict in the early years of the twentieth-century campaigns. Frequent joint membership of the two wings indicated that many suffragists felt their activities to be mutually reinforcing, and that some felt a merger of the two wings to be a realistic possibility. However, neither militancy nor constitutionalism was to remain unchanging in its content. While the underlying strategies of the two wings remained constant, new policies and modes of campaigning were developed in pursuit of them which were to bring increasing conflict and to destroy the earlier mutually advantageous nature of militant and constitutional activity.

A significant new departure first became evident in WSPU tactics in 1908. Alongside her attempts to dissociate the WSPU from its earlier socialist and labour-movement connections, Christabel Pankhurst was exploring an alternative aspect of the organisation of large demonstrations. Previously these had been intended as illustrations of popular support. In the summer of 1908 the WSPU had organised the largest women's-suffrage demonstration ever seen, in Hyde Park. Some estimates put the crowd at half a million persons. The Liberal government remained unimpressed by this massive but peaceable demonstration. It was from this time that militant demonstrations were increasingly organised in terms of threats to public order. It is this aspect of militancy that is still most widely remembered nowadays. At another demonstration a few months later, in October 1908, Christabel Pankhurst attempted to strengthen the force of WSPU demonstrations by linking suffragists' protest with that of the unemployed, whom she asked to join the women in 'rushing' the House of Commons.[75] The adverse attention this attracted no doubt convinced her that any further attempts to link working-class and suffrage protests in threats to public order would soon alienate the WSPU's increasingly important body of support among the influential and the wealthy. In contrast, it was found that the spectacle of hundreds of unthreatening, well-dressed women confronting ranks of batoned and mounted police aroused accusations of Czarism against the Liberal government, without creating any greater sense of insecurity in the community.

From 1908 WSPU tactics were increasingly built around such precisely calculated and limited threats to public order, rather than the demonstration of broad popular support. The latter had proved ineffective as a form of extraparliamentary pressure on the Liberal government, while any association between suffrage and working-class protest threatened to antagonise many among the WSPU's wealthier supporters. Thus, though the central features of militant strategy, an aggressive stance in relation to the Liberal government and the organisation of extraparliamentary pressure upon it, remained constant, the forms and expressions of militancy changed considerably. When militancy had centred on the embarrassment of the Liberal leadership through the demonstration of popular support, it had not been inconsistent with an involvement in working-class protest. But as it increasingly came to turn on carefully calculated and strictly limited threats to public order, so the arguments for dissociating the WSPU from socialist politics further strengthened.

Up until 1908 violence on the part of militant demonstrators was not part of official WSPU tactics, though clearly these were devised with the possibility in view of a strong response from the authorities. The arrest of WSPU demonstrators was actively sought during marches on the House of Commons and when small groups of WSPU supporters undertook the disruption of Liberal public meetings. It was the government's persistent refusal to give the WSPU prisoners political status that first provoked some militants to attack government buildings. They then found that window breaking ensured a quick arrest and a safe escape from any hostility on the part of the crowds that came to view their demonstrations.[76] Once it was an already established practice, window breaking received the endorsement of the leadership. More serious attacks on property began, again spontaneously, as a response to the government's resort to the forcible feeding of hunger-striking militant prisoners in 1909.[77]

Constitutional suffragists' response to militancy changed as its modes of expression involved the increasing use of violence by the demonstrators themselves. Originally militants had only suffered, and perhaps provoked, violence on the part of the authorities and bystanders. Many constitutionalists had been impressed by the bravery required to participate in such agitation. Mrs. Fawcett wrote to Lady Frances Balfour: 'The physical courage of it all is intensely moving. It stirs people as nothing else can. I don't feel it is the right thing and yet the spectacle of so much self-sacrifice moves people who would otherwise sit still and do nothing'.[78] But the developments of 1908–9 began to arouse serious doubts in the minds of constitutionalists. At this time Mrs. Fawcett wrote to an American suffragist: 'I have felt great anxiety and perturbance about the increasing violence of the "militant" societies ever since the 30th June.' She particularly disliked what she viewed as Christabel Pankhurst's misuse of the anger of other disaffected groups. By her account, before the WSPU's recent call on demonstrators to 'rush' the House of Commons handbills had been distributed amongst those she characterised as 'the lowest classes of London roughs and the dangerous hordes of the unemployed'.[79] Yet despite such fears Mrs. Fawcett hesitated to protest publicly against these developments in militant activity, and declined to join the Men's League for Women's Suffrage in a letter of censure. She explained that she was 'disinclined to encourage one set of suffragists to denounce another set' though she foresaw that 'It may be necessary sometime soon to formulate our views on the subject. I feel that law and order are essential to all that makes life worth living and that they are especially and peculiarly vital to women.'[80] To a friend she wrote: 'It seems to me that there is only a slight distinction between their recent actions and positive crime.'[81]

It was actions by the Women's Freedom League that eventually provoked the National Union's leadership to consider publicly dissociating its organisation from militancy late in 1909. They had had serious reservations about the actions the previous year of WFL demonstrators who chained themselves to the Ladies' Gallery of the House of Commons. Other militant 'outrages' from both WSPU and WFL members followed. Finally, during a by-election in Bermondsey in 1909, two Women's Freedom League demonstrators threw acid in a polling booth, slightly injuring two officials. A statement was issued to the press dissociating the National Union from the action, and an embargo was placed on any further joint membership of the two bodies.[82] The National Union had already withdrawn its support from the independent suffrage journal *The Women's Franchise* because its owner refused to exclude Women's Freedom League reports.[83] It was as a consequence of this dispute that *The Common Cause* was established to provide an independent voice for constitutionalist opinion.[84] In 1909 the new journal attacked both militant and government attitudes (forcible feeding had recently begun) in an article entitled 'Outrages, Legal and Illegal'.[85]

But it is clear that among the rank and file of the provincial societies many did not share the leadership's view on this issue. Helena Dowson, of the Nottingham Society, wrote regretting the public stand against militancy, pointing out that many of her members were also militant sympathisers: 'Meanwhile they give their work and money to us and before long, I feel sure, will leave the S & PU altogether. Is it wise to hurry them too much? and for something that is not of vital importance . . . above all the militants are disliking and apologising for their tactics, and by degree leaving the SPU for us.' She pointed out that two of her executive had only recently left the militant organisation.[86] Mrs. Fawcett replied that she was inclined to turn a blind eye to those societies that were ignoring the council's resolution, though she insisted that recent developments in militancy represented more than just a few individuals taking matters into their own hands. She believed the violence was now 'definitely premeditated and arranged beforehand. And the worst of a policy of revolutionary violence is that it is bound to go on and become more and more violent.' She too believed that an increasing number of suffragists would leave the WSPU as a consequence. In the meantime, she commented: 'the ineptitude of the Government is beyond all words. They prosecute the unknown and friendless and release Lady Constance Lytton and Mrs. Brailsford because their relations are influential people.'[87]

The growing division between the two wings of the movement had a disruptive effect on some National Union branches during 1909, notably the London Society. Those who had earlier been working for unity between the two bodies, and who had disagreed with the public condemnation of militancy in 1909, made a final attempt to win the London Society over to the militants' election policy, and to exclude Liberal women from its executive. They were defeated on both counts, and the society decided in future to exact a pledge from all new members to oppose militant tactics and policy. The National Union executive ensured that subsequently it had majority representation on the London Society's executive.[88] Mrs. Fawcett noted the recruitment by the London Society of 293 new members in the three months following these events, compared with 133 resignations, and declared: 'I think there is no doubt that it will very greatly strengthen us to finally get rid of the militants within our gates.'[89]

Such internal tensions within the National Union reflected both continuing sympathy for militancy and growing dissatisfaction with constitutional political policies among some of the membership. The Glasgow Society, for example, had seen a succession of resignations by the militant sympathisers within its leadership.[90] Such dissension within the National Union usually focused on the issue of election policy. But the central Executive Committee continued to resist all efforts to change its election policies, and allegations of undue Liberal Party influence proliferated. This had been one of the main grievances among the pro-militants of the London Society. In two successive years they sought to win over the general meeting of the branch to WSPU election policy. Flora Murray's resolution to the 1907 Annual Meeting called on the executive not to put party interest before the interests of suffrage.[91] When Mrs. Fawcett placed amendments to this resolution, she received a letter of protest from another member, Winifred Ball, outlining her grounds for suspecting undue Liberal bias in the National Union. She cited the use of the National Union's offices earlier in the year for a Women's Liberal Federation meeting, and insisted it was no answer to tell those out of sympathy with the National Union's election work to resign. 'Are those of us who agree with the Society [London Society] and Union [National Union] so far as its constitution and legal activities is concerned but object to its Party bias to resign?' The Women's Liberal Federation meeting had been called by Marie Corbett, wife of a Liberal MP and mother of the National Union's secretary at that time, Marjory Corbett. Winifred Ball concluded: 'I should feel I was not acting fairly in asking anyone save a strong adherent of the Liberal Party to join the London Society.'[92]

In 1909 Ethel Snowden, a socialist suffragist, tackled Mrs. Fawcett on a similar controversy in the Birmingham Society, where she had attended a meeting to protest at the exclusion of women from the audience of one of Asquith's meetings:

The awfully dispiriting thing about it was this. I found that the President of our Society there and some of the members were actually occupying seats on Mr. Asquith's platform.

You will see what this means – party before their own cause. This is what makes disloyal members of the National Union and no wonder.

She suggested it was now necessary that members of the National Union executive resign from their party organisations (she herself was soon to withdraw from active work in the ILP): 'It is no use those of us who belong to another Party declining to help and support it though with much more reason and justification, if Liberal women intend to let us down again and again in this appallingly undignified way.'[93] The Birmingham controversy also brought public protests from two leading Lancashire women Liberals prominent in the National Union, Margaret Ashton and Bertha Mason. Caroline Osler, president of the Birmingham Society, subsequently resigned from her position in the local Women's Liberal Federation.

Thereafter, in 1910, the National Union rules were changed so that National Union officers and Executive Committee members had to pledge themselves to 'put the interests of suffrage before party considerations'. The following year it became necessary for candidates for these positions to provide societies with information on their occupation or special social-work interests and any official position in the political party to which they belonged. This resulted in the resignation of several women active in both Liberal and Labour politics.[94] It is doubtful whether this development significantly weakened the influence of women Liberals within the National Union. Much more important was the increasing disillusion evidenced among such suffragists over the prime minister, Herbert Asquith's, persistent hostility to their cause. Caroline Osler of the Birmingham Society had been joined in her resignation by three other officers of the local women's auxiliary Liberal association shortly after the controversy there, and reports of similar resignations are frequent in the columns of *The Common Cause*.[95]

Constitutional suffragists, anxious to pursue more effective policies yet unprepared to involve themselves in active attacks on a Liberal government, suggested a number of other tactics, notably tax resistance and the running of suffrage candidates in by-elections. National Union leaders remained wary of tax resistance as a national policy, doubting that it could be carried through in sufficient numbers to be effective. They fought the adoption of this policy on a number of occasions while giving tentative support to individual tax resisters. The idea of women's-suffrage parliamentary candidates had been initiated by the textile workers, in Wigan in the general election of 1906. Other suffragist candidates followed – Bertrand Russell in the Wimbledon by-election of 1907, and another textile workers' candidate in Rossendale in 1910.[96] The policy was popular among the rank and file of the National Union, and pressure from below finally overwhelmed the opposition of the leadership when the National Union's council voted to make the running of suffrage candidates official election policy in 1909.

The operation of the new policy in the general election of 1910 was an overall disaster, for the suffrage candidates polled a very insignificant number of votes.[97] It did appear to have worked to good effect in the South Salford by-election shortly after. Here the National Union began an active campaign on behalf of the radical journalist, H. N. Brailsford, who was running as the women's-suffrage candidate. The antisuffragist Liberal candidate, Hilaire Belloc, was soon persuaded to stand down in favour of a pro-suffrage Liberal, Charles Russell. With the adoption of a pro-suffrage Liberal, Brailsford withdrew from the contest.[98] But in general the elections of 1910 revealed the complete inadequacy of National Union election policy. Brailsford, whose wife was a prominent militant, offered the following analysis to readers of *The Common Cause:*

It is true . . . that I have been impressed by the success of the National Union in dealing with private MPs. Your policy is well adapted to secure their adherence as individuals. You can get them to vote pretty steadily year after year for the second reading of a Suffrage Bill, or even to sign memorials in its favour. But there I am afraid the zeal of most of them ends. With some notable exceptions, they do not work resolutely for your Bills, or force the Government to give them a real opportunity of becoming law. And why should they? Your policy leaves them perfectly comfortable so long as they have once performed their duty of going into the right lobby during an academic debate. . . . The root of the matter may be put in a sentence. At present you make candidates suffer for failing to pledge themselves; you have to make members suffer for failing to pass your Bill. In other words, they must be made to suffer for the sins of the Government they support.[99]

Such an analysis further indicated the pressing need by 1910 for a complete review of suffragist political strategy. Not only were existing policies causing dissension and disunity within the movement, they were also failing to produce any sympathetic response from the Liberal government. In fact, hopes for votes for women were being further undermined by the government's increasing commitment to a reform of the franchise on manhood-suffrage lines. In proposing such a reform the Liberal Party expected the support of adult-suffrage opinion, especially that organised within the Labour Party. By this time significant groups of suffragists were actively promoting the adoption of a new political strategy which aimed to unite women's suffrage with socialist and labour-movement campaigning for franchise reform. They argued this would better realise the political potential of the popular support for votes for women which the suffrage organisations had so successfully built up. Supporters of such a strategy were often themselves already combining suffrage activities with their work for the labour and socialist movements. But, as LCTOWRC and early WSPU campaigning had already demonstrated, achieving a conjuncture of feminist and working-class politics was never to be an easy task. Those suffragists who advocated a feminist–labour alliance were continually to be hampered by the mutual suspicions existing between the two movements. They had to attempt to reverse the unsympathetic stand of the Labour Party at this time towards votes for women. They had also to try to moderate the hostility of many women's suffragists to any attempt to broaden their own de-

mand, beyond an equal-franchise law for men and women to a challenge also to the existing property qualifications. Their overall task, then,
was to bring the labour and suffrage movements each to a truly uni-
versalistic, and fully democratic, perspective on franchise reform. Only
in this way could a labour–feminist alliance become a political reality.

CHAPTER 3

ADULT SUFFRAGE OR
WOMEN'S SUFFRAGE?

In Britain in the 1900s the right to vote was based upon the ownership or occupation of property of a minimum value, and it has been estimated that only about 59 percent of adult males had a vote at this time. Alongside this property restriction, which operated along class lines, there was the exclusion of all women by virtue of their sex. Only about a third of the adult population, then, was enfranchised in the early decades of the twentieth century.[1] Women had been continuously campaigning for the removal of the sex disqualification since the introduction of the 1867 Reform Bill. In contrast there had been very little organised demand for the removal of those property qualifications remaining after the passage of the last Reform Act in 1884, or for a change in the registration provisions which also served to disenfranchise many.

The earliest conferences of the Labour Representation Committee (LRC), as the future Labour Party was initially known, had supported resolutions in favour of equal voting rights for women. It had been formed from three distinct and not always harmonious elements: the Independent Labour Party (ILP) with its ideological roots in nonconformist religion and the utopian socialist tradition which had re-emerged with figures like William Morris; the marxist Social Democratic Federation (SDF); and the trade unions.[2] Women's suffrage was one of the issues which were to provoke disagreement among Labour Party supporters. In the 1890s ILPers had given much sympathetic consideration to 'the Woman Question'[3] Though not all ILP leaders were to prove unambiguous in their support of equal votes for women, the party's conferences consistently passed resolutions supporting the removal of the sex disqualification as the most pressing aspect of franchise reform. The ILP view had dominated the LRC's earliest consideration of the issue, but from 1904 LRC support was turned to opposition by leading SDFers and trade unionists who advocated instead the demand for *adult* suffrage. These elements in the Labour Party gave priority to the removal of the property qualifications in the existing franchise laws. They opposed equal votes for women as a purely middle-class demand. For SDFers it was also one which, inasmuch as it fostered sex solidarity among women,

53

threatened the unity of working-class men and women and hence the struggle for socialism. Labour Party advocates of adult suffrage argued, too, that this form of alteration to the franchise was necessary if the new party were successfully to establish an autonomous parliamentary presence. Only with adult suffrage would the new party be able to develop its potential constituency among the industrial working class and build up an election machinery independent of the Liberal Party.

The reformulation of the Labour Party's demand for an extension of the suffrage in terms of adult enfranchisement might appear to have incorporated the call for votes for women, and to have provided a good basis for a feminist–labour alliance. In fact it was to become the root of much suffragist resentment against and suspicion of the labour movement. The formulation 'adult suffrage' remained ambiguous in the context of a property-based franchise. It could connote either universal suffrage with both the property and sex disqualifications removed, or merely the extension of the existing sexually exclusive franchise to all adult males. Women's suffragists believed, with good reason, that the political ambitions of many within the labour movement would be satisfied by a reform limited to manhood suffrage. In the view of socialist suffragist Charlotte Despard, for example, support for adult suffrage was frequently a mask for sexual prejudice among members of the labour and socialist movements. She felt this so strongly that in 1906 she withdrew from her previous involvement with adult-suffrage societies, and thenceforth committed herself to the women's-suffrage campaign.[4]

Universal suffrage at a single stroke was considered an impracticable demand by most women's suffragists, and they suspected that many proponents of 'adult suffrage' shared their assessment of its unrealistic character. If universal suffrage had, then, to be achieved in stages, women's suffragists maintained that the removal of the sex disqualification should be given priority. It was, after all, the only absolute disqualification in existing franchise law. A woman could never become a man, though a child could expect to reach adulthood, a lunatic might become well, and a working-class man might acquire sufficient property to qualify for a place on the electoral register. Women's suffragists felt that the Labour Party's abandonment of its formal support for votes for women in favour of the adult-suffrage demand represented the expression of narrow, sectional interests at the expense of a more fundamental principle. There were, too, some women's suffragists who did not favour political democracy, who opposed adult suffrage in itself, and who promoted the enfranchisement of property-owning women as a bulwark against such trends.[5]

Suffragists' suspicion of, and hostility towards, labour-movement support for adult suffrage had its counterpart in widespread Labour prejudices against the suffragists' demand for equal votes. Labour Party supporters who rejected the priority women's suffragists demanded for their cause did so for a variety of reasons that went beyond a purely sectional interest in transforming the electorate. Some, like the ILP's chairman, Bruce Glasier, were apparently reacting to attitudes among the suffragist leadership which they found incompatible with their own political ideals. Recording a meeting with Christabel and Emmeline Pankhurst, he wrote:

A weary ordeal of chatter about women's suffrage from 10pm to 1.30am – Mrs. and Christabel Pankhurst belabouring me as chairman of the party [the ILP] for its neglect of the question. At last get roused – speak with something like scorn of their miserable individualistic sexism, and virtually tell them that the ILP will not stir a finger more than it has done for all the women suffragists in creation. Really the pair are not seeking democratic freedom, but self-importance. . . . They want to be ladies, not workers, and lack the humility of real heroism.[6]

In the first chapter it was suggested that British socialist thought in this period increasingly disavowed the sexual radicalism of an earlier period. It defended the existing constitution of the family in monogamous marriage as a haven and retreat from the economic ravages of wage labour and capitalism.[7] Such a viewpoint would seem to have informed the attitudes of another ILP leader, James Ramsay MacDonald, towards feminist demands. He expressed particular resentment at suffragists' involvement in attempts to reform family law in ways he would not countenance. When Katharine Bruce Glasier tried to persuade him to moderate his attacks on the suffrage movement, he replied:

In view of what is happening – of the fact, for instance, that our beloved WLL [Women's Labour League] has passed a resolution declaring that when a husband and wife feel they are not getting on so well as they expected and would like a change, they ought to be able to get a divorce – must we not say some plain things in the Labour Party? This development of the Women's Movement and this capturing of our own by prepared resolutions, is a very great menace. By and by we shall not be safe unless we too protect ourselves by wire-pulling and night marches; and it is all very hateful and unclean. If we had but one member in each branch who thought critically we should be perfectly safe. But our people feel and do not think. There is an interesting tussel going on behind the scenes just now. If our matriarchy friends ever succeed they must get babies classified with drains as they see it. So they are at the Local Government Boards to take over Schools for Mothers and Baby Clinics, and not the Education Department. . . . We must try and put things on common sense lines. . . . Keep the WLL straight.[8]

MacDonald's explanation of his antagonism to the suffrage movement indicates also a degree of jealousy concerning the impact the votes-for-women campaign was making on labour-movement women. Sylvia Pankhurst, in her autobiographical account of these years, suggests that the Women's Labour League was established by ILPers to stem the flow of women out of socialist and labour organisations into those of the suffrage movement.[9] Opponents of women's-suffrage resolutions at Labour Party conferences certainly made reference to the attraction of what one termed 'this artificial agitation' for labour-movement women.[10] Ramsay MacDonald recalled that his wife, Margaret, a founding leader of the Women's Labour League, also resented the suffragists' successful attempt to focus interest on one issue of social inequality at the expense of all others. He explained her abandonment of an earlier involvement with suffrage activities as being partly a result of her impatience with the single-mindedness of suffragists. MacDonald also noted the disapproval his wife felt for the manner of many WSPU demonstrations.[11]

As we have already seen, early militant demonstrations were frequently viewed as a working-class initiative, and labour-movement women out of sympathy with militancy particularly resented this association. Mrs. Fawcett's papers contain a letter from Esther Roper in her capacity as secretary of the LCTOWRC that provides evidence of such a reaction even among committed working-class suffragists. Following a WSPU demonstration outside the House of Commons in October 1906, Esther Roper asked that Mrs. Fawcett not repeat her earlier public statements linking the advent of militancy with the entry of working-class women into the movement. She stressed:

Our members in all parts of the country are so outraged at the idea of taking part in such proceedings that everywhere for the first time they are shrinking from public demonstrations. It is not the fact of demonstrations or even violence that is offensive to them, it is being mixed up with and held accountable as a class for educated and upper class women who kick, shriek, bite and spit.[12]

Such resentments could only have been intensified when Christabel Pankhurst decided to abandon the WSPU's existing associations with the ILP at the end of 1906.

Socialists' resistance to the suffrage demand sometimes reflected nothing more than plain misogynist prejudice. Such attitudes can be found in extreme form in the attack made by Belfort Bax, a prominent member of the SDF, in his book *The Fraud of Feminism*.[13] Bax roundly asserted the physical and mental inferiority of women, and took up the claims of a leading member of the medical profession, Sir Almroth Wright, that menstruation and the menopause rendered women periodically mentally unstable and thus unfit to make political decisions.[14] Malcolm Muggeridge has also recalled the attitudes of his father's circle of friends in the South London SDF:

My father, an early socialist, felt in duty bound to be theoretically in favour of Votes for Women, but in private conversation with his cronies treated the subject with a certain derision. I feel sure that he neither hoped nor expected they would get the vote in his lifetime. The same went for his cronies, who were all fellow-socialists, or socialist sympathisers. They were on the whole a very masculine lot, and spoke with scarcely veiled contempt of male supporters of the suffragists like Pethick-Lawrence.[15]

However, the most forceful socialist opposition to the women's-suffrage demand became that organised around the call for adult suffrage, and as the cause of women's enfranchisement grew in prominence in the early years of the century, so it attracted ever more vehement opposition from committed adultists. At successive Labour Party conferences from 1904 adultists defeated the women's-suffrage resolutions by arguing that it would be a 'retrograde step' whose 'tendency would be to increase the power of the propertied classes'.[16] A woman trade unionist, Miss Hope, spoke admiringly of the courage of much of the suffragist campaigning, but insisted that 'they had created a sex antagonism instead of a class antagonism, and it was contrary to the spirit of socialism that that should be so'.[17] Similarly Margaret Bondfield, previously assistant secretary of the Shop Assistants Union, and Mary Macarthur of the National Federation of Women Workers rejected participation in the women's-suffrage campaigns in favour of campaigning with the Adult Suffrage Society, the main body organising the adult-suffrage demand at this time. The Adult Suffrage Society consistently followed the Social Democratic Federation line in opposing women's suffrage as a middle-class demand. At the International Socialist Women's Congress in Stuttgart in 1907, the deep divisions within the British socialist movement regarding women's suffrage were once again evident. The votes of the SDF and Adult Suffrage Society delegates helped defeat the ILP's equal-suffrage amendment to an adult-suffrage resolution.[18]

Socialist support for the women's-suffrage demand was, of course, informed by a very different analysis of the issue from that of the adultist opponents. Socialist suffragists accepted much of the ideology of the suffrage movement concerning women, and their commitment to the women's cause often reflected an optimistic romanticism concerning women's likely impact on political life.[19] Socialist suffragists frequently appealed to essentialist arguments for feminism. They invested womanhood with sex-specific virtues and aptitudes such as nurturance and altruism which they held to be essential both for the furtherance of reform and in the defining of a truly socialist society. To this extent many socialists were echoing the suffragists' demand for the 'feminisation of democracy'. Society could only be reformed with the recognition of female values. Socialist suffragists often also accepted aspects of the feminist analysis of women as a sex class. The ILPer Victor Grayson expressed such a viewpoint when speaking in support of the women's-suffrage resolution at a Labour Party conference. He argued that socialist suffragists recognised 'the degradation of womanhood in England, they knew that in London that night there would be 86,000 women and girls selling body and soul upon the streets. . . . women were economic slaves and needed political freedom to emancipate themselves'.[20]

At the heart of the disagreement between adultists and suffragists was the question of whether economic-class or sex-class subjection was more fundamental in the construction of social inequality. These issues were explored in a public debate in 1907 between the socialist suffragist Teresa Billington Greig (who had helped lead the breakaway from the WSPU to form the Women's Freedom League) and the socialist adultist Margaret Bondfield.[21] The claim that women formed a sex class by virtue of their universal economic and sexual subjection to men led Teresa Billington Greig to argue that the priority adultists gave to extending the working-class franchise represented a deformed version of the democratic principle: 'To base your arguments upon an assumption that by talking about the working class you are talking about democracy is showing a want of universalism in thought as well as in action.'[22] While only some men were denied the franchise, women's exclusion was total, and their claims ought to be pre-eminent in any truly democratic demand: 'Be the franchise [as] stupid as you like, it is good enough for men to vote under. If it is not illogical for men and undemocratic for men to use this stupid franchise, then it is not for us to use it.'[23] Teresa Billington Greig insisted that women had interests particular to their sex and distinct from the interests of men: 'The quicker you give women the power to care for women's interests, the quicker all women will have redress.'[24]

In reply Margaret Bondfield argued that the equality to be secured through votes for women on the existing property basis 'would only be nominal, theoretic, academic if you like, but not a real equality'[25] because it ignored the economic inequalities between women of different classes: 'Mrs. Billington Greig spoke as though she could count on all women being united. That is an entirely erroneous view to take of the women of the present day. . . . I protest against the striking of the sex-note every time.'[26] Margaret Bondfield acknowledged the danger presented by the possibility of a manhood-suffrage bill but insisted, for her part, she would resist any such measure as adamantly as she did the suffragists' equally limited demands. The only way forward was to work for a universal-suffrage measure which would enfranchise all men and all women.

Nonetheless the fact remained that many in the adultist ranks did not share such a strong commitment to the principle of universal suffrage and exhibited none of the universal suffragists' concern for issues of sexual equality. Moreover, socialist suffragists like Keir Hardie argued that universal suffrage was not yet practical politics: 'If the workers were prepared to lay every other reform on the shelf, and begin an agitation for adult suffrage [by which he meant universal suffrage] they might, if specially fortunate, be successful and get it about the year 1929.'[27] His estimate proved well judged, for universal suffrage was not to be enacted in Britain until 1928. Hardie argued that while manhood suffrage could probably be secured at once and for the asking, the complete enfranchisement of all men and all women in one reform would be bitterly resisted by both the major parties. For pragmatic reasons, then, it was necessary that socialists make a choice whether to work for adult suffrage in the form of a manhood franchise, or on an equal-votes-for-women measure. To work for adult suffrage on the existing basis of the franchise was to ignore women's claims to sexual equality. Socialist suffragists also believed they could demonstrate that the large majority of voters under an equal-votes bill would be working women.[28]

Yet between 1904 and 1909 the adultists succeeded in repeatedly defeating women's-suffrage resolutions at Labour Party conferences. Such opposition to the principle of sexual equality at one point provoked Keir Hardie's threatened resignation as chairman of the Parliamentary Labour Party. Eva Gore Booth also expressed resentment at the adultist challenge to the equal-votes demand on behalf of the women textile workers. She did so despite the LCTOWRC's formulation of their demand in terms of *full womanhood* suffrage, which on the surface would seem to ally the textile workers with the adultists:

It is no exaggeration to say that among the more progressive workers there has grown up a deep feeling of bitterness and disappointment, a feeling which culminated this year when the Labour Party, led away by a theoretical inclination for the very stale red herring of immediate and entire adult suffrage, refused to fulfil their written pledge and press forward a measure for the enfranchisement of women. . . . Their position is absolutely indefensible. They have built up the whole of the Labour Party on what they are pleased to call a property qualification, a qualification that, according to their own often repeated statement, no democratic person could accept or even compromise with as a temporary instalment of justice. . . . In fact they have eaten their cake and enjoyed and digested it; it is only when a hungry beggar asks for a slice that they find out that it is poisonous.[29]

When adultists interrupted a demonstration by the West of Scotland Men's League for Women's Suffrage with the cries of 'blacklegs' and 'traitors', one suffragist was prompted to ask: 'Is there then in the male sex a kind of instinctive trade unionism?'[30] Adultist insensitivity to women's claims for sexual equality could only lend further credence to suffragists' analysis of women's social position as that of a sex class, and their argument that women of all economic classes needed to unite in order to secure the representation of women as a distinct interest group vis-à-vis all men. Some such conviction was expressed by a former women's trade union organiser, Ada Nield Chew. She wrote to *The Common Cause* to explain why she had turned her activities to suffrage campaigning:

I have not changed my opinion as to the immediate value and wisdom of trade unionism for women workers, but it has been forced on my consciousness more and more that whilst women are at a political disadvantage trade unionism is necessarily limited (which does not detract from the value of trade unionism, but emphasises the importance of the vote). But I could not see that anything less than Adult Suffrage would be of any use to the working woman, and therefore opposed a limited measure as being reactionary. Now, after many months of anxious thinking, I have come to the conclusion that we cannot get on at all whilst women have no means of even presenting their point of view, and that we shall be at a standstill till this necessary 'first step' is taken; and that to be determined to wait until all women can vote is as reactionary and as impracticable as to oppose all reform because it does not go as far on our way as we wish it to go.[31]

Nonetheless, though most socialist supporters of an equal-votes measure accepted the suffragist analysis of women as a sex class, many felt uneasy within the largely middle-class suffrage societies. The expense of membership, the middle-class ambience of the garden-party and drawing-room meeting, and the political conservatism of some leading suffragists must all have played a part in such unease.[32] In the period between 1906 and 1912, then, many working-class suffragists found themselves torn 'between a socialist movement which denied feminism, and a feminist movement which dismissed socialism'.[33] Involvement in either entailed minimising respectively their sense of sexual and of class oppression. Organisations like the LCTOWRC and the Women's Cooperative Guild were founded on just such a consciousness. The Women's Cooperative Guild's general secretary expressed the problem thus: 'From my general experience I have found that, so long as there is class and sex inequality, it is necessary that working women should have their own separate and affiliated organisations.'[34] From such bases working-class feminists were to work both to democratise the women's suffrage demand and to bring the labour and socialist movements to a firm commitment to the principle of sexual equality in political rights. In the context of the women's-suffrage campaigns between 1906 and 1912 this entailed an attempt to unite the adult-suffrage and women's-suffrage demands.

A major initiative towards this end was undertaken by the Women's Cooperative Guild (WCG) in 1907. By this time the WCG had been actively campaigning for women's suffrage for over a decade.[35] It had participated in the collection of the textile workers' petitions around the turn of the century, and had taken part in the campaign behind the private-member women's-suffrage bill introduced in 1905.[36] At its 1905 conference an adultist resolution was passed, but a manifesto issued at the same time made it clear that the Guild's support for women's suffrage had not been tempered in any way: 'While womanhood [and therefore adult] suffrage is their goal, the Guild leaves itself free to support any measure which would be a step in the direction of this goal.' The Guild continued to participate in activities organised by the suffrage societies.[37] However, the vote on equal terms with men would have enfranchised mostly widows and spinsters among the working class. The WCG's membership was composed largely of married working-class women, few of whom could have qualified for the franchise on the basis of an independent occupation or ownership of property. In recognition of this hindrance to her members' full-hearted support for women's suffrage, the Guild's president, Margaret Llewelyn Davies, initiated a campaign to change the nature of the private-member suffrage bills which were now regularly being introduced in parliament. She sought the inclusion of a provision for the enfranchisement of married women on their husbands' property qualification. This formulation had first been suggested at the Labour Party's Annual Conference in 1904.[38] It is not clear why the Guild took such an initiative at this particular time, although it did coincide with the beginning of the breach between the WSPU and the Labour Party and the potential for yet further disillusion with women's suffrage among working-class women. The WSPU, like the National Union, now formulated its demand in terms of an equal-votes measure, and some of its spokeswomen who had earlier shown explicit sympathy with the adult-suffrage cause had now departed from the organisation or changed their position.[39] It would appear that the Guild leadership believed a fresh attempt was now required to link the women's-suffrage and adult-suffrage demands, and that this might best be achieved by broadening the basis of the women's-suffrage bills.

The WCG's broader formulation of a women's-suffrage measure was introduced by W. H. Dickinson in 1907, and from the beginning it met resistance from the suffrage organisations. A National Union spokeswoman insisted: 'The franchise law does not distinguish between married and unmarried men, and it must not do so between married and unmarried women.' Such opposition was linked to suffragist suspicion of adultist demands. It was suggested that the best course for the Guild to follow would be to secure an amendment to a more limited bill, if and when it reached committee stage, rather than undermine the formulation of the demand according to the principle of sexual equality.[40] The class-antagonistic nature of some suffragist attacks on the Dickinson bill must have disturbed many working-class suffragists. Typical was such a comment as this: 'There are many of us who, while fully recognising that a socialistic tendency in Government is necessary to the betterment of the working classes, are yet strongly opposed to a state socialism as shown in the programme of the ILP, the SDF, etc.' This suffragist opponent argued that Dickinson's bill would increase the danger of the socialist vote. The franchise, in her view, should first be extended to the educated women, then the 'better class' of working women, and finally 'it may become general'.[41] Similarly another suffragist argued against the bill as 'the worst form of class legislation, in no way redeemed by benevolent intention'. She insisted that 'with every increase of the electorate the individual voter becomes of less obvious account. . . . we have little warrant for believing that adult suffrage . . . would be an improvement'.[42] Even those suffragists who were sympathetic to adult suffrage frequently opposed the bill on the grounds that it was bad tactics. One

such, Marion Holmes, argued: ' "Half a loaf is better than no bread."
The women of this country are in the position of political starvation at
the present time.'[43]

Such attacks created considerable resentment among the women of
the WCG. Rosalind Nash pointed to working-class women's willingness
to compromise with the equal-votes demand: 'No genuine suffragist
wished to create difficulties, and the Guild deferred to the prejudices
against asking for adult suffrage so far as to state the claim in a form
suitable to a limited bill.'[44] Margaret Llewelyn Davies demanded: 'Is it
not time, too, that we should agree to cease the parrot cry of "Traitor"
against any one who dares to speak of adult suffrage? . . . Women should
leave out no women from their demand for citizenship. The excluding
can quite safely be left to the men.'[45] The Dickinson bill met the usual
fate of women's-suffrage bills – a satisfactory majority in the House of
Commons, but a refusal by the government to allow it any further facilities – and thereafter private-member bills reverted to the more limited
form of votes for women on the same basis as the male franchise.

The WCG's attempt to broaden the suffrage demand and unite the
women's-suffrage and adult-suffrage forces had failed. It had been hin-
dered by some women's suffragists' antagonism to the adult-suffrage
demand, and by the WSPU's increasing hostility to the Labour Party. Its
failure only lent credibility to the adultist contention that votes for women
was a middle-class demand that ran counter to the interests of the labour
and socialist movements. As a consequence the issue remained controversial within the Labour Party. At its Annual Conference in January
1908 the ILP's women's-suffrage solution was once again defeated by
the adultists. The ILP paper, *The Labour Leader*, commented: 'The [La-
bour] Party is not hostile to women's suffrage, but only to the present
mode of obtaining it – the only immediately practical mode.' It reiterated
Eva Gore Booth's argument that adultists opposed the limited bill on the
grounds that it was based on a property qualification, 'regardless of the
fact that no man present had any other kind of vote'.[46]

The WCG did not renew its attempts to broaden the formulation of
the demand for votes for women, for in 1908 there became evident an
even more pressing threat both to the interests of its membership of
married working-class women and to its hopes for uniting adultists and
women's suffragists. This threat lay in the increased likelihood of a government manhood-suffrage measure in the not-too-distant future. In
February 1908 Herbert Asquith, the newly appointed antisuffragist leader
of the Liberal government, announced his commitment to the introduction of such a measure. This served to stimulate further the organisation
of adult-suffrage forces and the Social Democratic Federation called a
conference on the payment of MPs, the payment of election expenses,
proportional representation, and adult suffrage (the Independent Labour Party refused to attend, as women's-suffrage amendments were

not to be in order at the conference). All the women's-suffrage organisations were incensed by Asquith's announcement of a manhood-suffrage bill, seeing it as an attempt to block the advance of their own cause. They were similarly angered when, shortly afterwards, a number of women-suffragist MPs who were also adultists sought to assess the support which universal suffrage might command by introducing a private-member bill for full adult suffrage.[47] The bill was passed by a majority, though smaller than that for earlier women's-suffrage bills, so that suffragists might claim that a universal franchise was less popular with the House than votes for women. The bill then lapsed for lack of government support. It had been introduced without prior consultation with the suffrage organisations, and suffragists' suspicions of such manoeuvres now extended to a new adultist organisation promoted by a number of labour-movement women.

With Asquith's promise of a manhood-franchise bill, women adultists had confronted the very real possibility, always predicted by women's suffragists, that adultist opinion would not hold firm for a universal franchise. Some new initiative was clearly essential to strengthen the commitment of the adultist forces to sexual equality. Women trade unionists joined together with women from the WCG to sponsor the formation of a new adultist organisation, the People's Suffrage Federation (PSF). Its founders included Margaret Llewelyn Davies, Margaret Bondfield, and Mary Macarthur, as well as most of the Parliamentary Labour Party and many Liberal Party adultists. Its demand was for full adult suffrage regardless of sex on a three-month residential qualification. It sought to unite women's suffragists and adultists by ensuring that the enfranchisement of women form an integral part of any forthcoming franchise reform. The PSF described its own origins thus:

It was the outcome of a strong belief on the part of the promoters that the enfranchisement of women – being a part of the movement towards a truly representative and democratic government – could best be carried through in alliance with the progressive forces in politics – and could only be realised in a really effective manner by the reform of the franchise in the sense of ADULT SUFFRAGE.[48]

The leading role of the WCG's general secretary in the formation of the PSF did not reflect any lessening of the Guild's commitment to women's suffrage. Its annual report insisted: 'It should be understood that no opposition would be offered to a smaller suffrage measure if it became practical politics.'[49] Despite the defeat of its attempts to broaden the women's-suffrage demand in 1906–7 the Guild had continued to participate in major suffrage demonstrations and to issue suffrage pamphlets.[50] This remained the case even after the formation of the PSF.[51] But it is evident that this same period had seen a waning of interest in the issue among the rank and file of the Guild's membership, largely because of the increasingly violent nature of much militant activity.[52] Guild affiliation to the PSF represented both its leadership's conviction that the announcement of a future manhood-suffrage bill necessitated fighting for women's suffrage within a wider demand for universal suffrage, and an attempt to revitalise rank-and-file interest in the issue of franchise reform.

Response to the formation of the PSF from women's suffragists was not uniformly negative, but even the more sympathetic among them expressed only cautious interest. The WSPU leadership's reaction was forthrightly hostile: 'Those who are anxious to obtain votes for women at the earliest possible date will have nothing to do with the new Suffrage Federation. The record of Adult Suffragists in the past . . . is such that not only does it not inspire confidence, but that it actually inspires suspicion.'[53] *The Common Cause*'s response was more moderate. Nonetheless it indicated the complex issues that remained to be clarified between universal and women's suffragists. It argued that women's suffragists should be able to work with the universalists on the government's proposed bill, provided that it was clear the PSF would not in the meantime oppose more limited bills, or support the passage of a purely manhood-suffrage bill.[54] Less conciliatory was the attitude of Mrs. Fawcett, the president of the National Union. She refused to receive a deputation from the PSF, and insisted:

I do not believe there is much genuine demand for universal suffrage. I certainly have not met with it when I have been about the country speaking. . . . In any case our position is clear. We have nothing to do, and can have nothing to do, with a general alteration of the franchise as it affects men. . . . Any change in the direction of adult manhood suffrage would make our task infinitely more difficult of attainment.[55]

Nonetheless the formation of a new adult-suffrage organisation expressly sympathetic to sexual equality did find some support among constitutionalist suffragists. The reception of a PSF deputation had been suggested by the National Union's secretary at that time, Marion Phillips. Marion Phillips was closely associated with the labour and socialist movements through both the Women's Labour League and the Women's Trade Union League. Shortly after this she resigned from her post with the National Union, and her own commitment to adult suffrage was almost certainly a factor in her resignation.[56] Other women's-suffrage sympathisers, like Bertrand Russell, resigned from the National Union at this time because of the leadership's unbending attitudes toward adultist opinion.[57] PSF founders had hoped to bring together women's suffragists, their sympathisers in the labour and socialist movements, and committed universal suffragists behind a single campaign to secure the abolition of both property and sex qualifications for the vote. The resignation of figures like Marion Phillips and Bertrand Russell from the

National Union indicated that there was indeed a current within the women's-suffragist movement favourable to such a solution.

In a letter to *The Common Cause*, Margaret Llewelyn Davies sought to rally this body of opinion among those she identified as 'democratic suffragists':

> Those who have initiated this joint movement of men and women believe that the effective political strength and the fighting force of the women's suffrage movement will be greatly strengthened by showing that it is in harmony with democratic sentiment. . . . To combine the splendid uprising of women against their subordinate position with the democratic demand that the suffrage should be placed on a human and not a property basis is the way to secure the passing of a great Reform Bill. . . . There is no reason why democratic suffragists should not welcome the Federation and join it as well as their own special women's societies. . . . The only practical course for women is to work along the lines of least resistance, and let our demand be for a measure in keeping with democratic principle.[58]

On another occasion she insisted that suffragists must take heed of the Liberal and Labour parties' shared conviction of the need for a democratic franchise:

> The real danger lies in a refusal to demand an extended franchise for women. . . . The PSF is not just playing men's games with blindfolded eyes. If its women members want manhood as well as womanhood suffrage, they strengthen their demand for the vote for themselves, because the argument for Adult Suffrage is comprehensive and inspiring.[59]

Issues of class inequality had become the major threat to that sense of sexual solidarity to which women's suffragists increasingly sought to appeal by the turn of the century. In identifying and attempting to rally what she recognised as the democratic current within the movement Margaret Llewelyn Davies sought to remove this growing source of disunity. Her appeal for a democratic-suffragist initiative highlighted both the increasing radicalism of many middle-class Liberal suffragists and the new opportunity for joint Labour–suffrage campaigning offered by the promise of a forthcoming government-backed Reform Bill. There were good grounds for believing that there was within the suffrage movement a significant strand of opinion which would welcome greater opportunities for cooperation with the labour and socialist movement. Many women's suffragists were socialists or progressive Liberals who believed in the principle of universal suffrage. They concentrated their efforts on the issue of sexual equality only because of the danger of a manhood-suffrage bill, which many estimated would set back the women's cause for at least another generation. One democratic suffragist, Helena Swanwick, recalled the frustration she felt with this situation. For her, feminism was but a partial expression of her broader humanist perspectives.[60] She explained how she decided on the title of the National Union's journal in these terms: 'I chose the name *The Common Cause* to indicate my conviction that women's cause was men's, but also because I was frankly sick of "Woman this" and "Woman that".'[61] In its early issues the paper's cover bore a group made up of man, woman, and child to give further expression to such views.

Other evidence of a democratic-suffragist impulse had already been offered in the textile workers' campaigns and the formulation of their demand in terms of *womanhood* suffrage (though they did, in practice, stay closer to the position of the suffrage societies than to that of the adultists of the PSF). The early years of militant organising had already illustrated the very real possibilities for labour–suffrage cooperation. Between 1907 and 1913 those among the militants whom Margaret Llewelyn Davies would undoubtedly have identified as democratic suffragists were increasingly excluded from WSPU policymaking. They left to form dissident militant organisations like the Women's Freedom League, the East London Federation of Suffragettes, and the United Suffragists. Though their campaigns have been little researched, they too must be reckoned as significant expressions of democratic suffragism. But beyond these still-little-explored expressions of democratic suffragism, there was a further possible source of support for a labour–suffrage alliance at this time among many of the constitutionalists of the National Union. It is probable that Margaret Llewelyn Davies was aiming her appeal especially at this section of suffrage opinion, for the WCG had always worked most closely with the National Union. In the preceding two years Newcastle, Manchester, and Edinburgh constitutionalists had begun to press for a revision of National Union election policy in favour of the Labour Party. They argued that such an initiative would serve to strengthen the case of those within the socialist and labour movements who sought to uphold the principle of sexual equality.

Material on the Newcastle Society of the National Union is scant. What does exist makes it clear that in this locality there was a quite determined effort to join rank-and-file socialists and suffragists in a united campaign for sexual equality and independent labour representation. The Newcastle Society was led by Dr. Ethel Bentham and Dr. Ethel Williams. Ethel Bentham was a Fabian and a leading member of the Women's Labour League, and Ethel Williams headed the local Women's Liberal Federation. From 1907 the Newcastle Society consistently worked in close association with the local labour movement. In that year it decided to support the Labour candidate, Pete Curran, in the Jarrow by-election. In so doing it ignored the National Union executive's decision that the Liberal and Labour candidates were equally 'good friends' to the suffrage cause, and that consequently only propaganda work need be undertaken. *The Labour Leader* recorded that 'the movement has deep reason to be grateful to the woman suffragists for their help in canvassing and lending motor cars'.[62] Joint labour–suffrage organisation was again evident during a local strike in early 1908.[63] In the same year, during the Newcastle by-election, the local ILP chose to work with the suffragists rather than support the SDF candidate, who refused to promise opposition to any future franchise reform restricted to manhood suffrage.[64] Open-air and works meetings were a routine part of the society's activities,[65] and were reminiscent of the work of the North of England Society around the turn of the century.

It was the Newcastle Society that led the movement within the National Union for a change of election policy in favour of the Labour Party. Ethel Bentham first put a tentatively worded resolution to a provincial council meeting in 1907: 'In the event of one political party distinguishing itself from the others by officially adopting as one of its principal objects the immediate abolition of the sex disqualification, in parliamentary elections the NUWSS would give active electoral support in by-elections to candidates belonging to that party.'[66] It embodied a veiled reference to the efforts of those suffragists in the labour and socialist movements who were seeking to bring the Labour Party to a more supportive stand on the women's-suffrage issue. The resolution met with firm resistance from the National Union leadership, but at the following council meeting the Newcastle Society did win permission to explore the possibility of running a joint Labour–suffrage candidate in the South Shields constituency.[67] With the support of the Manchester and Edinburgh societies it continued to press for a general revision of the National Union's election policies in favour of the Labour Party, and was eventually to meet with success, in 1912.[68]

The Manchester Society had revived its earlier popular style of campaigning with the arrival in 1908 of a new secretary, Kathleen Courtney, and a new organiser, Margaret Robertson. Both were university women, but with an evident sympathy for working-class politics. Once again open-air speaking and factory-gate meetings became a regular part of the work of the society, while a one-penny subscription was introduced to open up the membership to less-wealthy women.[69] Helena Swanwick, who was closely involved with the work of the Manchester Society at this time, recalled: 'The encouragement we got from the poor and the inarticulate was best of all. Said one, "What you bin sayin', Ah bin thinkin' long enough, but Ah never getten t'words reet." '[70]

There is no direct evidence of labour–suffrage campaigning this early in either Manchester or Edinburgh (where even fewer records of the National Union's branch society survive), but these societies' sympathy with such a policy can be inferred from their support of the Newcastle Society proposals at National Union councils, from their subsequent involvement in Labour election activity in the 1910–11 period, and from their commitment to the Election Fighting Fund policy from 1912. The organisation of working-class support was the main emphasis in the Manchester Society's campaign behind a women's candidate in the South

Salford by-election of 1910, for example.[71] In the Kirkdale by-election of 1910 Lancashire suffragists again worked for the Labour candidate, and in the Middleton by-election of 1911 they were helped by local socialists to run a propaganda campaign. Moreover many socialists decided to abstain from voting in this election when neither the Liberal nor the Conservative candidate would pledge full support for the women's-suffrage bill then before parliament.[72] Similar suffrage–labour cooperation was evident in Scotland in the Kilmarnock Burghs by-election of 1911. Here the Edinburgh Society's organiser, Alice Crompton, helped run the campaign for the Labour candidate, Thomas McKerrell.[73] She was assisted by the Newcastle Society's organiser, Clementina Gordon, and her sister, Lisa Gordon, an active member of the Edinburgh Society. Both were to be prominent in labour–suffrage campaigning between 1912 and 1914.

This pro–Labour alliance strand of opinion within the National Union was organised by a younger generation of its middle-class leadership, whose bases at this time were still in the provincial societies. Between 1909 and 1912 however they moved rapidly into prominence in the national leadership. Kathleen Courtney became National Union secretary in 1910. Helena Swanwick became the founding editor of the national Union's journal *The Common Cause*, which began publication in 1909. She, together with other prominent members of the Manchester, Newcastle, and Edinburgh societies like Margaret Ashton, Ethel Bentham, and Elsie Inglis, was elected onto the National Union's Executive Committee during this period. Many were beginning their move away from earlier Liberal Party commitment to involvement in the Labour Party. They found sympathisers among those socialists and socialist sympathisers, like Maude Royden, Isabella O. Ford, and Ethel Snowden, already established in the National Union leadership as speakers or members of the executive. Catherine Marshall, who became acting parliamentary secretary in 1911, was to prove yet another firm proponent of the new policy. Further support was to come from the National Union's increasing numbers of working-class organisers in the provinces, women like Ada Nield Chew, Selina Cooper, Margaret Aldersley, all of whom possessed considerable experience of labour-movement organisation. The labour–suffrage alliance advocated by the democratic suffragists of the National Union was eventually to be realised in the establishment of the Election Fighting Fund in 1912. Through the work of this fund women's suffragists became deeply involved not only in campaigning for Labour candidates, but also in helping to build an independent election machinery with which the Labour Party might better challenge the Liberals.

A more general acceptance of this new direction in suffragist political strategy followed from two developments. First, there was the ever-growing disillusion with the Liberal government among the Liberal women who formed the backbone of National Union branch life. Secondly, the mutual suspicions between the old guard of the National Union leadership, especially Millicent Fawcett, and prominent Labour politicians, like Ramsay MacDonald, began to dissipate. Labour Party support for votes for women had generally become less and less equivocal as the likelihood of a government-backed manhood-suffrage measure grew. At last those earlier efforts of labour-movement women to secure Labour Party adherence to the principles of class *and* sexual equality began to bear fruit. The immediate context of Liberal women's growing disillusion with their government and the rapprochement between Labour and suffragist leaders were the 1910–11 campaigns behind what were known as the Conciliation Bills. It was the ultimate failure of these bills after significant initial successes that drove women's suffragists in both wings of the movement to reconsider their political policies. Their fate demonstrated the intensification of the political complexities surrounding any attempt at franchise reform during this period, complexities that were even to defeat the government's own plans for a manhood-suffrage bill.

David Morgan has provided a detailed analysis of these complicating factors, and interpreted their impact as bringing about the failure of the women's-suffrage campaigns prior to the First World War.[74] Such an assessment underestimates the considerable achievement the Conciliation Bill campaigns represented and suffragists' subsequent success in turning such apparent failure to good effect. For though none of these bills was ever enacted, they were to prove the most successful women's-suffrage measures ever introduced into the House of Commons. The pressure they exerted on the Liberal cabinet forced some among it, notably Lloyd George, for the first time to give consideration to how the demand for women's enfranchisement might be enacted, and precipitated the government's introduction of its own manhood-suffrage Reform Bill. It was this advance for the cause of franchise reform that was to prepare the way for an effective suffrage–labour alliance, and it was this alliance that ensured the inclusion of women in any future Reform Bill.

The Conciliation Bills were so named because they were drawn up by the Conciliation Committee, a committee of MPs representing all shades of suffrage opinion in the House of Commons. Its chairman was the Conservative the Earl of Lytton, brother of Lady Constance Lytton, a leading member of the WSPU who had recently endured imprisonment and forcible feeding after posing as a working-class militant. Its secretary was the radical journalist H. N. Brailsford, whose wife, Jane, was another prominent member of the WSPU.[75] Together with H. W. Nevinson he had recently resigned as leader writer for the *Daily News* when the paper offered editorial support for the forcible feeding of WSPU hunger strikers in prison.[76] Brailsford had initiated the formation of the committee after consultation with the National Union leadership.[77] The Conciliation Committee sought to find a simply formulated measure that would compromise between the universal-suffrage solution – regarded unfavourably by many Conservative suffragists – and the equal-votes solution, which the Liberal and Labour parties feared would strengthen the propertied vote.

The resulting bill aimed at reproducing the same franchise as then existed for women on the local government registers. To quiet Liberal and Labour fears of faggot voting – that is, the parcelling up of property among female relatives by the wealthy to secure the maximum representation of their own particular interests – the bill excluded the ownership, lodger, and joint-occupier qualifications of the existing male franchise.[78] The criterion the Conciliation Bill adopted for the enfranchisement of women was the independent occupation of property, even where this was only part of a house. The Conciliation Committee argued: 'Our basis has satisfied a Committee which includes both supporters and opponents of Adult Suffrage. It does not preclude a further advance towards Adult Suffrage; but neither does it render such an advance inevitable.'[79] It was claimed that 82 per cent of those enfranchised under such a measure would be working-class women, though these would mostly be widows and spinsters.[80]

The first Conciliation Bill passed its second reading with a large majority, and even the antisuffragist prime minister, Asquith, felt that this obliged the cabinet to consider providing the bill with further facilities in the next session of parliament.[81] The cabinet's discussions however indicated that some of the bill's firmest opponents were among those, like Lloyd George, who wished to see more sweeping franchise reform.[82] Outside cabinet, National Union leaders found that many of their sympathisers among the rank and file of Liberal MPs were also looking for a bill which was 'thoroughly democratic', and that in such a stand they frequently had the support of the Liberal women in National Union branch societies.[83] The People's Suffrage Federation's support had been no more than nominal,[84] and the Women's Cooperative Guild had taken no official part in the very considerable popular campaigning which the constitutionalists organised behind the bill.[85] Nor was the Parliamentary Labour Party prepared to press for further facilities for its passage, although thirty-two Labour MPs had voted for the bill.[86]

As a consequence its promoters undertook several modifications to the bill in its 1911 version. These left it open to widening amendments and removed the one remaining possibility of faggot voting in its earlier provisions.[87] By this time, too, the National Union had undertaken surveys to demonstrate that the majority who would be enfranchised under the bill were working-class women.[88] One of its pamphlets explaining the bill insisted: 'The Conciliation Bill is small, but it is democratic. The qualification is not *property*, but *residence*.'[89] Philip Snowden, a leading Labour MP who earlier in his career had shown little sympathy for votes for women, supported such claims and emerged as one of the bill's principal champions.[90] In the summer of 1911 the revised Conciliation Bill received an even larger majority than that obtained after its 1910 reading.

The Liberal government finally yielded to such pressure behind a women's-suffrage measure and conceded further facilities for it in the next parliament, should a third such Conciliation Bill again successfully pass a second reading. It was this advance for the cause of women's enfranchisement that prompted Lloyd George to open negotiations with the Conciliation Committee and the National Union. His go-between was C. P. Scott, the editor of the *Manchester Guardian,* and himself a committed supporter of sexual equality.[91] Lloyd George feared the implications of the government's promise both for the long-term electoral interests of the Liberal Party and for the present cabinet's unity.[92] He put it to Brailsford that a preferable form of franchise reform would be the enfranchisement of all householders, with married men and women able to qualify jointly on the same property.[93] As a democratic suffragist, Brailsford welcomed such an opportunity to unite the women's-suffrage and adultist demands.[94]

Democratic suffragists in the National Union leadership were to prove similarly positive in their response to Lloyd George's eventual formulation of his proposal. This sought suffragist support for the introduction of a government manhood-suffrage bill which would be drafted in such a way that it might be open to an amendment also enfranchising women.[95] In return he offered his own support for the Conciliation Bill should the government's measure fail, and his own opposition to any purely manhood-suffrage legislation.[96] Scott recorded that during these negotiations both Kathleen Courtney and Helena Swanwick 'hailed the proposal as opening up a new and far better prospect of success', and predicted the full support of Mrs. Fawcett, 'her principle being "the more suffrage for women the better." '.[97] The formal announcement of this proposed Reform Bill was made to a deputation from the People's Suffrage Federation on 7 November 1911.

Lloyd George's scheme, however, was soon to founder. It had been based on the assumption that the government's measure would be heard before the introduction of the third Conciliation Bill, which would then provide a fall-back should the broader measure fail. In the event, continuing cabinet disunity over the issue caused the introduction of the Reform Bill to be postponed for over a year,[98] and the Conciliation Bill was reintroduced ahead of it in March 1912. By this time its all-party support had been seriously weakened by the government's own initiative on franchise reform, and it narrowly failed to gain a majority. A mass-window-breaking raid by the WSPU in London's leading shopping centre was generally held to be the immediate cause of its failure, though the constitutionalists' analysis of the voting patterns was to suggest a more complex explanation. Originally the WSPU had joined the constitutionalists in promoting the Conciliation Bill, and had undertaken two lengthy 'truces' on antigovernment agitation in 1910 and 1911 to facilitate the campaigning behind them.[99] But its leadership had become increasingly frustrated with what it saw as the cabinet's unnecessarily lengthy prevarications concerning further provisions for the bill. They were increasingly suspicious, too, of what they saw as a male conspiracy in Brailsford's intriguing with Liberal politicians.[100] Brailsford for his part was increasingly unsympathetic to the impatience of the WSPU leadership.[101] Militants' anger had been further fuelled by the extremes of police violence endured by their demonstrators on 'Black Friday' during a brief intermission in the truce, and by the continuance of the savage practice of forcibly feeding hunger-striking militants in prison.[102]

Nor had the WSPU leadership been party to the negotiations that preceded the announcement of the new Reform Bill, and the militants' organisation had been thrown into serious internal confusion and dissension over what response was most appropriate. At first it took up the call for full adult suffrage, but then quickly retreated to the demand for a government bill limited to equal votes for women.[103] As a corollary, it campaigned violently against both the government's bill and the third private-member Conciliation Bill. The government's response was to move against the leadership of the WSPU. Christabel fled to Paris; her mother and the Pethick-Lawrences received lengthy prison sentences for conspiracy, from which they had to hunger-strike temporary escapes. Antagonism to male involvement in suffrage campaigning greatly intensified among the militant leadership at this time. The Women's Freedom League initially also experienced serious internal divisions over whether to follow the WSPU leadership into an escalation of violent demonstration or to follow the constitutionalists' new political policy.[104]

The consequences of the failure of the third Conciliation Bill proved equally significant in terms of reforming constitutionalist political policies. Trust in Lloyd George had been undermined by the decidedly erratic nature of his promised support for the final Conciliation Bill.[105] The National Union had also taken due note of the voting on the 1912 bill. This indicated that its former supporters among the Irish Nationalists were no longer prepared to vote for it. The Irish MPs feared that its successful passage would seriously endanger the unity of the Liberal government on which they were depending for the success of their own cause, Irish home rule.[106] This turnaround in the Irish Nationalists' commitment held considerable implications for suffragist political strategy. Since the 1910 elections the Liberal government had depended on the support of both the Irish Nationalists and the Labour Party to stay in office. If one element of this informal coalition, the Irish nationalists, was now reneging on considerable former support for women's suffrage, it became of critical importance to strengthen that of the other minority party to it.

Moreover, in contrast to the Irish Nationalists, the Labour Party had put up a strong vote in support of the Conciliation Bill, even though a number of its MPs had been absent because of the widespread industrial unrest at the time. Equally important, since Asquith's announcement of a forthcoming manhood-suffrage bill, Labour Party support for women's suffrage had become noticeably more positive. At its Annual Conference in January 1912 the Labour Party had made a firm commitment to votes for women, despite opposition from the miners' unions, and declared that it would find unacceptable any measure of franchise reform that excluded women.[107] Mrs. Fawcett had responded with a letter to Ramsay MacDonald that declared: 'I wish you were double your present strength in the House of Commons.'[108] It was from this time that she became openly sympathetic to pressure from democratic suffragists within the National Union for an electoral alliance with the Labour Party.

At least one Liberal democratic suffragist sought a quite different outcome. Eleanor Acland was on the executive of the Women's Liberal Federation and in contact with the National Union's leadership through her friendship with its new parliamentary secretary, Catherine Marshall. She expressed her gladness at finally being free of the 'dishonest' Conciliation Bill and advocated a new campaign behind a womanhood-suffrage bill which would enfranchise 'all classes of women'. In the meantime she urged: 'Do let us plump for the Liberal Party (even if it means manhood suffrage has to be passed first).'[109] Many women Liberals, however, were not feeling so generous towards the government, and in canvassing for a change in constitutionalist election policy National Union leaders were able to build upon their disillusion. *The Common Cause*, for example, suggested to its readers that the Liberal government's record on women's suffrage indicated the bankruptcy of the Liberal Party as a force in reform politics:

The Fall of the Liberals

If the Liberal Party has nothing better to do than to keep up what one party correspondent [a reference to the MP for Holmfirth] complacently called 'Liberal *tradition*', and if this means, as it clearly does with some, that they are content to rest on what their fathers achieved and absolve themselves from the need of progressive thinking, there is no question whatever that power will pass from them. We express no opinion as to the merits of parties as parties, but for Liberalism to become 'traditional' is to cease to be Liberal. No better example of the dangers of 'traditional' thinking could be given than the hopeless bog into which anti-suffragist Liberals have wandered so that they are gradually enticed into a practical denial of every truly Liberal principle while loudly proclaiming the same with their lips. It is the business of the master of Elibank [the Liberal Chief Whip] to keep his forces together; he will find this canker destroy them unless he meets it.[110]

Such arguments met with sympathy from many disenchanted women Liberals. After the defeat of the Conciliation Bill one such had written to *The Common Cause* calling on Liberal Party women to resign and concen-

trate on suffrage work: 'Signs are not wanting that the already numerous defections of Liberal women are causing anxiety at headquarters.
No party woman likes to withdraw; in fact it must always be a most
painful duty. But must not non-militants use *every* means in their power
at the present extreme crisis in suffrage affairs?'[111] Not surprisingly proponents of a suffrage–labour alliance were to be among the most active
in organising this disaffection among women Liberals. One such was
Ethel Williams of the Newcastle Society. She led a local Women's Liberal
Association of which she was president to pass a resolution that at the
next election it would not work for any party that did not include wom-
en's suffrage in its programme. She achieved a similar commitment from
the Gateshead Women's Liberal Association.[112] When the new election
policy in favour of the Labour Party was put to the National Union council in May 1912 it was welcomed by many such disillusioned Liberal
suffragists. One, on resigning from her local Women's Liberal Association, wrote: 'I am throwing my whole energies and substance into the
support of the new development of the NUWSS policy – viz., the providing of a Labour candidate in all constituencies where either Liberal
or Unionist has not proved himself a supporter of our cause not only in
name but in deed.'[113]

It was the failure of the 1912 Conciliation Bill that demonstrated con-
clusively to such suffragists the inadequacy of existing consitutionalist
political strategy in the parliamentary situation then prevailing, and the
need for a more aggressive policy in regard to the government. At the
same time it appeared imperative to constitutionalists that their own
campaigning be completely dissociated from the more recent outrages
of the WSPU. While they generally stressed the government's responsibility for provoking such a response, they nonetheless felt that their
own role in maintaining popular goodwill had become in consequence
of even greater importance.[114] The desire of democratic suffragists, middle-
class and working-class, Liberal and Labour, for an electoral alliance with
the Labour Party offered a promising solution. It provided both a constitutional way in which to attack the Liberal government and a more
effective means of harnessing popular support for the cause. The Liberal
Party could be hurt by the active support of Labour candidates and by
the encouragement of more three-cornered fights during elections, for
the 1903 election agreement between the Liberal and Labour parties was
becoming less and less workable. Rivalry between the two parties, particularly for industrial seats, was developing rapidly.[115] At the same time
the Labour Party's increasingly sympathetic stand on women's suffrage
could only be reinforced by such an alliance, while its support was critical to the success of any women's-suffrage amendment to the government's forthcoming manhood-suffrage bill. Such a policy also promised
to moderate some of the antagonism to women's suffrage created by

the WSPU's anti-Labour policy. The deliberations that preceded the establishment of the National Union's Election Fighting Fund Committee, however, were to indicate that many problems still surrounded such an alliance.

CHAPTER 4

A SUFFRAGE–LABOUR
ALLIANCE

Following the defeat of the third Conciliation Bill in March 1912, H. N. Brailsford, on behalf of the National Union, opened discussions with Labour Party head office regarding a possible election alliance.[1] By the end of April, Kathleen Courtney, the National Union's secretary, was involved in formal negotiations with Arthur Henderson, secretary of the Labour Party.[2] The Manchester and Newcastle societies, the leading provincial proponents of the new policy, called a special council of the National Union for its ratification.[3] The plan was to raise a fund, the Election Fighting Fund, especially to support Labour candidates during by-elections and in this way to attack the Liberal government by promoting more three-cornered contests.[4] Such a scheme involved delicate issues for both sides. The promotion of such an election policy had been made easier by the significant degree of disaffection among women Liberals. Nonetheless the National Union leadership remained anxious concerning possible internal dissension among those constitutionalists who remained loyal to the Liberals. Initially it was stated that Labour Party candidates would not be supported against 'tried friends' of the suffrage cause (principally committed suffragists among the Liberal MPs). By such means the National Union sought to maintain a nonparty posture even while pursuing the new policy. Writing to Arthur Henderson to outline the proposed scheme, Kathleen Courtney stressed: 'From our point of view it is important that this proposal should not prejudice the non-party character of the National Union.' The administration of the fund was to remain completely under the control of the National Union.[5]

Despite such careful representations of the policy, reservations were still expressed by some among the National Union's membership. These sprang largely from doubts concerning the strength of certain Labour MPs' support for votes for women. In particular it was noted that 'the miners' representatives are usually a little shaky'.[6] Eleanor Rathbone of the Liverpool Society was eventually to lead some of the future opposition to the Electing Fighting Fund policy. She indicated the significant degree of reciprocation she and others felt such a commitment would require from the Labour Party to make the policy worth while. She sug-

76

gested for example that the Labour Party might threaten to withdraw support from Irish home rule should the Irish MPs not agree to support a women's-suffrage amendment to the government's Reform Bill.[7]

Many among the Labour leadership were also hesitant about the proposal. They feared for the parliamentary party's independence of action. In their view it was essential that there be no appearance of the Labour Party having been 'bought' by the suffragists, or acting as the tool of interests other than those of the labour movement. Such reservations were voiced by Ramsay MacDonald early in the negotiations. H. N. Brailsford tried to assuage such anxieties, but his response confirmed that the National Union did expect the new policy to have some impact on the Labour Party's choice of constituencies to be contested: 'In practice it will of course mean that our support, if as considerable as I expect it will be, must put some premium on your choice of Liberal anti's as your opponents. But this will not be put in any crude way which could expose you to legitimate criticism.'[8] In return, Brailsford suggested, the Labour party might expect an extra £10,000 to £20,000 for its election campaigning, together with zealous, experienced help in constituency organisation. He undertook the engagement of socialist organisers for work on the scheme, so that it might 'run from the first on harmonious lines'. He argued also that the scheme had significant implications for future Labour Party growth in terms of membership. He believed many nonparty or Liberal women might be won for socialism through its operation.

Some of the main issues between the two organisations were discussed when a subcommittee of the Labour Party executive, consisting of Keir Hardie, Ramsay MacDonald, Arthur Henderson, and Labour chief whip George Roberts, met with National Union officers on 30 April.[9] The National Union sought clarification concerning Labour Party policy on votes for women. It was confirmed that women's suffrage was party policy, and that Labour remained pledged also to adult suffrage. The Labour leaders were not yet ready to give a specific pledge on their party's future actions in parliament regarding any bill which removed the sex disability but yet came far short of adult suffrage. It was clear only that the party would be willing to accept some limited form of women's suffrage if an adult-suffrage measure had already been defeated. Nor would they make any pledge to vote against the third reading of a Reform Bill that did not include women, though Keir Hardie made this commitment on his own behalf.

The National Union do not appear to have put their planned questions about possible Labour Party ideas 'for dealing with the Irish' on the issue of women's suffrage, or any proposals it might have to secure the introduction of a Reform Bill that session.[10] The suffragist leaders' apparent satisfaction with the Labour Party's response to their questions suggests they held very moderate expectations of the influence they might

exercise on the party's policies. For their part, the Labour leaders repeated their concern that the new policy be formulated in a way that did
not suggest their party had been 'bought' by the suffragists. It was agreed
that funds should be offered to individual Labour candidates, not to the
party as such.[11] Even so the Labour leadership continued unhappy with
the wording of the relevant resolution for the special council meeting
called to ratify the new policy. This read:

That the National Union raise a sum of money for the specific object of supporting individual candidates *standing in the interests of Labour* in any constituency
where Liberal Anti-Suffragists may successfully be opposed, and that the Union
also support such candidates by the organisation of a vigorous campaign on
their behalf [my emphasis].[12]

Henderson's request that the underlined phrase be removed brought
an angry response from Brailsford which also indicated that serious reservations continued among many within the National Union:

You will not be surprised to hear that there is a good deal of doubt and opposition to the scheme inside the National Union. Some say that the Labour party
does not really mean to do anything. Others fear the loss of moderate support
all round when it is said that 'suffragists are all socialists'. I leave you to guess
the effect on these critics of the news that the Labour Party while apparently
quite glad to take women's money refuses to accept their support publicly. If
the officers of the Union have to convey that message to the Council, the plan is
killed and incidentally all who have been urging that the Labour Party scheme
should be trusted and helped are made to look ridiculous.[13]

Again Brailsford promised great long-term gains for Labour if the policy
were implemented. He argued: 'The Liberal women are in the midst of
a split, and all the more active of them are prepared to back our plan.'[14]
He again suggested that the suffrage movement might prove a valuable
recruiting ground for the Labour Party once such an alliance was forged.

The National Union replied to Henderson more temperately, explaining that his amendment had not been received in time to alter the agenda
of the special council, and that anyway it had been felt that it 'would
convey a false impression'. There was also a veiled threat: 'It is of course
by no means certain that it will be carried, nor indeed do I know whether,
in view of your attitude, the Executive will wish to press the matter.'[15]
A meeting between Ramsay MacDonald and Mrs. Fawcett and Kathleen
Courtney one week later restored friendly relations. MacDonald here
outlined his complex reservations about the scheme. His comments indicated that by this stage in the negotiations the Labour Party had made
some commitment to oppose any Reform Bill which excluded women,
though he doubted if its organisation and discipline were strong enough
to enforce it. An explanation for what seemed to be a continual wavering
on this question by MacDonald and other Labour leaders was also offered. To make such a commitment public, he suggested, would be a

tactical error. It would strengthen the hand of those in the government who wanted to abandon the bill. It would also encourage Conservatives to vote against the women's-suffrage amendments, in the hope of thereby ensuring the defeat for the whole bill through the resulting loss in Labour support. The three agreed on a formulation of the new policy that they felt both preserved the national Union's nonparty identity and did not in any way compromise the Labour Party's independence in relation to the suffrage issue. This presented the new policy as but a refinement of the National Union's former practice of supporting 'the best friend' to women's suffrage. The only real change was that not only 'the personal views of the Candidates but also of the official attitude towards Women's Enfranchisement of the Party to which he belongs' were to be taken into account.[16] The policy would be directed particularly against Liberal antisuffragists, but again it was stressed it would not be implemented against Liberal MPs whose individual record on women's suffrage was satisfactory.

In explaining the proposed new policy to the National Union's membership, Catherine Marshall emphasised that it should not be referred to as an alliance, for this was prohibited by the Labour party's constitution. She presented it as 'a very slight modification of our present election policy', aimed mainly at attacking Liberal 'Antis' and 'Wobblers'. She suggested that it also offered 'some chance of securing the Irish Vote or part of it', and dismissed fears that the new policy might be interpreted as 'additional proof of suffragist leanings to socialism'. This argument had already been run by antisuffragists for all it was worth, in her view.[17] Catherine Marshall also assured members that the special fund would be kept quite separate from other National Union income, and that those who did not wish to support the scheme would not be expected to subscribe to it. On the other hand, she suggested, the new scheme could expect to attract money from those who were looking for a fighting policy but who were unhappy with the present practice of both the National Union and the WSPU.[18]

Nonetheless committed Liberals in the National Union continued to challenge the policy. They argued that the potential loss of Liberal support for women's suffrage far outweighed the value of the help the Labour Party seemed prepared to offer. Eleanor Rathbone passed on to Mrs. Fawcett 'several questions which all the more intelligent of my Committee [North Lancashire, North Cheshire, and North Wales Federation] kept asking me'. These concerned the effect of the policy on Liberal rank-and-file opinion and on long-time friends of the cause in the Liberal and Conservative parties. Their scepticism was also based on the smallness of the number of Liberal antisuffragists who had slim enough majorities to be threatened by the running of a third candidate. Eleanor Rathbone indicated that such doubts might be diminished if she could report that Brailsford had succeeded in obtaining Labour abstentions from the second reading of the Irish Home Rule Bill.[19] Such doubters of the new policy clearly felt that it could be justified only if its potential impact on the Irish MPs could be demonstrated. The Cardiff Society led the firmest opposition to the new policy by attempting to postpone the holding of the special council meeting which was to ratify it.

In fighting this resistance a circular letter from National Union officers to the membership stressed that their organisation was not to be 'sacrificed'. It denied there was any 'proposal to identify the National Union with the Labour Party'.[20] It repeated that the EFF policy was no more than an elaboration of the National Union's formula of supporting the 'best friend' to the cause, and the organisation's continuing nonparty identity was insisted upon. The National Union's press statement, issued after the special council had voted in support of the new policy, also emphasised this view:

In recommending that preference be given at elections to candidates who were not only themselves in favour of women's suffrage, but belonged to a party which also identified with it, they were acting simply in the interests of women's suffrage, and they were perfectly ready to extend the same principle to other political parties which might in the future offer similar conditions.[21]

Henderson greeted the news of the acceptance of the new policy with a friendly letter to Kathleen Courtney.[22] She in turn was able to report that £1,000 had been raised at the council meeting for the support of Labour candidates.[23] Shortly after the inauguration of the new policy, the WFL, the smaller of the two militant organisations, announced that in future it, too, would support Labour candidates in three-cornered fights.[24] Its associated group, the Men's League for Women's Suffrage (in which H. N. Brailsford was a leading member), had declared a similar change of policy a month before.[25]

The Election Fighting Fund Committee, which was to administer the fund raised for the new policy, was controlled by the executive of the National Union, and was responsible to it. A large majority of the early committee were national Union members, eight of them members of the National Union executive. As had been hoped, the new fund attracted the support of some who had previously worked more closely with the WSPU.[26] The records of the EFF Committee exist only for the first six months of its operation, and an account of its work thereafter has to be based upon reports in *The Common Cause*, the minutes of the National Union Executive Committee, to which it reported regularly, and material among the papers of Catherine Marshall, who was to act as its secretary. As we have seen, by the time of the foundation of the EFF Committee the National Union leadership contained a group which was already dedicated to the success of the new policy. The orchestrators of the new policy were also to prove exceptionally able. Margaret Robertson, formerly organiser for the Manchester Society, became chief EFF organiser. She was evidently a brilliant political campaigner. Fenner Brockway believed she might have gone on to become one of the leaders of the ILP if she had not left national politics on her marriage.[27] Margaret Robertson's skills were matched by those of Catherine Marshall, the National Union's recently elected parliamentary secretary and now also EFF secretary.[28] They were supported in their EFF activities by the secretary of the National Union, Kathleen Courtney,[29] who had also begun her career with the Manchester Society. These three directed and consolidated the EFF policy, with the support of other democratic suffragists within the National Union's executive – notably Helena Swanwick, Margaret Ashton, and Maude Royden. They were eventually to be joined by Alice Clark, who assisted Catherine Marshall with the administration of the EFF Committee's campaigns. Alice Clark had already made a successful career in her family's shoe business, and was later to write a pioneering history of women's work in the seventeenth century.[30]

As H. N. Brailsford had promised, the local organisation of EFF work was undertaken by labour-movement suffragists like Ada Nield Chew, Selina Cooper, Annot Robinson, Margaret Aldersley, Hilda Oldham, and Annie Townley, or middle-class socialist sympathisers like Wilma Meikle, Edith Hilston, Alice Low, and Lisa and Clementina Gordon. Some of their experiences in joint labour–suffrage campaigning will be recounted in Chapter 5.

Enthusiasm for the new policy clearly ran high at this time – £1,115 was collected in the three weeks between 3 and 24 July, and only two months after its formation the EFF had reached £3,629.[31] The rate of financial support eventually died down in late summer. Only £255 was collected between 2 August and 20 September, bringing the total contributions to the fund in its first four months to £4,394.[32] The EFF Committee hoped donations would reach £10,000 by the reopening of parliament in October, and a large demonstration was held at the Albert Hall to encourage further support. The special council that had ratified the EFF policy had also agreed to the establishment of the Friends of Women's Suffrage Scheme, which was to become an increasingly important accompaniment to EFF activity. The scheme was aimed largely at demonstrating working-class support for women's suffrage. Existing National Union members undertook responsibility for organising a specific district. There they canvassed each of the streets, and as supporters of women's suffrage were located they were asked to sign a Friends of Women's Suffrage card. Thereafter these supporters were informed of all suffrage activities in the district and encouraged to participate in them. They were also kept supplied with suffrage literature, including the Friends of Women's Suffrage Newssheet, which stressed working-class interest in, and support for, votes for women. The scheme was also operated at National Union public meetings, particularly works and factory-gate meetings. No membership fee was involved. In the two and a half years between its inception and the outbreak of war 39,500 Friends of Women's Suffrage were enrolled.

The urgency which the National Union attached to the new policy had been evidenced in its regret that suffragists were not able to begin work at once. Labour had decided not to fight the by-election in North-West Norfolk in May. The list of possible constituencies where the policy might be employed, supplied by the Labour Party shortly after the ratification of the new policy, must also have been something of a disappointment. None were the seats of leading Liberal antisuffragists.[33] The earliest EFF campaigns took place in the by-elections at Holmfirth, Hanley, Crewe, and Midlothian. All these by-elections reflected the current disagreement between the Labour Party and the Liberal government over which party should represent industrial seats, and Labour MPs withdrew from the House of Commons, and therefore as parliamentary support for the government, during these contests.

The National Union always employed Labour sympathisers for EFF by-election campaigning. At Holmfirth for example the campaign was worked by Annot Robinson, Selina Cooper, and Ada Nield Chew, all women with considerable experience in trade union or socialist organising. Ada Nield Chew had first entered labour and socialist agitation after the publication of a series of letters by her signed 'Crewe Factory Girl' in 1894. Between 1900 and 1908 she had worked as an organiser for the Women's Trade Union League. Former millworker Selina Cooper had also been active in local socialist politics in Lancashire since the late 1890s and had taken part in the textile workers' suffrage campaigns. Annot Robinson had been active in suffrage and ILP agitation in the Manchester area since the early 1900s.[34] At Holmfirth they undertook speaking, canvassing, and the distribution of literature in cooperation with the Labour party's organiser. Isabella Ford, who had a long experience in women's trade unionism, and was a founder member of the ILP, also went down to speak for the National Union. At an EFF meeting in the constituency Annot Robinson held a crowd of over a thousand despite the arrival of the Liberal candidate. Although Holmfirth was a Liberal stronghold, and the result was the expected Liberal victory, the former majority was halved and the Labour vote almost doubled from 1,643 to 3,195. The EFF campaign had succeeded in making women's suffrage an issue in the election, and had created enough interest to support the formation of three new suffrage societies. The National Union claimed: 'Our workers were valuable chiefly because they brought with them the habits and experience of skilled organisers.'[35]

In Hanley the suffragists found the Labour organisation in a particularly poor state, for the seat had previously been held by a Lib-Lab member who had relied entirely on the Liberal Party for his election machinery. The Labour poll was disappointing – 1,694 votes. *The Common Cause* asked:

What is the moral of Hanley? The 'machine' was a Liberal organisation. The plain moral which we have always tried to drive home is 'organise and organise now'. The spirit and fire of the Labour Party is wonderful, but you can't mobilise forces without the machine of mobilisation. . . . We should now like to see Labour and suffragists sit down in the Hanley division and plot it patiently out.[36]

Such hopes were not realised, and EFF organisation did not continue in this constituency. The Crewe by-election was altogether more successful from the suffragists' point of view, leading to the defeat of the Liberal candidate and the establishment of longer-term working relationships between local suffragists and labour organisations. The National Union had made £1,000 available for the conduct of the campaign. The previous Liberal majority of 1,704 was converted to a Unionist majority of 966, and the Labour vote nearly doubled to 2,485. Afterwards *The Common Cause* foresaw the formation of 'a great working class suffrage society'.[37] Catherine Marshall put to Arthur Henderson the suggestion that the resources of the EFF be used to support and continue Labour Party organisation in this constituency. Henderson was agreeable. He pointed out, though, that James Holmes had proved a very good candidate and might be moved elsewhere. He added the hint that this candidacy might be retained 'if by any chance we had some new machinery for securing an extensive vote'. The EFF subsequently made a grant to Holmes of £125 per annum on condition that he remain Labour's candidate at Crewe.[38]

The last EFF by-election campaign of 1912, at Midlothian, was seen as a similar success for the new policy. The Labour Party candidate, Robert Brown, was instructed by his head office to issue a stronger statement in support of women's suffrage. A grant of £250 was made available by the EFF, and a campaign was organised by Margaret Robertson and Annot Robinson. The Edinburgh Society also took an active part, supplying two more organisers very sympathetic to EFF policy, Alice Low and Lisa Gordon. Two cars were provided for the campaign by Countess de la Warr (formerly more closely associated with the WSPU) and Margaret Ashton. Again a former large Liberal majority was converted to a small Unionist majority with labour recording 2,413 votes in its first contest in the seat. One member of the Labour Party estimated that EFF intervention had been worth a thousand votes to the Labour candidate.[39]

The National Union's experience during these 1912 by-elections highlighted a major hindrance to the EFF's effectiveness – the rudimentary nature of Labour party election machinery and the frustration it brought suffragist organisers. Moreover the limited return to be expected from such occasional and unpredictable contests compared with the work and money invested soon became clear. By-elections ceased to be the centre of EFF activity after 1912. In the light of Labour's generally poor preparations, and the suffragists' desire to concentrate on seats represented by leading Liberal antisuffragists, EFF activity was increasingly concentrated on the more routine and long-term organisation of Labour sup-

port in constituencies specially selected by the suffragists. Nor was Labour's poor election machinery the only problem that confronted EFF
work at this time. The EFF organisers had gone to great lengths to master the elaborate procedures that preceded the adoption of a Labour Party
or an ILP parliamentary candidate.[40] Nevertheless, very soon after its
establishment the EFF inadvertently became involved in a 'renegade'
Labour candidacy at the Ilkeston by-election, which almost led to a complete breach with Labour Party head office. When the Ilkeston Labour
Representation Committee had adopted J. T. White, the EFF had offered
a grant of up to £500 and an added loan of £200 for his campaign before
he had been officially endorsed by Labour Party head office. The Labour
leadership subsequently decided that the 'organisation and general situation are certainly not of a kind to justify a candidate being entertained
at present', though the fact that White would be opposing the re-election
of a Liberal minister was no doubt a greater factor in this decision. In
the meantime, news of the National Union's offer had leaked to the
press, causing considerable embarrassment to National Union leaders,
and even greater irritation to the Labour leadership. The ILP decided to
continue with White's candidacy on their own, but the EFF's offer of
help was withdrawn and the Labour Party leaders mollified.[41]

If National Union activity could sometimes embarrass the Labour Party,
Ramsay MacDonald proved a considerable thorn in the flesh of the constitutionalists' leadership. He had become ever more alienated from the
suffrage movement as the WSPU resorted to increasingly extreme forms
of violent demonstration, and he now frequently made their exploits the
occasion for derogatory comments on the suffrage movement in general.
In early July 1912 he published another such statement, and Catherine
Marshall prepared to hold up the flow of funds into the EFF until he had
publicly recanted. Some of her notes from this time read, 'R. M. must
make unequivocal declaration that party will vote against third reading'
(of the Reform Bill, should women be excluded). She pressed Arthur
Henderson for some such statement from MacDonald with some success. She was able to report to the National Union's provincial council
on 11 July 1912 that the Labour leader had made a strong women's-
suffrage speech during the Crewe by-election, and had invited Margaret
Robertson to join his platform.[42]

October 1912 saw yet a further threat to the Labour–suffragist understanding when the WSPU announced that in future it would extend its
attacks to Labour Party candidates and leaders on the grounds that they
formed a part of the Liberal government's 'coalition' of support. The
WSPU hoped by this means to pressure the Labour Party into giving
priority to votes for women in its parliamentary programme.[43] George
Lansbury's attempt to achieve such a position had been defeated a few
weeks earlier at a meeting of the Parliamentary Labour Party. Such actions provoked a statement from the Labour chief whip, George Rob-

erts, that the Parliamentary Labour Party did not favour limited women's suffrage. There were also at this time recurrent rumours that Ramsay MacDonald had reached a new election alliance with the Liberal chief whip, Percy Illingworth, which would completely undermine the central aim of EFF policy, the promotion of more three-cornered contests.[44] A further rumour suggested that the parliamentary Labour Party had refused to stand by Ramsay MacDonald's pledge to oppose the third reading of the Reform Bill should women be excluded from it.[45] Arthur Henderson sought to allay some of these fears by sending Catherine Marshall a copy of the resolutions passed by the Parliamentary Labour Party to 'resolutely press' for a women's-suffrage amendment.[46]

But Ramsay MacDonald continued to cause disquiet by repeatedly attacking the WSPU and asserting the middle-class basis of the women's-suffrage movement.[47] He also refused EFF help to improve the election organisation in his own constituency of Leicester. Catherine Marshall wrote to him stressing the sacrifice that many contributions to the EFF represented, most of which, she claimed, were 'made up of the savings of business and professional and working women'. She reported that many were going without holidays, medical treatment, food, and new clothing in order to contribute to the work.[48] Catherine Marshall detected class antagonism at the root of MacDonald's lack of commitment to women's suffrage, yet, she claimed, many middle-class suffragists shared similar aims with himself. They too wished

to concentrate on breaking down this big monopoly of political power which stands in the way of all progress. If you think I am exaggerating ask Miss I. O. Ford. She can tell you something of what this struggle means to the middle class women for whom you have so little kindly feeling. Why do you hate us so? I have been reading your book on Socialism again to try to discover. Your accusation of class-feeling on our side, against the working women, wounds – and shows that you have missed much of the significance of the Women's Movement.

She insisted that, together with the peace movement, it had done a great deal to

break down the business of class between one group of human beings and another. And I believe the spirit of solidarity it has created among the women of all classes is going to be one of the most important and beneficial factors in the social development of the future .,. . these are things on which I feel very deeply, and the attitude I have been vaguely conscious of when talking to you, and which appears in your letter today [in the *Daily Citizen*] really *hurts*.[49]

Katharine Bruce Glasier also urged more tolerance from Ramsay MacDonald towards the middle-class women they encountered in their joint campaigning with the constitutionalists:

We are a *stage army* everywhere and can't help being till this suffrage business is out of the way . . . the suffrage muddle will right itself too – and we mustn't be jealous. It makes us look so ugly. I am a poor plain sparrow myself and feel a bit queer with Birds of Paradise queening it beside me in an election where the Labour fight is real and earnest – but skillful handling, such as Peters is capable of and eager for, will use the plumage for the real work – perhaps put some soul inside it too.

After a recent election campaign, she herself 'rejoiced in all the United Suffrage work I saw – M. Robertson was splendid'.[50] Finally, she pointed out that both she and Ramsay MacDonald had daughters and should give some thought to how they would see their parents' reactions to the women's-suffrage issue in the future.[51]

The antisuffragist outbursts of MacDonald only strengthened the resistance of those within the National Union who opposed the new policy. The constitutional societies in Wales were dominated by loyal women Liberals who consistently fought the operation of the EFF Committee in their constituencies. In East Carmarthen, in the by-election of August 1912 for example, the recalcitrance of the local suffrage branch and the muddle surrounding the adoption of the ILP candidate, Dr. Williams, caused the EFF Committee to abandon its hope of fighting the election. Instead National Union headquarters sought to avoid provoking further controversy by offering to support the ILP candidate as 'the best friend' to the cause.[52] Similarly, although the South Wales Federation declared itself anxious to fight the antisuffragist minister, Reginald McKenna, it resisted the introduction of EFF organisers to his constituency in North Monmouth. A compromise was reached whereby the National Union began preliminary organising, but not under the supervision of the EFF Committee. The South Wales Federation agreed, in return, to reconsider its opposition to the EFF when it had seen how the Labour party voted on the third reading of the Reform Bill.[53] The local National Union branch in the constituency of another antisuffragist minister, Charles Hobhouse, in Bristol, also resisted the introduction of EFF organisers. It seems most likely that a new branch of the National Union, the East Bristol Society, was created by local sympathisers for the new policy specifically to circumvent this problem.[54]

Despite such difficulties and tensions, the National Union leadership was clearly satisfied with the effect of its new policy and had recommended to the council meeting in July 1912 that it consolidate its operation by encouraging the formation of local EFF committees within the federations. Throughout the summer and autumn Catherine Marshall was reporting favourably the impact of the new policy on the Labour Party leadership to the executive of the National Union.[55] Subsequently at the October council the leadership declared itself sufficiently impressed with the results of the first six months of the EFF activity to recommend that the policy be extended in a number of ways. EFF campaigning thereafter involved the continuous organisation of election machinery in constituencies where Labour candidates had already been supported, and similar work in the constituencies of sitting Labour MPs who were themselves strong suffragists and who were under possible threat of attack from a Liberal candidacy. Further, it was now made clear that once EFF work had begun in a constituency it would not be abandoned if the Liberal Party decided at some later date to put up a strong suffragist candidate.[56]

Gradually, then, the EFF policy was increasingly formulated explicitly in terms of support for the Labour Party, and EFF activity was extended to election preparations in the seats of sitting Labour MPs and in those other seats which the National Union hoped to persuade Labour to fight, that is, in the seats of leading Liberal antisuffragists. Catherine Marshall wrote to Arthur Henderson in mid-October outlining the new plan of work.[57] Each National Union federation that contained an existing Labour seat was to be asked to enrol volunteers to prepare for the next election. Only those with Labour sympathies would be employed as canvassers and speakers; the National Union's own organisers would be put through a course of reading to familiarise themselves with the main lines of Labour Party policy. Other volunteers would be used for more routine work like tracing removals, organising cars for polling day, etc. Catherine Marshall recommended that a preliminary Suffrage–Labour Week be organised in each such constituency during the coming winter as 'a sort of test mobilisation of forces'. The EFF was now to be made available for the maintenance of Labour agents both for defensive work in existing Labour constituencies and to attack other seats which the National Union wanted to see the Labour Party fight. These were the seats of leading Liberal antisuffragists in Rossendale, Accrington, East Bristol, Rotherham, North Monmouth, Ilkeston, Glasgow, Bridgeton, East Bradford, and North Leeds. Catherine Marshall stressed that though the EFF had raised £4,500 since its inception, a continuation of this scale of support very much depended on the Parliamentary Labour Party's attitude to the women's-suffrage amendment to the Reform Bill.[58] In the meantime National Union societies and federations were advised to concentrate all election preparation on Labour-held constituencies 'so as to counteract the harmful effects of the Militants' policy on the Labour Party'.[59] Ramsay MacDonald felt able to turn down the EFF's offer of help in constituency organisation, but other Labour MPs, including Philip Snowden and Arthur Henderson, took immediate advantage of it. Such activity strengthened the National Union's hand with the Labour Party and eventually secured the running of Labour candidates in five of the constituencies the suffragists wished to fight – East Bristol, North Monmouth, Accrington, Rossendale, and Rotherham.[60]

The National Union's success in achieving Labour Party pressure on the Irish Nationalists was more mixed. In October 1912 the Parliamentary Labour Party sent a deputation to the Irish Nationalist leader, Redmond, to press him to withdraw his opposition to the women's-suffrage

amendment to the Reform Bill.[61] In November, Philip Snowden introduced a women's-suffrage amendment to the Irish Home Rule Bill. Although it did not receive official Labour Party backing, Ramsay Mac-
Donald made his first speech on women's suffrage on this occasion. The
majority of Labour MPs voted in favour of the amendment, but the National Union was clearly disappointed by the eight Labour abstentions
and five Labour votes against.[62] Labour Party pressure on the Irish Nationalists, however, had always been but a secondary aim of the EFF
policy for its leading proponents.

By this time the National Union had devised a means of checking the
flow of funds into the EFF when it felt the Labour Party was not being
as helpful as it might be. A Transferable Fund was established for donations whose ultimate use was to be left to the National Union executive. For the first months or so after its inception at least, it is clear that
direct donations to the EFF dwindled to very little. Between the end of
October 1912 and early February 1913 the EFF rose only from £4,115 to
£4,197, whereas £869 had been placed in the Transferable Fund at its
inauguration on 5 November, a sum that had risen to £1,164 only one
week later.[63] No detailed breakdown of EFF expenditure during its first
six months is possible, but *The Common Cause* reported in February 1913
that of the £5,293 received (it is not clear whether this sum included
donations to the Transferable Fund) £2,349 had been spent on EFF campaigns, and £2,000 was being held on deposit to fight the next general
election on behalf of Labour candidates in specially selected constituencies.[64]

By the end of 1912 the National Union had also established a fruitful
working relationship with the ILP leadership. Links were first established when the National Union consulted with ILP organiser James
Mylles over his party's Political Equality Campaign in early 1912. At this
stage both organisations remained shy of an open alliance, and Mylles
advised Catherine Marshall to keep their negotiations private for the
present.[65] One of the EFF Committee's first actions after the inauguration of the new election policy had been to send Annot Robinson to the
ILP conference in May 1912 to organise a women's-suffrage demonstration. She had also been instructed to explore the possibility of running
ILP candidates in the constituencies of a number of antisuffragist Liberals.[66] Though the ILP had been slow to respond to the National Union's
early offers of help, by the end of the year a meeting had been arranged
among H. N. Brailsford, Catherine Marshall, Isabella Ford, W. A. C.
Anderson, and the ILP's treasurer, Benson, to establish how 'the National Union could influence the selection of candidates'.[67] Another
meeting, between Isabella Ford and Benson, resulted in an agreement
that the ILP would accept National Union contributions if they were
paid into its general fund and from there transferred to particular constituencies for the support of ILP candidates.[68] In return, ILP MPs were

committed to oppose the third reading of the Reform Bill should it exclude women (though Ramsay MacDonald's statements continued to be changeable on this matter).[69] It was the advice of Benson at this meeting that led to a major restructuring of EFF activity in 1913 with a new concentration on the organisation of rank-and-file opinion within the Labour Party, particularly within trade union branches, in favour of women's suffrage. This aspect of EFF activity will be explored in Chapter 5. It is necessary first to look briefly at the parliamentary context to such National Union campaigning in 1912 and more especially at the progress of the government's Reform Bill. Constitutionalists' experience in working for a women's-suffrage amendment to this bill only served to further strengthen their adherence to the EFF policy.

Following the announcement of the forthcoming Reform Bill in November 1911, the National Union had consulted with the Conciliation Committee, the Women's Liberal Federation, and the Conservative and Unionist Women's Franchise Association as to the best means of securing the safe passage of a women's-suffrage amendment to what was essentially a manhood-suffrage bill.[70] As a result of these meetings the National Union established a Parliamentary Committee to unite all who supported such an amendment on a broad, democratic basis – the position of Conservative suffragists on any possible amendment remaining unclear.[71] This committee first met on 14 December 1911, and each of the organisations involved was invited to send one delegate to a Central Committee to organise work throughout the country. Significantly, the committee took an office at the People's Suffrage Federation headquarters. At this stage it appears to have acted largely as a clearing house, arranging for MPs willing to speak in support of a women's-suffrage movement at meetings up and down the country.[72] By February 1912 the committee had acquired the title of the Women's Suffrage Joint Campaign Committee, with its main objects the establishment of a list of MPs prepared to speak on the issue, the coordination of major suffrage demonstrations, and the organisation of campaigns behind the amendment in those constituencies where pressure on the MP was thought to be important. This committee recommended that suffragist MPs should follow a coordinated plan: first, to work for an equal-suffrage amendment (that is, womanhood suffrage); if this failed, to work for an amendment on the lines of the Conciliation Bill with the addition of the wives of voters (that is, the formulation advocated by the Women's Cooperative Guild in their 1907 initiative); and failing both these, simply to work for an amendment on Conciliation Bill lines.[73]

A list of constituencies was drawn up where it was considered most useful to work up support for a women's-suffrage amendment, and an organiser was appointed.[74] Though the ILP had declined to join the Joint Campaign Committee, it did consult with the National Union on the planning of its own Political Equality Campaign, which also was aimed

at securing the inclusion of women in the promised Reform Bill.[75] The
work of the Joint Campaign Committee in the constituencies was to illustrate even more clearly the comparative weakness of Liberal commitment to securing votes for women. Demonstrations were planned in
Poplar, Bishop Auckland, Huddersfield, Hoxton, Sunderland, Spen
Valley, Devonport, Sheffield, Southampton, Dundee, Midlothian, and
Greenock to pressure local MPs to support the women's-suffrage
amendment. However, when the National Union sought help from local
branches and federations it found that its Liberal members were sometimes lukewarm. Dr. Elsie Inglis of the Scottish Federation had to report
to Kathleen Courtney: 'I have written to the secretaries of Dundee and
Greenock. Dundee I know will be quite ready to help. Greenock will
find it a good deal more difficult as the society is more Liberal there. I
have written a strong letter and will let you know what happens.'[76] As
predicted, the campaign was successfully organised in Dundee, but the
National Union found it necessary to send one of its national organisers
to undertake the necessary work in Greenock. Such local Liberal opposition was, of course, occurring against the background of the National
Union's move towards an increasingly close working relationship with
the Labour Party.

The Joint Campaign Committee continued to operate throughout the
rest of 1912. It agreed to ask MPs to support the extension of the franchise to women on the lines of the local government register but became
increasingly concerned that women's suffrage should not be lost through
demanding too wide a measure. In October, Brailsford was writing to
Kathleen Courtney urging the National Union to pressure those Liberal
and Labour MPs who were supposed to be sound suffragists to be prepared to accept a limited women's-suffrage amendment and to oppose
anything wider should it 'seriously divide the supporters of women's
suffrage'.[77] On 4 November there was a large Joint Campaign demonstration at the London Opera House to demand the inclusion of women
in the Reform Bill 'on broad and democratic lines'. The National Union
Executive Committee minutes record that Labour supporters had sought
to exclude this last phrase from the conference agenda in order to evidence commitment to the general principle of women's suffrage rather
than to any particular form. They had been outvoted by those Liberals
taking part.[78] At this time, too, the People's Suffrage Federation organiser was lobbying adult suffragists within the House of Commons while
the Joint Campaign organiser was at work in their constituencies to ensure that they would support more limited women's-suffrage amendments if necessary, as well as the broader ones. But while the People's
Suffrage Federation showed itself ready to work for less than its own
full demand if necessary to safeguard votes for women, Liberal Party
adultists were proving to be less flexible. The increasing evidence of
Labour's firmer support for women's political emancipation on what-

ever terms could serve only to stimulate and strengthen support for the new election policy within the National Union.

The government's slowness in proceeding with its own Reform Bill reflected growing fears that the women's-suffrage issue threatened the stability and unity of the cabinet. Significant bodies of opinion within the Liberal Party would be alienated should a women's-suffrage amendment either pass or fail, and Asquith's personal 'credit and authority' were felt by many, especially the Irish Nationalists, to be at stake.[79] Four women's-suffrage amendments were planned. The first to be taken would be that to omit the word 'male' from the bill. This was essential before any consideration could be given to specific women's-suffrage amendments. It was to be put by Sir Edward Grey, a Liberal suffragist; Arthur Henderson, a Labour suffragist; and Alfred Lyttelton, a Liberal Unionist suffragist. The three further women's-suffrage amendments were to be taken in the following order: first, a universal-suffrage amendment, to be put by Henderson and Snowden (of the Labour Party); second, the 'Norway' amendment, to be put by W. H. Dickinson and Francis Acland (both of the Liberal Party), which would enfranchise wives of electors as joint householders; and finally, the Conciliation Bill amendment, to be put by Alfred Lyttelton and another Unionist MP. From papers on the committee-stage discussions of the bill it is clear that an age restriction was also much favoured for women's-suffrage amendments, and an age limit of over twenty-five was part of the 'Norway' amendment.[80] It was estimated that as it stood the bill would add three million new male voters to the electorate. Henderson's amendment would add ten and a half million women voters; the 'Norway' amendment would allow about five million women to vote; and the Conciliation Bill amendment would enfranchise about one million women.[81]

Preparations for the reading of the bill itself involved the National Union in very complex lobbying. This was necessary if suffrage opinion were not to be ruinously divided by the different options represented in the various amendments. In essence it sought to trade Liberal support for the narrowest amendment in return for some Conservative support for the Norway formula. Catherine Marshall also aimed to attach every suffrage MP to one of three groups being organised around each amendment, and to ensure that no suffragist MP voted against any one amendment, but that all would vote against a purely manhood-suffrage bill.[82] Within the parties Francis Acland made an almost complete canvass of Liberal MPs. Lord Robert Cecil undertook the same work among Conservative MPs, and had hopes that a considerable number would be voting for the Norway amendment, and even a few for the universal-suffrage amendment. The Labour Party organised a special whip behind the Conciliation Bill amendment, should the broader ones be defeated. They also interviewed all the Irish Nationalist MPs in the hope of exerting what little pressure they could. Nonetheless constitutional suffragists held small hopes in that quarter, and optimism was clearly waning as the time approached for Grey's initial amendment to be taken.[83] Among the militants, Evelyn Sharp had persuaded her leadership to declare a temporary truce. Nevinson recorded that she had believed this to be 'the only way of saving the Union, though personally she dislikes the amendments'. He himself remained anxious, nonetheless: 'Danger still is that the Pankhursts will find means to fufil their prophecies of disaster.'[84]

As the debate on the Reform Bill finally got under way, the *Manchester Guardian*'s correspondent reported: 'Political excitement over the result of the debate which began on Friday ran higher than ever today. One would have to go back nearly ten years in the history of Parliament to find its parallel.'[85] However, all this debate, lobbying, and excitement came to nothing when Bonar Law raised a point of order on the bill. He questioned the exclusion of the occupier franchise, present in the second reading, from the final form of the bill. At this point the Speaker refused to give an immediate ruling, but he let it be known to Liberal ministers shortly afterwards that he was considering ruling the bill incapable of the proposed women's-suffrage amendments. Although the ruling was generally described by the government as a bombshell, Arthur Thring, the civil servant in charge of drafting the bill, had written to Pease on 8 January 1913 pointing out that it remained unclear whether women's-suffrage amendments to the bill would be in order. He had suggested that the matter might be resolved by means of questions in the House.[86] It seems very unlikely, then, that the government had not been expecting just such a reversal for its own bill. The Conservatives, certainly, had felt the problem with the bill to be an obvious one. Some among them had discussed the relative advantages for their party of this measure or a Plural Voting Bill, which, they assumed, would replace the present bill were it declared out of order. They concluded that a Plural Voting Bill would involve less damage to Conservative Party interests, and might also provoke a rebellion among disappointed women's suffragists. To these Conservatives 'it was obvious that the Government must have been fully prepared for the situation'.[87]

The Speaker's ruling, in fact, offered the government a way out of a situation that had proved ever more embarrassing for it. With the withdrawal of the Franchise Bill, Pease, the antisuffragist minister in charge of it, hoped to be able to press right ahead with a quite new bill to simplify registration and abolish plural voting. He maintained that Asquith's promise of full facilities for a women's-suffrage bill could be properly met by the offer of facilities for another private-member bill the following session. This view did not prevail, however, for Asquith had to make commitments to his suffragist ministers which prohibited such a course.[88] According to *The Times*'s correspondent, 'The Suffragist Ministers desired that since women suffragists have lost their Parliamentary opportunity the Government for their part should make a sacrifice – a propitiatory sacrifice.'[89] The diaries of Charles Hobhouse, an antisuffragist member of the cabinet, indicate that it was unanimously agreed to introduce a Plural Voting Bill, but not until the following March,[90] by which time a further women's-suffrage measure would have been put to the House. Another account of events in the cabinet was offered to Conservative Party chairman Arthur Steel-Maitland on behalf of Austen Chamberlain:

Apparently the Suffragist members of the Government have now made it a condition that there should be no extension of the male Franchise unless at the same time the vote is extended to some women. If, therefore, women's suffrage can be defeated next session [in the private-member bill], it would appear that we shall have no male suffrage bill at all. In any case a year has been gained.[91]

By failing to resolve its own disagreements regarding women's suffrage, the Liberal government had allowed the Conservative Party the opportunity to destroy its Reform Bill. As a result a stalemate was established between opposing factions within the cabinet. Antisuffrage opinion in the cabinet had brought about a situation where the government could not for the moment pursue measures of electoral reform that were in the interests of its own party. For their part, the pro-suffrage forces had ensured that when the Liberal government did once more come to consider franchise reform, women's suffrage would have to be part of the agenda. The National Union's advisers in parliament, including Philip Snowden of the Labour Party, Francis Acland of the Liberal Party, and Lord Robert Cecil of the Conservative Party, all advised that the suffragists should have nothing to do with the private member's measure for which facilities were to be made available. They all agreed the National Union should now concentrate its campaign behind the introduction of a _government_ bill which included votes for women.[92] The National Union executive decided to follow such advice, though they planned no definite action to oppose any private-member bill.

Catherine Marshall explained the executive's position in a circular to all National Union societies, and prefigured a further strengthening of the commitment to the Labour Party:

When facilities are offered to us in exchange for the incorporation of an amendment in a Government Bill, we turn indignantly from the counterfeit coin and say to Mr. Asquith: – This does not discharge your debt . . . if the best that the Suffrage members of the Cabinet can get for us is a worthless offer . . . we have nothing to hope for so long as the present Government remain in power. If this is the conclusion the Council comes to, its course will be clear and the shaping of a new policy easy.[93]

The validity of this analysis was confirmed by Lloyd George and Sir Edward Grey in their meeting the National Union leaders to review the situation. The burden of Grey's advice, in fact, was that the National

Union should continue both an antigovernment policy and a campaign for a new government bill; Lloyd George agreed to press for such a measure.[94] The continuing adherence of the Labour Party to women's suffrage was clearly critical to the success of any such strategy. For the preceding months much of EFF campaigning had been aimed at strengthening official Labour backing for the women's cause at the forthcoming Annual Conference in January 1913. Margaret Robertson and Ada Nield Chew had campaigned among Labour rank and filers for support of a resolution urging the Parliamentary Labour Party to vote against the third reading of any Franchise Reform Bill that excluded women. A suffrage supplement had also been arranged to appear with the *Labour Leader* issue for 9 January, paid for by the EFF. This was also sent out to all WCG branches and all delegates to the Labour Party conference. Free literature on the suffrage issue was also made available, 'on the understanding it should be distributed among working people'.[95]

Benson's advice on the need to win trade union support, particularly among the miners, had been heeded. Before the Annual Conference Margaret Robertson had visited miners' leaders Hartshorn, Smillie, and Winstone, all of whom she found sympathetic to the pro–women's-suffrage resolution. Although a miners' MP, Stephen Walsh, led the opposition to it, miners' delegates abstained at the actual vote. This represented a significant, if limited, success for the suffragists. Philip Snowden's resolution, 'to oppose any Franchise Bill in which women are not included', passed with a two-thirds majority of 870 to 437 on a card vote.[96] *The Common Cause* declared: 'Women know henceforth that one body of men will make a united and self-sacrificing stand on their behalf. There is the less ground for bitterness, the less excuse for the extremist tactics of anger and despair.'[97] This was a reasonable assessment. The vote at the Labour Party conference strengthened the position of the pro-suffrage Liberal ministers and made it impossible for any solely manhood measure to be introduced by the government. Snowden wrote to Mrs. Fawcett:

The importance of this vote is tremendous. It has killed any Franchise Bill which might have been intended. I may tell you that I was talking to two members of the Cabinet yesterday (George was one) and they quite fully confessed that it had put the idea of re-introducing a man Franchise Bill into the region of the impossible.

He confidently asserted: 'Women's suffrage now absolutely dominates home politics.'[98] *The Common Cause* commented: 'The Reform of the Franchise is inevitable. It has become an intolerable chaos, and no patching for party motives at plural voting will solve the problem. Liberalism must reform or perish.'[99]

The National Union leadership had hoped that its more aggressive stance in relation to the Liberal government might offer the possibility of renewing concerted action by militants and constitutionalists. A meeting was arranged with Annie Kenney and Flora Drummond representing the WSPU, but they refused the National Union's proposal that militancy in its present form now be abandoned in favour of joint campaigning for a government measure.[100] Confusion and demoralisation continued to grow among the militants. Late in 1912 Emmeline and Frederick Pethick-Lawrence were expelled from the WSPU after they had begun to question the use of violence in demonstrations. The first WSPU demonstration of 1913 was held on 28 January, but Nevinson recorded it was 'not like the old deputations. Indeed the organising and inspiring spirit has gone, the implicit confidence and faith, ever since the split [with the Pethick-Lawrences].'[101] C. P. Scott, too, expressed his growing doubts concerning the value of the WSPU's approach: 'Militancy no good unless on a great scale – 100,000 women in the street would mean something. At present a mere handful and greatly declining.'[102] The government's response to renewed militancy was rapid and ever more repressive. The cabinet had discussed the possibility of the Cat and Mouse Act as early as February 1913, and despite doubts as to its efficacy, from Asquith among others, McKenna was soon instructed to proceed with the bill.[103] This allowed for the release of hunger strikers, and their rearrest once their health was restored. The government went on to raid the WSPU offices, to attempt to suppress *The Suffragette*, and to threaten WSPU sources of financial support. As Morgan comments, 'Myopia and exasperation over suffrage was making the Liberal government ever more illiberal', a point that was frequently made by suffragists at the time.[104]

The National Union took no part in organising support for Dickinson's private-member suffrage bill, which was introduced in May 1913. This token opportunity to advance the suffrage cause involved giving the vote to women householders and wives of householders over the age of twenty-five. Predictably the bill was lost. Nonetheless it remained clear that franchise reform was an increasingly pressing question for the Liberal Party and that no future measure could exclude women and succeed. The two issues were now inextricably tied, and, in Grey's words, this had 'given the whole question an actuality which it had not had before'.[105] The National Union's organisation of pro-suffrage opinion within the Labour Party was critical to creating and maintaining this position. Its ability to undertake such work was founded on the preparedness on the part of many constitutional suffragists to conceive of women's suffrage as part of a broader movement for a more democratic society. It was only this development in suffragist political strategy which prevented a complete disintegration of the women's-suffrage campaigns after the defeat of the final Conciliation Bill and the withdrawal of the Reform Bill. Such a disintegration was increasingly evident within the

WSPU, whose leadership continued to pursue its narrow sectarian approach to the issue, and in so doing completed its isolation and marginalisation.[106] It was to take another year and more for dissident militants, out of sympathy with their leadership, to begin successfully regrouping their wing of the movement. This aspect of suffrage organising in the months immediately preceding the outbreak of war will be examined in more detail in Chapter 6. In contrast, the National Union's policy had ensured that women's suffrage became an integral part of any discussion on franchise reform, and its work among the rank and file of the labour and socialist movements served to make suffragist campaigning an important aspect of radical reform politics and to secure the Labour Party's commitment to the enfranchisement of women.

CHAPTER 5

SUFFRAGE–LABOUR CAMPAIGNING 1913–14

The decision that it was now tactically necessary to campaign for a government measure of franchise reform confirmed the National Union leadership in its commitment to the EFF policy. In their view joint campaigning with the Labour Party represented the most effective pressure suffragists could exert on the Liberal government to this end. Their position was upheld at the National Union's Annual Meeting in February 1913, which agreed to yet further extensions of EFF activity. In future no government candidate would receive National Union support, however good a suffragist he might be, though 'tried friends' would not be actively opposed. Preparations for possible future elections were to continue, in order both to be able to defend the seats of certain sitting Labour MPs and to attack the seats held by leading Liberal antisuffragists, particularly those in the cabinet. Any candidate receiving National Union support had to affirm that he would include women's suffrage in his election address, would urge the government to introduce a women's-suffrage bill with full facilities, would oppose any extension of the franchise which excluded women, and would work to make women's suffrage part of his party's general election programme. The purpose of this extension of EFF activity was twofold; first, to embarrass antisuffragist cabinet ministers by ensuring they were challenged by Labour at future elections, and secondly, to strengthen the numbers of the Labour Party in the House of Commons.[1]

EFF Committee estimates for the six months from mid-May 1913 would indicate that the National Union was spending something over £3,000 per annum in the routine organisation of Labour support. Though sizeable donations had started to come in again by early 1913, at the end of the year they were apparently no longer adequate to meet this planned level of expenditure.[2] The committee's work was, by this time, beginning to disturb some Liberal MPs. In April 1913 Francis Acland had a meeting with Catherine Marshall at which he confirmed that the government had now dropped all ideas of a franchise-reform bill within the life of the existing parliament. However, his main object in the meeting seems to have been to elicit information on the progress of EFF activity. Catherine Marshall's notes on the meeting included this item:

Our Relations with the Labour Party. He talked a great deal about this. Said of course people would say the Labour Party resolutions [at its recent Annual Conference] were bought. Tried to draw me as to extent of help we were giving them. Made wild assumptions which I neither agreed to nor contradicted.
I said anyone who knew anything of the Labour Party must know it was impossible to buy them. . . . He was impressed when I told him of the keenness among the younger Labour men, the Scotch Miners, Blackburn, etc. (He had begun by saying no working men came to his meetings. I assured him they came to ours.) I told him of their reluctance to accept our help till they were assured it was 'clean money'. Of our care about the sources it came from, rapidly growing trust and good feeling between the Labour Party and us.[3]

At the National Union's May council, Catherine Marshall warned that many Liberals were now beginning to fear the effect of EFF policy, and were doing their best to break up the association between constitutional suffragists and the Labour Party: 'This anxiety on their part is significant testimony to the effectiveness of that policy. We must be on our guard against rumour, suspicion, and so forth.'[4]

The pattern of EFF activity for the remainder of the period before the First World War was concentrated on two objects: the building up of suffrage support among the trade unions, notably the miners' union, and the development of Labour Party constituency organisation in general, with a special effort in selected constituencies. These were the seats of antisuffragist Liberal ministers in Accrington, Rossendale, Rotherham, East Bristol, and North Monmouth, which it was hoped to persuade the Labour Party to contest, and also the seats of sitting Labour MPs Philip Snowden, Arthur Henderson, Tom Richardson, Fred Jowett, and Jack O'Grady. Emphasis was put on registration, canvassing, and the tracing of removals on behalf of the Labour Party. Such activity was extended to further similar constituencies in the summer of 1913, on the understanding that it did not necessarily commit the National Union to *general* election support in these particular seats.[5]

After the suffragists' success at the 1913 Labour Party conference, effort was concentrated on securing an equally satisfactory resolution at the next Trades Union Congress (TUC) conference in September 1913. The National Union had been disappointed by the Trades Union Congress's resolution on women's suffrage at its 1912 Annual Conference, having attempted, unsuccessfully, to influence its content. Catherine Marshall's notes for the new trade union campaign included the item 'Get a good man to move a suffrage resolution; a miner would be best', and the fact that Holmes, the Labour candidate in the Crewe by-election, was to get his branch of the railwaymen to recommend such a resolution to its national executive. Copies of the Labour Party resolution were sent to trade union branches asking them to endorse it and send it up to their executives for inclusion in the TUC conference agenda.[6] This work of obtaining women's-suffrage resolutions from trade union branches continued throughout May with obvious success. Despite her reservations about the EFF policy, Eleanor Rathbone was sufficiently impressed to offer to contribute towards the salary of another organiser to join the work, and the secretary of the West Lancashire, West Cheshire, and North Wales Federation advised that Miss Thompson's trade union work in their area had been 'remarkably successful', obtaining resolutions from about forty trade union branches in six weeks. Eleanor Rathbone urged some weeks later that one of the organisers concerned should visit one constituency in every federation to show how to organise such activity. In the North-East, that federation's plans included trade union work in Gateshead, Houghton, Mid- and South-East Durham, and possibly North-West Durham, and in particular 'an attack upon the Miners Lodges, in view of the forthcoming Trade Union Congress'.[7]

The National Union found the trade unions' leaders as sensitive to deal with as those of the Labour Party and drew on their newly acquired allies among the women's trade union leadership. Margaret Robertson, the EFF's chief organiser, gave this advice to Catherine Marshall concerning the organisation of a women's-suffrage resolution at the TUC conference:

No, please *don't* see Thomas, Wardle and Henderson. If it is well to see them (which I rather doubt) Miss Bondfield and I will do it at the right moment. Nothing can be done at present, except by way of approaching those whom we *know* are with us all the way, and whom we can trust with 'confidential' information. I am convinced that *the* essential is that the National Union should not appear in it at all. It's not like the Labour Party conference where the ILP, Fabians, WLL etc. are represented. This is *pure TU* and *very* jealous of outside interference. Bowerman made me realise that. I wished I had made Miss Bondfield go to him alone. I did next time.[8]

Even then the National Union's plans for the TUC conference did not go altogether smoothly, and there was no women's-suffrage resolution on the initial agenda.[9] National Union workers found themselves confronted with a hard task at the conference itself. Afterwards Margaret Robertson wrote to Catherine Marshall: 'Did I tell you of the agonies of the TUC? How the miners actually decided to vote *against* and I had to chase them all round and see them individually and get them to meet again and reverse it (deadly secret of course that I had anything to do with it).'[10] The resolution was finally successful.[11]

Pressure on the miners was kept up at their own Annual Conference a few weeks later. A National Union demonstration was planned to take place during the conference in Scarborough. A theatre holding 1,500 was taken, and Margaret Robertson reported: 'I want Mrs. Cooper, who has still lodges to visit in Yorkshire, to spend the next month more or less working the meeting up. . . . I have great hopes of its political effect, and of its effect on binding the Miners to us.'[12] Miners' leaders Brace, Smillie, Stanley, and Robertson appeared on the platform along-side National Union speakers. Robert Smillie declared his own readiness to back a general strike on the issue and promised that 'Women would have all the power the Miners' Federation could bring to bear on Parliament in order to secure this measure of justice.'[13] Such support was used to strengthen the claim that suffragists were working in the general interest of a wider democracy. *The Common Cause* declared: 'The question of the vote is no longer a question of sex; Cabinet Ministers who delude themselves with this belief – if any exist – are lamentably out of touch with public feeling, and particularly with the labour movement. In the Scarborough speeches the note continually struck was: "This is a question of democracy".'[14]

With such arguments, democratic suffragists sought to offer an alternative perspective on their claim to the sex-war attitudes increasingly fostered by the WSPU leadership. The success of the trade union campaign continued, and culminated in a large demonstration at the Albert Hall on 14 February 1914. The main intention was to show Asquith that he did indeed have a mandate to introduce women's suffrage, and that there was a large popular demand behind the women's cause, particularly among organisations of working-class men. Trades and Labour councils and ILP branches were strongly represented, as well as a broad section of trade union branches, with an especially large number of delegates from the Engineers and the Railwaymen. Arthur Henderson and Fenner Brockway were among those who spoke. *The Common Cause* reported: 'A large space had been reserved for men, and it could have been filled again and again. The Hall was sold out, and every ticket returned was sold as fast as it came in.' The crowd outside, of those hoping to buy a last-minute ticket, did not disperse until 9.30 p.m. By the end of the meeting over £6,000 had been pledged for the new Women's Suffrage Mandate Fund, which was to be used to fight the next general election.[15]

The second main emphasis of EFF activity from the beginning of 1913, the development of Labour Party election machinery in selected constituencies, proved far more controversial within the National Union. The extent of such work in any one area largely reflected the enthusiasm and interest of the local federation or branch society regarding the EFF in general. The regionality of support that had become evident in 1912 continued in a similar pattern. *The Common Cause* claimed that suffragist support for the new policy in any particular area reflected 'the extent to which organised Labour has locally shown itself active in support of our claims'.[16] It is clear, however, that the pre-existing political loyalties of a branch's membership were an equally significant factor. Nor was the new policy successfully pursued in areas where it might have threatened the cause of progressive politics in general. The EFF policy found its strongest support among suffragists in constituencies where the Liberal Party was secure in relation to the Conservative Party, like those in the east of Scotland, north-east England, and the textile districts of Yorkshire, or where the Labour Party was already establishing itself as an effective alternative to the Liberal Party, as in the Manchester area. That is, it was strongest where an intervention on behalf of the Labour Party was not likely to damage the interests of reform politics in that area by splitting the progressive vote and perhaps letting in a Conservative candidate.[17]

In areas where the Liberal Party itself was weak, as in Merseyside, or seriously threatened by Conservatives in a number of marginal seats, as in the west of Scotland, the EFF policy was frequently opposed by the local National Union branches.[18] Opposition from Eleanor Rathbone's federation, that comprising West Lancashire, West Cheshire, and North Wales, also continued. It sent the London executive a resolution that EFF policy not be implemented in its areas 'in view of the special national conditions existing in North Wales' (a reference to the strength of Liberal opinion among suffragists there). This request was refused, though the executive pointed out that no active steps to implement an EFF campaign were ever taken without first consulting the local federation.[19] K. O. Morgan has argued that the maintenance of a strong loyalty to the Liberal Party in the early decades of the twentieth century in Wales reflected the continuation of community politics there, as opposed to class politics. The Labour Party was not yet a real presence in the Welsh constituencies.[20] It has also been contended that Scottish Liberalism was more antisocialist, and anticollectivist, than that in England.[21] Certainly the dominance of loyal Liberal Party workers in the National Union's Glasgow Society and South Wales Federation was to hamper the participation of constitutional suffragists in Labour politics in those areas.

The National Union's claim to be nonparty had often been subject to question, as we have seen. In those areas where constituency work on behalf of Labour was developed and extended, the purely nominal nature of this claim became more and more evident. For whereas the WSPU's partisanship was of a negative kind, the National Union's policies now involved a positive and continuing involvement with the interests of one particular party. Whereas WSPU policy involved attacking the Liberals as the party in power and the Labour Party as a partner in an informal coalition which kept them in power, National Union campaigning involved the active promotion of Labour Party interests. As the EFF policy was developed and extended in 1913 and 1914, there became more clearly evident certain tensions between different understandings of what it signified among members of the National Union leadership. For some it was simply a question of expediency, of the use of the most effective means, in their judgment, to the given end of putting pressure on the Liberal government. But for others it had a far greater significance as the embodiment of their particular perspective on feminist campaigning. In working with and for Labour in the cause of franchise reform they were able to give expression to their concern with questions of both class and sex inequality. For them the EFF policy was more than a temporary, tactical ploy. The possibility for conflict contained in such very different views of labour–suffrage campaigning was soon being realised in the constituency work and election organisation undertaken by the EFF.

The Manchester Federation, for example, continued to be one of the firmest advocates of the EFF policy. It established its own EFF Committee which undertook considerable responsibility for Labour Party organising within its area. This involved constituency work in the seats of six sitting Labour MPs – in North-East Manchester, East Manchester, Gorton, Blackburn, Ince, and Stockport. Such activity was supported in a number of ways. Joint labour–suffrage campaigns took place – one week's activity in Blackburn resulted in a final labour–suffrage demonstration of 2,000 persons. New Suffrage Clubs, along the lines of that established during the 1910 by-election in South Salford, were started in Hulme and Didsbury, and achieved 'excellent propaganda work in the working class districts of the city'.[22] Others followed in Ancoats and Bradford, at the request of the local Labour MPs. Midday suffrage meetings outside works became commonplace, and 1,147 Friends of Women's Suffrage were enrolled in 1913.[23] Finally, the trade union campaign in this area proved very successful, with Manchester providing the largest contingent outside London to the Albert Hall demonstration in February 1914.[24]

The Manchester Federation also organised the EFF campaigns in Accrington and Rossendale, by which it was hoped to persuade Labour to contest those seats at the next election. Here the suffragist stimulus to Labour organisation was considerable. In February 1913 deputations of working men in support of women's suffrage were organised to call on the two antisuffragist ministers who held the constituencies. The work in Accrington proved sufficiently successful for the National Union executive to report by mid-1913 that the Labour Party was now considering running a candidate there, 'EFF work in the constituency having made it worth while for the Labour Party to fight this constituency'.[25] Arthur Peters wrote to Catherine Marshall of his pleasure in hearing that Mrs. Darlington was to begin registration work under the direction of the EFF in Accrington. The opening of another Suffrage Club in Accrington, which soon attracted four hundred members, contributed to this advance, and the Manchester Society could record: 'The understanding between the Suffrage and Labour movement has been strengthened and to this influence we may in part ascribe the formation of the LRC [Labour Representation Committee] in Accrington on February 19th to consider the question of a Labour candidate.'[26] At about this time two EFF organisers, Annot Robinson and Ellen Wilkinson, the future Labour MP, were invited to join a local LRC, and it would seem most likely that this was the Accrington committee.[27]

The work in Rossendale was to match this effort, though not with quite the same degree of success. Ada Nield Chew, the EFF organiser there, had found an unpromising situation to begin with. She reported: 'I took Peters to Rossendale on Monday. . . . The industrial organisation is strong – the political organisation does not exist. The Labour Council has been financially crippled for several years owing to running a paper which got them frightfully into debt. They have also been unfortunate in their Secretaries.' But the LRC was now out of debt, expecting to appoint a new secretary soon, and planning a big demonstration in the autumn. In Ada Nield Chew's preliminary assessment: 'The idea of them asking for or adopting a Labour candidate until there is some political organisation is out of the question, but Peters thinks a year of Labour organisation might make it possible. Perhaps I am saying too much in committing him to this (you know what a dark horse he is) but I think the estimate will not be far short of the mark.' She advised against sending a woman to initiate the Labour organisation and recommended that 'a man the equal of Monk the Liberal Agent' should be employed initially. Thereafter the National Union's Miss Dring might follow up once 'it became sufficiently realised that business is meant'. Margaret Robertson supported this view: 'We've got to give the impression in the division that the *men* are moving, and a man agent, at first at any rate, is essential.'[28]

At this time the Labour Party secretary, Henderson, refused the £100 offered by the EFF for an agent in Rossendale, on the grounds that his party never put an organiser where there was no MP or candidate. He had no objection to the local Labour organisation taking the £100 if they wished. Margaret Robertson responded that this would not be possible, as it was still so small, 'and it would not do at all for it to be known that we were doing so'.[29] Ada Nield Chew continued to work Rossendale despite this setback, and by the spring of 1914 the Manchester Society could record that a local meeting called to discuss the running of a Labour candidate had voted for the proposal by 69 to 10. It was believed that a Labour candidate was now likely, providing the general election did not occur before the autumn.[30] Certainly Rossendale appears on Peters's list of constituencies which the Labour Party was considering fighting at the general election. Together with Accrington it appears under the heading 'Uncertain'. McKibbin notes that this generally indicated that only the issue of financial responsibility remained to be clarified, and that it can be assumed that in 'the usual rush of sanctions' which preceded a general election Labour would have fought most of these 'uncertain' seats.[31]

The North-East Federation, too, continued its commitment to the EFF

policy and established its own EFF Committee. Labour Party organisation was undertaken in Gateshead, South-East and Mid-Durham, Barnards Castle, Bishop Auckland, South Shields, and Chester-le-Street,
with a special campaign among the miners' lodges.[32] The federation's
area also saw several by-elections in which the EFF was employed, and
during which the degree of interpenetration of the local labour and suffrage movements began to disturb both the National Union and Labour
Party leaderships. The first was at Houghton-le-Spring, in March 1913,
where Margaret Robertson and Clementina Gordon had already undertaken preparatory work during February, in case it should become a
three-cornered contest.[33] The campaign demonstrated the conflicting
understanding of the EFF policy that was beginning to emerge between
some of the National Union's leadership and the democratic suffragists
involved in the day-to-day work of putting that policy into practice. Mrs.
Stanbury and Chrystal Macmillan complained at the language of the National Union's address to the electors 'as not confining support of the
Labour candidate on Suffrage grounds'. Some others in the executive
agreed, and took particular exception to one paragraph and a reference
to the class dimensions of the campaign. The EFF Committee was asked
to remind its organisers that addresses to electors in support of Labour
candidates should base that support on the suffrage issue only.[34] Other
than this, the National Union gave the campaign its full support, providing £75 for the hire of cars for the election. The Liberal retained the seats,
but Labour, fighting for the first time, polled 4,165 votes. It was again
estimated by a member of the Labour Party that the National Union's
intervention had been worth a thousand votes to their candidate, and
another was sufficiently moved to pen a series of poems 'for the lady
workers in the division, whose labours resulted I'm confident in converting many to Labourism'.[35]

It is clear that through EFF work in this area many suffragists were
pursuing their joint commitment to Labour politics. In Mid-Durham the
National Union's organiser, Miss Dring, went to the Revision Court as
Labour agent. Catherine Marshall's notes on the state of organisation in
the Houghton constituency after the by-election show that eleven new
ILP branches had been formed, largely at the instigation of suffragist
workers, and had weekly joint meetings with the five suffrage societies.
The local suffragists also had two representatives on the Houghton LRC
(this was clearly still an 'unofficial' LRC; nonetheless it provides evidence of the close relationship that existed between the labour and suffrage movements locally).[36] Labour Party records show that in October
1913 its executive received a request from the North-East Federation of
the National Union for 'Head Office to take the lead in initiating a local
LRC in the Houghton-le-Spring Division'. Head office decided to consult with the Miners' Federation on their intention of continuing to support a candidate before taking further action. The following year the

Labour Party executive's Organisation and Electoral Subcommittee reported that two National Union branches had sent representatives to the conference on 25 April, preliminary to establishing a local LRC. It was resolved that 'the attendance of such organisations for the purpose of the selection of a candidate would be an irregular proceeding, and the convenors of the conference be informed accordingly'.[37] Meanwhile suffragists in the North-East were actively encouraging Labour candidatures elsewhere in their areas – in Bishop Auckland, Mid-Durham, and Chester-le-Street.[38]

During this period the National Union struggled to retain some degree of control over the local EFF committee in the North-East. In February 1913 the London executive decided that the members of all local EFF committees should be subject to the approval of the central EFF Committee,[39] but it appears never to have succeeded in pinning down the north-eastern committee on this subject.[40] Clementina Gordon, the EFF organiser in the Newcastle area, argued that she did not have EFF committees of the same type as other federations:

We tried at Gateshead, but have found by experience that such are not the best methods of getting work out of the Labour Party. Hence we now have committees for organisation only, formed of representatives of the branches of the ILP and of the National Union in the constituency concerned. Should certain members be unable to attend through the three-shift system or for any other reason, proxies are sent. Thus though the majority of the committee remain the same there are slight variations in its personnel. Hence it is impossible for us to send an exact list of members to headquarters.

She requested that her committee be exempted from the ruling, as it was responsible for organisation only, not policy. Any doubt or difficulty was always referred back to the officers of the federation, and their ruling passed back to the local EFF committee. There is no record of the matter being resolved.[41]

In other National Union federations the EFF policy continued to encounter less emphatic support. The secretary of the West Riding Federation, Helena Renton, favoured the EFF policy but found herself at odds with other suffragists in her area when she tried to form a local EFF committee.[42] She had to report a further disappointment in Holmfirth, where the National Union had hoped to maintain the organisation begun in the 1912 by-election. The secretary of the local society had told her 'that things are not going well, indeed the society appears to be going to pieces'. The organiser, Wilma Meikle, was 'of the opinion that it will be quite impossible to have a strong non-party society in view of the EFF work that will be done'. Helena Renton asked whether it might not 'be better to concentrate on forming a good local EFF committee rather than to try to bolster up the present society'. Interestingly, Catherine Marshall underlined this passage and annotated the margin with the answer 'Yes'.[43] A nonparty stance was clearly impossible to maintain where EFF policy was being actively pursued.

Holmfirth was eventually dropped from the EFF's operations, presumably because of lack of local support. In the meantime Helena Renton carried on with the plans for a campaign among miners' lodges and other trade union branches. Her trials come not only from those local suffragists opposed to the new policy. The activities of the EFF organiser in Rotherham, Mrs. Oldham, became a cause for concern to her, too.[44] Rotherham was the constituency of J. A. Pease, one of the antisuffragist cabinet ministers the National Union wished to see opposed in the next election. But when the possibility of running a Labour candidate in Rotherham arose in 1914, Helena Renton began to feel that Mrs. Oldham's commitment to Labour representation outweighed that to suffrage interests. This EFF organiser became involved with what Helena Renton perceived as a conspiracy on the part of the local Labour supporters to ensure a Labour candidate for their constituency.[45] Mrs. Oldham reported in July 1914 that she had been assured that 10 per cent of the election expenses could be found locally but that finding the £50 a year being demanded by the main union in the area for an agent's salary would be very difficult. The union official concerned had suggested the National Union might make a secret contribution to fund this.[46]

Catherine Marshall explained that such an arrangement would be impossible. The TUC and ILP required that local labour organisations should provide an adequate share of an election fund as a guarantee that they would back up a Labour candidate effectively. She insisted: 'For any outside organisation, or even for any wealthy individual who was in sympathy with the Labour demand, to supply these funds would frustrate this purpose; and for us to supply this money in some roundabout way which would not be accepted by the Labour Party if it were done openly would be an unfriendly as well as dishonest action.'[47] She added that if a local fund were opened the EFF might contribute a 'reasonable share towards it', but 'we cannot be a party to supporting a *fictitious* demand for a candidate'. When Mrs. Oldham continued to urge that hers was the only way to ensure a Labour candidate in Rotherham, Catherine Marshall telegrammed: 'Impossible to agree to suggestion. Please do nothing in the matter.'[48]

Soon after, however, Mrs. Oldham was able to report that at a recent local meeting it had been agreed that Walker, of the Steel Smelters' Union, should be adopted. The money for the agent's salary had been guaranteed, and £120 for election expenses was to be raised by local trade unionists, at 6 old pence a head for the election and 3 old pence for the agent. She planned to collect the new register the next day and to concentrate on this aspect of organising the Labour vote. Helena Renton sent an independent report of the meeting, including the information that twenty local trade union representatives had been unanimous in selecting Walker, and she 'felt he would be a most popular candidate'. He was to receive a deputation from the local National Union branch, and a joint campaign was being planned for the autumn.[49] As in Manchester and the North-East, EFF organisers in this area were increasingly being absorbed into local Labour organisations, and this in itself offered further potential for disunity within the suffrage organisations. The East Leeds Labour Party, for example, had already put the EFF organiser, Miss Hilston, on its executive. Helena Renton recorded: 'They would have asked me too had I been a member of the party but for the sake of the Federation I don't feel justified in joining.'[50]

There is evidence of similar tensions in other local National Union organisations over EFF work in their areas. The reactions of the Bristol Society, for example, to the adoption of East Bristol as an EFF constituency had been variable. When the society had finally agreed to cooperate with the new policy at the end of 1912, three members of its committee resigned.[51] No local EFF committee was formed, and the organiser, Mrs. Townley, worked directly under the London committee. A special campaign during April 1913 was followed by registration work in the constituency. Mrs. Townley reported that the campaign had been a success, 'especially among the Committee [of the National Union branch] themselves who never before had heard Labour speeches, or met Labour men. . . . You will be glad to know I am billed for the Great Labour Demonstration hear [sic] on May 4th representing women's suffrage.' She had hopes that a joint suffrage–labour committee would be formed to further the organisation of Labour opinion in the constituency.[52] In July it was reported that the situation was 'still rather critical and difficult owing to the withdrawal of the candidate'. Another was found, but again finance proved a source of problems. It appears that the EFF hoped to fund the ILP's candidate, Walter Ayles, through a grant to the local ILP branch, and thus preempt attempts to secure Ben Tillett the Labour candidacy in this constituency.[53] The Bristol Society's continuing reservations about EFF work were clear when at first it refused to take part in a planned *Daily Citizen* week in December 1913 (the *Daily Citizen* was a paper recently founded by the Labour Party).[54] Alice Clark, now assisting Catherine Marshall with EFF administration, reported that in the end 'we coaxed them round and are going to try to persuade the *Daily Citizen* to have something about us in during that week. I wanted to help Labour if we possibly could.'[55] EFF activity most certainly helped to maintain Labour organisation in this constituency and to strengthen Labour's hopes for running a candidate there in the next election.[56]

The Scottish Federation, though it undertook a considerable amount of EFF work, was particularly seriously divided on the issue. While a number of the Edinburgh Society were deeply involved in operating the new policy, the Glasgow Society proved to be one of its most consistent opponents. Tension between the two factions grew as the Edinburgh suffragists increasingly felt themselves hampered by the attitudes of their opponents among the Scottish Federation officials. Alice Low, a supporter of the EFF policy in the society, wrote to Catherine Marshall in November 1913:

I am worried about EFF work altogether, and a discussion with you would probably clear the air. I feel that we should be making some plans for the General Election. . . . Miss Gordon, Miss Pressley-Smith and I are the only people who know anything whatever about EFF work, and my own private impression is that the Officers of the Scottish Federation are all against the policy.[57]

Another member of the Edinburgh Society, Lisa Gordon, advised Catherine Marshall that all EFF grants should be forwarded direct to her society, rather than through the Scottish Federation's EFF committee, which would adversely interfere with the intended campaigning. She also argued that EFF work in Scotland should be managed either from London or through the Edinburgh Society, for the Scottish Federation's practice was instructed to work the constituency on ordinary propaganda lines organisation.[58] Other material in Catherine Marshall's papers indicates that relations between the Glasgow Society and the Scottish ILP were particularly poor, and that she suspected that society of putting forward candidates for the Scottish EFF committee who were quite out of sympathy with its activities.[59]

Despite such divided councils and determined opposition, some successful EFF campaigning did take place in Scotland.[60] In Midlothian, work continued after the by-election of 1912. Alice Low argued that the constituency held 'an important strategic position. If worked well the Liberal would not be returned again, but if left it could be won back by them.'[61] Labour organising had also been begun in Leith Burghs, where it was believed EFF work could influence the attitude of the antisuffragist Liberal MP, R. Munro Ferguson, and keep him 'up to the mark'. This work was intensified later in 1913 when it was heard that Peters was negotiating for a Labour candidate in the constituency and 'the working women there [were] most anxious that we should start regular fortnightly meetings'. When the Leith by-election occurred in February 1914 the EFF was able to run an active campaign in conjunction with the Women's Labour League. The result was the election of a Unionist suffragist by a majority of 16, Labour polling 3,346. The campaign continued after the election with registration work and joint propaganda meetings with Labour. Shortly before the outbreak of war the Edinburgh organiser could report there were twelve suffragists on local Labour ward committees in Leith and Musselburgh.[62]

The South Wales Federation of the National Union was to remain the most fixedly opposed to the EFF, though work in North Monmouth was continued nonetheless by an organiser sent from London. At first she was instructed to work the constituency on ordinary propaganda lines only, in the hope that the federation would eventually come round. But finally the National Union executive had to inform the federation that the work was 'too urgent to admit of further delay'.[63] The EFF organiser in North Monmouth, Miss Hilston, reported hopefully after early work in Blaenavon (which she described as 'the Gilbraltar of Liberalism in the constituency'). She had 'almost convinced' the president of the local Liberal women's organisation (who was also president of the local British Women's Temperance Association), a local curate, and the Wesleyan minister's wife that they should support an EFF campaign. The local Labour organisations, the ILP, WCG, and Trades and Labour Council, were also responding well, with several women's-suffrage resolutions passed.[64] The South Wales Federation attempted to regain the initiative by announcing a plan to form its own local EFF committee. When the National Union executive and Catherine Marshall stressed that its members would have to be sanctioned by the central EFF Committee, however, the idea appears to have been dropped. The South Wales Federation further embarrassed the National Union by announcing in its annual report: 'There has been no by-election in the Federation area, and we have received an assurance that the EFF policy will not be put in force in our area without our consent.' This prompted an angry letter from one of the strongest supporters of the policy, the North-East Federation, to National Union headquarters.[65]

Despite such attempts at sabotage by the local federation, Miss Hilston was able to report continuing good progress among Labour supporters in the area, though she stressed the need for better Labor organisation. Peters had suggested to her that suffragists might help in this by providing funds for an organiser. Miss Hilston stressed: 'It is so difficult to get them to work here, they always have committee meetings and conferences, nothing more.' She was initiating a women's branch of the ILP, as the WLL had not been able to afford to send an organiser to the area, and was also pressing the WCG to organise a new branch there. The antisuffragist minister, Reginald McKenna, had lost a lot of ground in the constituency, and it was rumoured that he would not stand there again. She enclosed an optimistic report from William Harris on the state of Labour support in the Western Valley. Peters supported this view of Labour's prospects in the constituency after a visit there: 'I was most impressed with the general outlook. . . . I am certainly of the opinion that the division should be contested in the interests of Labour.'[66] The EFF Committee felt able to claim: 'Until our organisers began their campaign the Labour forces in North Monmouth were content to be represented in Parliament by a Liberal. Our work has been twofold, in rousing discontent amongst Labour and converting the Trade Unions to Women's Suffrage.'[67]

Three by-elections in the 1913–14 period further illustrate the tensions and complexities that frequently surrounded the operation of the EFF policy. As in the earlier 1912 campaigns, by-election activity was to prove

by far the least satisfactory aspect of the EFF work. First, suffragists continued to experience considerable frustration with the primitive level of
much Labour Party election machinery. In the South Lanark by-election,
for example, Margaret Robertson decided that EFF organisers might as
well leave the constituency on polling day, as there had been no system-
atic canvass there. Nor had they been allowed to participate in what
casual canvassing had been undertaken. She reported to Catherine Marshall: 'We all stayed at Midlothian, and kicked our heels all day – the
same at Houghton and the same at Crewe . . . it is in vain for us to make
any suggestions with a man like Duncan Graham in charge. He will
listen to nothing and is absolutely incapable of organising.' Graham had
both failed to advertise Annot Robinson's three meetings and announced Keir Hardie's meeting only two hours beforehand, though he
had known of it for a week. Margaret Robertson's report concluded: 'It
is heart-breaking.' Another EFF organiser, Clementina Gordon, confirmed this impression: 'I do not think it is worth our while to stay, the
Labour organisation is so bad.'[68]

Even more significant however was the evidence in several of the by-
elections of a conflict of views within the National Union leadership concerning such involvement in Labour politics. To begin with, as we have
already seen, there was a growing fear among some National Union
leaders that many of the EFF organisers were allowing their commitment to Labour politics to overshadow their loyalty to the suffrage cause.
Such concern was evidenced in a resolution put to the National Union
executive in June 1913, that organizers, in speeches or letters to the press,
refer to their support for Labour on suffrage grounds only. Given the
background of most EFF organisers, this was clearly unrealistic, and after
discussion the resolution was amended.[69] Further evidence to support
such concern was forthcoming when the National Union executive decided not to run an EFF campaign on behalf of the Labour candidate in
the Keighley by-election in December 1913. The Liberal candidate, Sir
Stanley Buckmaster, was a committed suffragist, and the Labour Party
organisation was felt to be very weak. Consequently it was decided to
run a propaganda campaign only. EFF organiser Margaret Robertson
was much angered by the decision and argued that the National Union
should have taken no part at all in the election if Labour were not to be
supported. In response, headquarters pointed out that propaganda work
had begun two weeks before the Labour candidate, Bland, was announced.[70] The National Union's secretary, Kathleen Courtney, commented:

The Keighley business has been a nuisance but I don't regret it as it will have
opened the eyes of quite a number of people. Including my own which are open
to the fact that Gordon is more Labour than Suffrage, and that Margaret Robertson inclines that way. This is serious and may in the future be calamitous. What
are we to do about it?[71]

For their part Margaret Robertson and Clementina Gordon insisted the decision had been both a breach of National Union policy and a threat to good relations with the Labour Party.[72] A complaint also came from Dr. Ethel Williams of the North-East Federation:

We are in great trouble over Keighley here but hope to live it down. My belief is that the good Liberal women under the guise of propaganda did support Stanley Buckmaster. Our Labour friends are hurt and bitter to an extent hardly explained by the facts as we know them. I think the said ladies should be told what very serious harm they have done the cause.[73]

Margaret Ashton of the Manchester Society also wrote to Catherine Marshall: 'I am really relieved that *you* see the seriousness of the whole bother for I do not think Miss Clark does. We can't afford to be thrown by the Labour Party – we have only them to rely on (and a broken reed at that) for the next general election.'[74] In contrast Alice Clark upheld the official National Union view, and suggested that it might be wise to co-opt Margaret Robertson, together with a representative from the North-East EFF committee, onto the central body in order to 'a little detach her from the other organisers'. Alice Clark argued: 'They do so much work that I think their point of view would be valuable and I don't think people get so far away if they can discuss things point by point.'[75]

The next month the pursuit of EFF policy required that the National Union oppose one of its own members, Aneurin Williams, the Liberal candidate in the North-West Durham by-election. Mrs. Fawcett explained to Kathleen Courtney: 'I believe it would have been the end of the Labour policy if we hadn't supported Mr. Stuart [the Labour candidate]. . . . a good deal of work in preparation has been done in the constituency and our people up there are in close touch with the Labour Party.'[76] Alice Clark wrote in apology to the Liberal candidate's wife: 'The position is a most painful one for us and I trust you believe how deeply we regret appearing to oppose you. . . . I need hardly say that if Mr. Stuart fails we shall all be extremely gratified by your success.'[77] In contrast, when leading Liberal members of the Gateshead Society threatened to resign over the matter,[78] Ethel Williams made clear her whole-hearted support for the EFF campaign and attempted to strengthen Mrs. Fawcett's resolve in the matter by reporting an incident at a recent Labour meeting. When the suggestion of a joint suffrage–labour campaign was raised, one LRC member had remarked that they did not yet know Stuart's attitude to women's suffrage. At this point 'the meeting uprose and said "If Mr. Stuart is not the women's man, he is not *our* man, *we* don't want him." '[79]

The resistance to the EFF policy which the North-West Durham by-election provoked was further strengthened in January 1914 when the National Union executive made a statement on future EFF policy to the ILP's Annual Meeting in Glasgow. This indicated what would happen

to the policy should the Liberal Party decide to take up women's suffrage as part of its programme for the next general election. It guaranteed that even though the National Union would no longer feel able to
oppose the Liberal Party as such, in those circumstances it would nonetheless maintain its existing commitments to Labour candidates, and
would undertake not to support any candidates standing in opposition
to those of Labour.[80] Chrystal Macmillan and Eleanor Rathbone, at the
National Union's executive meeting, requested the withdrawal of such
statements as 'ultra vires,' inasmuch as they elaborated on National Union
election policy without the sanction of the National Union's council.[81]
Catherine Marshall, with a majority on the executive, resisted this request on the grounds that 'the Glasgow statement was an interpretation
of policy' (i.e. of what was implicit in the existing policy) and not a new
development of it.[82]

In the meantime Eleanor Rathbone and three other members of the
executive began to organise opinion within the National Union against
the operation of EFF policy at the general election. This brought a repri-
mand from Mrs. Fawcett, but the campaign continued. To settle this
crisis, the half-yearly council was moved forward from July to April. The
executive's resolution recommended that no further decision concerning
policy at a general election be taken (beyond that outlined in February
1913). If a general election were announced a special council would be
called to consider all possible courses. It also implied criticism of those
members of the executive who had involved themselves in organising
opinion in opposition to policy already decided by council.[83] The main
fear of Eleanor Rathbone and her supporters seems to have been that
proponents of the EFF policy within the executive intended to secure its
extension to the general election expected within the next year or so.
The dissidents insisted they were not against the pro-Labour policy in
the twenty-six or so constituencies where the National Union had already made commitments to Labour and agreed that 'the Labour Party
is undoubtedly entitled to preferential treatment by the services they
have already rendered us'. But they were opposed to an anti-Liberal
general election campaign, and feared that a pro-Labour policy went
hand in hand with support for Unionist candidates elsewhere.[84]

Even though this dissident section of the executive was defeated at
the National Union council, disquiet continued to be expressed, particularly among Liberal supporters of the National Union. M. A. Marshall
of the Haslemere Society reported that she and two others were now the
only EFF supporters on her local branch committee. Agnes Gill of the
Sheffield Society wrote to Mrs. Renton of the disaffection among Liberal
supporters, who claimed the National Union had become a Tory organisation. Maude Dowson of the East Midland Federation had a similar
story to tell:

All our Liberal members wrote to have their names taken off our books when the National Union adopted an anti-government policy. Of course we knew they would and it is only natural. We forfeited a tremendous amount of help by adopting that policy – I still get continual reports of resignations in the Branches (of *officials* and members).[85]

Such evidence, however, reflected a polarisation of attitudes within the National Union rather than simply a weakening of support for the EFF. Most democratic suffragists, like Margaret Ashton in Manchester and Ethel Williams in Newcastle, as well as the chief administrators of the EFF policy, Catherine Marshall and Margaret Robertson, had increased their commitment to joint labour–suffrage campaigning during 1912–14 period. Others, like the National Union's secretary, Kathleen Courtney, and Catherine Marshall's aide, Alice Clark, continued to support the work even though they experienced some unease as Labour organisation sometimes seemed to be taking precedence over suffragist interests. Such adherents of the EFF policy could continue to rely on the backing of Mrs. Fawcett on the purely pragmatic ground that her faith in its tactical value remained undiminished. But opposition to the policy was also intensifying, and there was a somewhat defensive note in Catherine Marshall's contention, after the Rathbone controversy, that the policy had lost no ground among the National Union's membership. She denied that a vote for a motion by Eleanor Rathbone at the council had been anti-EFF policy, and suggested it had simply indicated a desire for no further extension of the policy to any new constituencies in preparation for the general election. She countered this example with the fact that a Newcastle resolution at the November council to extend the EFF far more broadly had been lost by only ten votes. Further, she argued that the fact that EFF work had been entirely self-supporting, and had not yet had to draw on general National Union funds (though this was now possible), illustrated the scale of its support: 'Indeed it has carried out a large amount of propaganda among trades unions which might quite legitimately have counted as ordinary National Union work i.e. the National Union has practically received financial help from the EFF instead of giving it.'[86] Catherine Marshall might also have argued that the continual rapid increase in National Union membership was evidence that the EFF was not damaging National Union support – it was frequently stated that the National Union was enrolling at the rate of a thousand new members a month in this period.[87]

Closer inspection of both the membership figures and EFF finances modify such claims a little. If the rate of enrolment of a thousand a month is matched to the increase in total membership of the National Union for the years 1912–14, it is clear that there must have been a considerable turnover in membership – that is to say, if many were joining, many were also leaving.[88] While Catherine Marshall's description of EFF finances was true up to this time – spring 1914 – the estimated expenditure for the next quarter outstripped the funds in hand, and for the first time it was necessary to draw on the Transferable Fund and to set aside another £1,000 from general funds for probable expenditure in the quarter following that.[89] Though donations continued to come in, they were on a relatively small scale, with an occasional larger donation. In November 1913 it was announced that the EFF had raised £6,923 since its inception.[90] Over two-thirds of this had been collected by the end of 1912; but the extent of financial contributions to the EFF itself is an inadequate measure of support after the inauguration of the Transferable Fund and the Women's Suffrage Mandate Fund. The latter was specifically intended to finance preparations for the next general election, and therefore would have attracted similar subscribers to the EFF. Reports of EFF and Women's Suffrage Mandate Fund donations in *The Common Cause* indicate that the two were seen as interrelated.[91] It is not possible, in consequence, to assess the popularity of the EFF simply by the rate of donations that were coming directly to it.

It would seem that the approach of a general election, together with the work of the EFF committees, was intensifying partisan feeling among suffragists. A letter from three officers of the Highgate Society to Catherine Marshall made this clear. They had never been able to arouse much enthusiasm for the EFF, they claimed, and now found it increasingly difficult to raise funds or attract new members. In contrast, they argued, the party organisations for women's suffrage were attracting both, often among those who would previously have looked to their local National Union branch. 'Many of them refuse to accept our definition of "Non-Party" and unless some modification of the policy is agreed upon we fear that at a General Election we should lose some of our most active members, and only receive lukewarm support from others'. They agreed the EFF policy should be continued in constituencies where the National Union was already committed, but recommended that otherwise the National Union's local societies be allowed to support either a Conservative or Liberal candidate if he was a proved suffragist. Their own MP, W. H. Dickinson, had been involved with the Conciliation Bills and they would want to support him. 'It is hardly too much to say that the future of our branch depends on the attitude we adopt to this excellent friend to our Cause.'[92]

The effect of the EFF policy on the National Union itself in terms of membership and financial resources would seem, then, to present a very mixed picture. While many committed Liberals left over the policy, others welcomed the chance they felt it offered as a corrective to their party. One donor to the EFF sent her contribution in order 'to help purge my once beloved party – the party which still represents so much that is dear to me and is only going astray on *one* point – of those reactionaries and wobblers against whom I feel an indignation that no woman who is not a Liberal can fully share'.[93] By spring 1914, however, the enthusiasm of many such supporters was waning. No doubt there was a wide variety of reasons for this. Much of the initial anger at the defeat of the Conciliation Bills and the withdrawal of the Reform Bill would now have dissipated, and the approach of a general election would be reviving old party loyalties. Further, many were disillusioned by the continuing ambivalence, even hostility, of some Labour leaders, particularly MacDonald, towards the suffragists, and the performance of the Parliamentary Labour Party on issues like the Plural Voting Bill and the women's-suffrage amendment to the Irish Home Rule Bill.

The democratic suffragists, who were the most tenacious and consistent proponents of the policy, remained committed to a suffragist–labour alliance both as a long-term strategy and as an expression of their conviction of the interrelatedness of feminist and class politics. But they were dependent on the support of others who saw the policy only as a short-term tactic through which to express their displeasure with the Liberal government. This fundamental conflict of view over the standing of the EFF policy was to emerge clearly during the war years. If war had not broken out and, as seems likely, the National Union leadership had decided to maintain their commitment to the Labour Party in the next general election, they would almost certainly have had to confront a serious rebellion from the Liberal rank and file of their membership. At the same time, though, the evidence from the EFF campaigns indicates that democratic suffragists had successfully located a new and considerable source of support within labour groups and working-class communities, one that was outweighing losses to National Union membership in the form of departing Liberals.

CHAPTER 6

THE WOMEN'S-SUFFRAGE MOVEMENT AND THE IMPACT OF WAR

The Election Fighting Fund policy was the keystone of constitutional strategy in the two years before the outbreak of the First World War. During this same period, the pressure it served to exert on the Liberal government was intensified by a number of other political manoeuvres on the part of both constitutionalists and dissident militants. All of these evidenced the continuing vitality and ever-increasing political effectiveness of the suffrage movement in this period. It was not a time of dormancy, defeatism, or depression among suffragists.[1] Though the WSPU began to experience disintegration and decline, other sections of the movement had good grounds to feel in the weeks immediately preceding the outbreak of war that they were on the eve of victory. Nor can interpretations that see the suffrage movement as a spent force during wartime be sustained.[2] Suffragists were to be seriously split over a number of issues thrown up by the war, and significant realignments were to occur. Some suffragists were to immerse themselves almost completely in work for the war effort. Yet suffrage organisation was to be maintained to a remarkable degree during the first years of the war, and suffragist participation was to be a significant factor in the debates and campaigning that preceded the Representation of the People Bill of 1917. These contentions can be supported by a review of the course of suffrage politics in the months preceding August 1914 and the initial response of constitutional suffragists to the enormous disruption that followed the outbreak of war.

From the spring of 1912 National Union political policies had been aimed at securing the inclusion of women in any government measure of franchise reform. From January 1913 and the withdrawal of the Franchise and Registration Bill, their central object had been to make women's suffrage an issue at the expected general election. The Election Fighting Fund policy was intended to strengthen the efforts of the Labour Party in these directions. But at the same time National Union lobbying was intensified in two other respects. In the first place the pro-suffrage Liberal ministers were kept under constant pressure to increase their commitment to the issue, while pro-suffrage opinion among the rank and file of the Liberal Party was organised in order to strengthen their hand. Secondly, prosuffrage opinion within the Conservative Party was organised so as to create the threat of a possible Tory women's-suffrage measure, disadvantageous to Liberal Party interests. In parliament, National Union activity during this period ensured that 'the Government should find the women's suffrage confront them at every turn' – on the Scottish Home Rule Bill, the Plural Voting Bill, and the Welsh Disestablishment Bill (to which an amendment was placed to include women in the Synod).[3] In all these ways the National Union aimed to undermine the position of the antisuffragists in the cabinet.

Extraparliamentary activity during the summer of 1913 concentrated on the highly successful Women's Suffrage Pilgrimage, where suffragist marchers set off from a number of points around the country, converging several weeks later on London for a major demonstration. Even antisuffragists in the cabinet appear to have been impressed by the event.[4] Mrs. Fawcett requested that they receive a deputation from the 'pilgrims' with the assertion that suffragists could 'hardly believe that you and your Party can regard coercion [a reference to the Cat and Mouse Act] unaccompanied by any remedial measure as an adequate response to the demand of women to share in the advantages of representative government.'[5] Asquith agreed to receive the deputation, admitting: 'I quite recognise that the request which you put forward, after the recent law-abiding demonstration of your societies, has a special claim on my consideration and stands upon another footing from similar demands proceeding from other quarters, where a different method and spirit prevails.'[6] While he warned that he had nothing further to add to his recent statements on the intention and policy of the government, his tone was clearly conciliatory, and represented the first indication of a possible shift in attitude on his part.

The main thrust of the National Union's case during this meeting was the alliance of the women's-suffrage cause with that of democracy; and some speakers were clearly attempting to intimidate the Liberal leaders with evidence of working-class backing for the demand. Margaret Robertson asserted of the Anti-Suffrage League that 'Lord Rothschild had given £3,000' and its membership was 'running through the gamut of dukes and lords. . . . What I have found is that working men have discovered this and they are inclined to regard opposition to women's suffrage as a Conservative and Liberal Plutocracy against Democracy.'[7] In his reply Asquith both denied that he had been ready to defeat the women's-suffrage amendment to the Reform Bill and agreed that there was no hope for a private-member bill without government backing. Some present at the deputation believed that they had extracted a commitment from him to introduce a women's-suffrage measure in the next parliament, though others disagreed with this interpretation. All in all, the National Union was considerably heartened by its reception, claiming that Asquith 'had seemed genuinely impressed by the Pilgrimage and by the speeches made by members of the Deputation'. *The Common Cause* felt able to declare that the issue was at last being seen 'as a question, not of sex, but of democracy'.[8] Certainly this was the aspect of the matter that Asquith was to stress when he received a further suffrage deputation from the militant East London Federation of Suffragettes the following year.

The National Union was less satisfied with the response of the suffragist ministers to a similar Pilgrimage deputation and their continuing vagueness as to a possible timetable for government action on women's suffrage. The cabinet suffragists did agree, however, to make the women's-suffrage issue figure in their public speeches, and Lloyd George offered a place on his platforms for suffragist speakers. But any more definite commitment was refused until the Irish home rule and Welsh disestablishment issues had been successfully settled. Once this had been achieved 'the position of the suffragists in the Cabinet would be different' – a reference to the antisuffragist prime minister's ability to command their absolute loyalty for the present, but only for the present.[9] In subsequent correspondence with Lloyd George, Catherine Marshall made explicit her own commitment to securing women's suffrage as part of an adult-suffrage measure when she expressed her hope that the chancellor was 'going to do what I have always hoped you meant to do, start a really effective demand for Adult Suffrage (which there never has been yet) at the same time as your land campaign. It would be a grand programme on which to go to the country.'[10]

By this time Sir John Simon had also emerged as a leading cabinet supporter of women's suffrage. At a further National Union deputation which he received in Manchester, suffragists once again pressed their case for franchise reform becoming the next major government concern after its present programme was complete. Once again they were rewarded with the promise that women's suffrage would in future be one of the issues the minister would air in his major speeches. Referring to the present cabinet impasse on franchise reform, he, too, indicated that 'conditions might alter'.[11] The other minister on whom the National Union kept up persistent pressure was Sir Edward Grey. Catherine Marshall arranged a confidential meeting with Grey and Francis Acland on 15 December 1913, from which she kept a summary of the discussion. This shows that, once again, she stressed the danger of the EFF policy being extended to a 'policy of blind hostility' to the Liberals, and the importance of making women's suffrage a major part of any future programme if the present parting of the way between his party and the constitutionalists were to be resolved. She predicted that the National Union could get enough active support from its members to threaten the loss of a good many Liberal seats by helping to strengthen Labour Party organisation. She suggested, too, the danger that this present disillusionment with the Liberal government might 'easily turn to anarchistic policy'. In pointing to the links between the women's-suffrage movement, the labour movement, and the movements for colonial independence, she argued: 'It matters enormously to whole of future civilisation whether these three great movements run on sound and healthy lines or are driven into revolution.'[12] Such arguments were to become a significant theme in her promotion of democratic suffragism.

Catherine Marshall's assertion of Liberal disillusion was not overstated, and Liberal ministers were themselves receiving ample evidence to prove that it was so. One of Lloyd George's correspondents wrote to ask if he could stop forcible feeding, and enclosed a letter from a friend which commented: 'Surely Women Liberals can never stand this real gross injustice – even if men's Liberalism believes in it.'[13] Another woman Liberal suffragist wrote to Mrs. Lloyd George: 'I wish you would put before him some thoughts which we Liberal suffragist women feel about his speech on women's suffrage as reported yesterday.' She rejected his assertion that militancy was the cause of failure – that responsibility lay with the cabinet. The large majority of suffrage workers were peaceful, and must be taken to include the members of the National Union of Women Workers, the women's temperance organisations, the WCG, and the WLL.

Look at the bitter injured feelings of the women Liberals too, as shown in our summer metings all over the country, they are leaving in shoals, and joining the only party honestly pressing women's suffrage, a party which can refuse its own good, Manhood Suffrage until we get free. . . . Every bright and clever woman in my Liberal society has left us. I am the only one who spoke and took chairs of them left. It is hard to get our Liberal women to care to go to a meeting now – they laugh at the Government for calling themselves Liberals and democrats. . . . Can you wonder at our intense gratitude to men like Philip Snowden and Ramsay MacDonald and the Labour associations who value their women and really think they could help England and are needed. They don't talk to Englishwomen as if they were that tiny handful of reckless goaded militants, as Liberal speakers do.[14]

By this time the resignation of leading members of the Women's Liberal Federation (WLF) was becoming commonplace,[15] and the WLF itself was in the process of organisational decline. The year 1912 had seen the peak of an expansion which had been considerable since the early years of the century – between 1904 and 1912 membership rose from 66,000 to 133,215, and the number of branches had grown from 496 to 837. The annual report for 1912–13 – after the withdrawal of the Liberals' Reform Bill – noted that membership had dropped to 121,888 since the preceding year, while twenty branches had withdrawn and thirty had lapsed. It commented: 'There can be no real peace or concord in Liberal ranks until the women's suffrage question is settled righteously.' This process of decline continued the following year, and by 1915 there were only 749 branches with a membership of 106,997.[16] Early in 1913 Eleanor Acland, a prominent member of the WLF, wrote to her old school friend Catherine Marshall concerning plans for a new Liberal women's-suffrage society: 'We Liberal women must have a Liberal suffrage society, distinct (I think) from the WLF which can no longer be quoted as a suffrage society. I know heaps of Liberal suffragists who say how they can't join yours (because of Labour Party pact) and don't know what to join.' She suggested that the EFF policy should be restricted to the seventy-eight Liberal antisuffragist candidates, without attacking the one hundred faithful supporters. 'We must have a party Bill. Well then we must have a Bill of a party *strong* enough to carry it. That party will be a Radical–Labour one. . . . The cleavage in the Liberal Party is becoming clearer and in the main it's a double cleavage running on the same lines – Whig-Antis versus Radical-Suffragists.'[17] She estimated that a Liberal women's-suffrage society might organise ten thousand supporters before the next election.

The subsequent formation of the Liberal Women's Suffrage Union (LWSU) was an attempt to hold the loyalty of Liberal women who were also committed suffragists. The initiative for the new society had come from some members of the WLF executive, led by Eleanor Acland. They had been defeated at the recent Annual Conference of the WLF on their resolution that only those associations should be affiliated that would make women's suffrage a test question for Liberal candidates during elections. The new society's objectives were to seek the withdrawal of antisuffragists as Liberal candidates, while working to strengthen the cause within the Liberal Party, for 'in many places the Men's Liberal Association were putting great pressure on the Liberal women and endeavouring to prevent them from adopting a strong suffrage policy'.[18] Following the formation of the LWSU, Eleanor Acland wrote to Lloyd George asking his approval for 'this new movement which we as Liberal women are starting with the object of obtaining more support within the Liberal Party for a democratic women's suffrage measure *in the next Parliament*. Our policy is to bind together Liberal suffrage women to work for Liberal suffrage candidates only.'[19] Lloyd George responded with a public statement of support and a promise to work to make women's suffrage 'a Liberal measure of the first rank', though he did not publicly give approval to the LWSU's pledge to refuse to work for antisuffragist Liberals at the next election.[20]

The LWSU quickly began to make an impact on the national Liberal Party. The *Manchester Guardian* reported a protest from a group of Liberal MPs regarding methods of selecting Liberal candidates. They demanded an inquiry into persistent rumours that at Liberal Party headquarters the chief whip, Illingworth, and the Scottish chief whip, Gulland, were demanding that candidates should be pledged to suffrage.[21] From Lloyd George's papers it is clear that he was keeping lists of the women's-suffrage views of both Liberal MPs and prospective candidates. These were marked 'Private and Confidential' and it is most likely that they originated from National Union sources. One of his correspondents protested against his association with the LWSU and 'its endeavours to make the Suffrage question a shibboleth', believing that, if successful, it would lead 'as surely to disruption and disaster as did the similar policy of the Unionist Party on Tariff Reform'.[22] Lloyd George intervened on the LWSU's behalf in at least one constituency, Cheltenham, where the Liberal candidate, Rhys Williams, was an antisuffragist.[23] Frances Stevenson, as Lloyd George's secretary, wrote to a member of the Cheltenham LWSU: 'I do not think you need despair. The Chancellor does not intend to let the matter drop, and is going to see Mr. Rhys Williams when Parliament meets again.' There was 'every hope that he may be brought round'.[24]

The LWSU's first public meeting was held in March 1914, when it was claimed that five thousand members had been recruited in the nine months since its formation. Any Liberal society or woman prepared to abstain from election work for antisuffragist candidates might join. W. H. Dickinson, who addressed the inaugural meeting, summed up its position in words which echoed the statements of representatives of the National Union: 'After Home Rule and the Welsh Church, what follows? The reconstruction of democracy.'[25] The LWSU continued the struggle within the WLF for a more determined suffrage position and put a resolution to the 1914 WLF Annual Conference that members should strike against antisuffragist Liberals in elections. It was lost by 400 votes to 456 against. Nonetheless the National Union felt the meeting had gone very well for the suffrage cause. Those members who had come top of the poll for election to the WLF executive had all been involved with the LWSU. Further, the conference had passed resolutions calling for a government women's-suffrage bill, and another that it was the duty of the WLF to secure the selection of suffragist candidates.[26]

Predictably, when conflict did appear between the LWSU and the National Union, it concerned the EFF policy. The LWSU hoped to convince the National Union that it should restrict its EFF campaigning to the seats of antisuffragist Liberals, and to concentrate especially on those of the antisuffragists in the cabinet. They constantly argued against any greater involvement in Labour politics.[27] The National Union remained deaf to such pleas, however, and relations between the National Union and the LWSU deteriorated rapidly during 1914. After the National Union made its commitment to the Labour Party regarding the general election, Eleanor Acland resigned as one of its vice-presidents. She suggested a joint conference between the executives of the two organisations to see if some compromise could be reached between them, and this meeting took place on 27 July 1914.

Here the National Union leaders made clear their position: 'We regard a Conservative Government in the future that does nothing for women's suffrage as less injurious to suffrage than a Liberal government that does nothing for suffrage.'[28] They declared themselves unimpressed with the LWSU's claim that it had achieved the replacement or conversion of antisuffragist candidates in several seats – Colchester, Exeter, and Hampstead were cited. However, Catherine Marshall did suggest that if the LWSU could effect a change in certain constituencies, like Harrow, where the National Union had plans to oppose the antisuffragist Liberal, the National Union might no longer wish to intervene. The result of the meeting was inconclusive, but its record suggests the growing influence of the LWSU within Liberal circles, the strength of the National Union's commitment to its alliance with the Labour Party, and the polarisation among women suffragists that was developing with the approach of the general election.

Increasing National Union involvement in Labour politics did not provide the only cause for friction between it and organised Liberal suffrage opinion. In the autumn of 1913 the National Union had also commenced a lobbying campaign within the Conservative Party. This was the third aspect of its overall strategy for the future general election. For the next few months Catherine Marshall concentrated much of her attention on drumming up Conservative support, with apparent success. She wrote to Lady Selborne, of the Conservative and Unionist Franchise Association, that she had just heard 'on good authority that our attempts to frighten the Liberals with the argument that a Conservative Government might bring in an "equal terms" measure of women's suffrage are being surprisingly successful. They believed that such a measure would "keep them out of office for a generation".' She had been told, too, that the Liberal Party was as uneasy at the prospect of a predicted demand from the Labour Party for universal suffrage: 'Even Mr. Lloyd George is afraid of a measure which would put women electors in the majority.'[29] To reinforce these insecurities the National Union consulted with Conservative suffragists regarding the possible introduction of a House of Lords women's-suffrage bill with a property qualification. Catherine Marshall also began to collect information regarding pro-suffrage Conservative MPs, agents, and party notables. In the spring of 1914 she was engaged in secret negotiations with Conservative suffragists regarding a possible future Conservative women's-suffrage initiative. These efforts were closely connected with women's-suffrage amendments to the Irish, Scottish, and Welsh home-rule bills being heard at this time.[30]

The prompt to all this activity, of course, had been the growing expectation of a general election. In mid-June 1914 Catherine Marshall reported to her executive: 'The Conservatives appeared to be as much agitated as the Liberals lest the other Party should take up the women's suffrage question.' Arthur Steel-Maitland, the chairman of the Conservative Party, had sent to the National Union for information and leaflets on the women's-suffrage question. Lord Robert Cecil reported 'being approached by influential Conservatives, both in the House and the country, who were anxious that steps should be taken by the Party towards a settlement of the question'. He had recommended a strong women's-suffrage deputation to the leading Unionists in the House of Commons. By mid-July 1914 the National Union was preparing to announce Arthur Steel-Maitland's conversion to support for women's suffrage.[31] Among Liberals, Catherine Marshall detected a 'marked feeling of anxiety . . . lest the Conservative Party should begin to take action, with regard to women's suffrage, and should bring in a Bill in Conservative interests'.[32] A. J. Balfour had also spoken in support of the women's-suffrage clause in the Scottish Home Rule Bill, although he had opposed the bill itself. In a draft speech for the London Society Catherine Marshall presented the growing women's-suffrage movement within the Conservative Party 'as the most effective means of producing action on the part of the Liberals'.[33]

At the same time National Union propaganda kept up the theme of women's suffrage as an essential component of democratic government. A leaflet designed for the East Fife by-election in April 1914, where Asquith was standing unopposed, read:

SHALL THE PEOPLE RULE. ASQUITH says NO. He is trying to pose now as the PEOPLE's champion but when millions of unenfranchised PEOPLE ask for VOTES HE is the man to flout this request. Is this Democracy? In Opposing the Enfranchisement of Women Mr. ASQUITH advocates Taxation without Representation. Is this Democracy? Mr. ASQUITH advocates Government without the consent of the Governed. Is this Democracy? Mr. ASQUITH supports the MONOPOLY of political power by one sex. Is this Democracy? Mr. ASQUITH supports the maintenance of a section of the community in a position of privilege from which by the ACCIDENT OF BIRTH half the nation is permanently excluded. Is this Democracy?[34]

Working-class support for women's suffrage was continually stressed, particularly in dealings with suffragist ministers.[35] The direction of Catherine Marshall's own thinking is reflected in a question she framed for the Labour leaders: 'What do they think about a "Progressive Suffrage Party" – Labour and Radicals?'[36]

Meanwhile, with the general election in view, Catherine Marshall consulted with Henderson on how the Labour vote could best be used to support women's suffrage. She suggested the possibility of asking Labour supporters either to cast their votes for suffragists against anti-suffragists, irrespective of party, or to withhold their votes, if neither of the major parties put women's suffrage in their programme. Henderson advised instead that she write to the national Labour Party at the time of the general election suggesting that women's suffrage be made a test question for securing the Labour vote in constituencies, as was done in regard to the Taff Vale judgment in 1906. He thought it would almost certainly agree.[37]

By July 1914 Catherine Marshall could note that 'the foremost issue' in the General Committee of the TUC was the textile workers' resolution for universal suffrage for the forthcoming conference. It was hoped to make this a test question for trade union–supported Labour parliamentary candidates. Both Henderson and W. A. C. Anderson of the ILP were pleased with this development, and Henderson was confident it would be carried. There were further plans to raise the question of women's suffrage becoming a test question for the Labour vote at events like the Durham Miners' Gala, together with the idea of a general strike for women's suffrage: 'Even the suggestion of it would be of great value to Suffragists abroad.'[38] The cooperation of suffragists with the labour movement was clearly succeeding in ensuring that the Labour demand for adult suffrage involved a commitment to universal suffrage, not merely to a manhood franchise. Catherine Marshall confidently asserted: 'Women's suffrage is bound to come soon, Militancy or no Militancy, if for no other reason than because the Labour Party will insist on it.'[39]

Such a note of euphoria was commonplace in the correspondence of National Union leaders at this time, and their optimism proved not to be without justification.[40] By the summer of 1914 Lloyd George, with the knowledge and approval of Asquith, had begun negotiations with Sylvia Pankhurst and George Lansbury (who was close to the suffrage movement in the East End of London, and also a leading member of the newly formed United Suffragists). In early July Lloyd George wrote to the home secretary, McKenna, asking to talk with him before he took any action to rearrest Sylvia Pankhurst, at present free on licence under the provisions of the Cat and Mouse Act. 'She and her friends mean to throw in their lot with the constitutionalists against the Militants. This would be useful and unless she is guilty of some outburst – which is extremely improbable – would it not be desirable to leave her alone?' The letter was sent with a covering note which stated: 'Since writing enclosed letter, the Chancellor saw the Prime Minister who promised to see the Home Secretary and arrange matters with him.'[41] These moves were presumably a follow-up to Asquith's reception of the East End deputation on 20 June 1914. This event has generally been accepted by previous writers as a clear indication that Asquith was at last preparing to move on the issue.[42] Asquith had declared to this deputation: 'If the change has to come, we must face it boldly and make it thoroughgoing and democratic in its basis.'[43]

Such a statement has to be seen within the context of constitutionalist campaigning over the previous two years, especially its increasing concentration on evidence of working-class support and the association of the women's demand with the call for democracy. His statement also compares interestingly with points Lloyd George made in a letter to the Liberal chief whip in 1911 and Margaret Robertson's speech during the National Union's deputation to Asquith the previous summer.[44] Morgan suggests: 'With, seemingly, a General Election not too far away Asquith was firing the opening shot of the campaign.'[45] The negotiations which Lloyd George became involved in after the East End deputation, and the evidence of Asquith's knowledge of them, provide further support for this view.

On 21 July 1914 Sylvia Pankhurst wrote to Lloyd George outlining her response to his proposals and suggesting further development of them. Lloyd George appears to have offered a women's-suffrage clause in a government Reform Bill which would be left to a free vote in the House of Commons, along with the promise of his own refusal to join a cabinet that would not agree to the latter condition. Sylvia Pankhurst responded by asking for his promise to leave the cabinet if the women's-suffrage clause were voted out of the proposed bill, or better still to declare himself unable to join any cabinet that would not make itself responsible for the women's-suffrage clause. On the question of militancy she could see no cessation 'until some very definite guarantee of action has been given'. She ended with a suggestion that echoed the one made to him earlier by Catherine Marshall:

What a splendid rally there would be if a Franchise Bill for Manhood and Womanhood suffrage were carried in this Parliament! If the Lords were to throw it out, it wouldn't matter at all – it would only be a temporary delay that would make the enthusiasm the greater and it would be the best possible rallying cry for the General Election.[46]

George Lansbury later claimed that an agreement was reached with the Liberal government, with Lloyd George promising that he, Grey, and Simon would publicly pledge themselves to refuse office in any future government that did not take up women's suffrage. This opportunity was destroyed by Christabel Pankhurst's refusal to consider a truce.[47] What remains significant about these events, however, is that, only two weeks before the outbreak of war, negotiations between suffragists and government were taking place. The evidence suggests that with a general election in view the Liberal leadership had at last made up its mind to tackle women's suffrage in the context of an adult-suffrage reform bill.

The National Union's records provide no evidence of its involvement in such negotiations – in fact Catherine Marshall's correspondence with Lloyd George during this period would indicate the contrary. But they do provide one further piece of evidence on the state of the issue in the cabinet. Catherine Marshall's papers contain a report from a National Union member of an unofficial conversation with another suffragist minister, Haldane, when 'his extreme friendliness' to the suffrage cause was expressed in this declaration: 'I say to Lord Curzon and the Prime Minister that it doesn't matter whether they think it wise or not, it has simply *got to be* and nothing can ultimately prevent it. The real obstacle now is militancy.' Haldane suggested that if this could be halted then most probably some big concession would be forthcoming: 'I fancied though he didn't *say* so that the Cabinet would then insist on a step forward being made.'[48] Such an assessment corresponds exactly with the nature of the agreement Lloyd George was trying to reach with one group of militants. It seems unlikely that the WSPU leadership could ever have been persuaded to this pact, given Christabel's hatred and suspicion of the Liberal leadership, but equally it is debatable how much longer the WSPU could have continued as an effective organisation or retained its credibility as the voice of the militant wing of the movement.[49]

There remains the question why certain members of the government chose to open negotiations with what was, relative to the National Union or the Liberal women's organisations, a small group with far fewer claims on their attention. O'Neill and Morgan have pointed to the working-class composition of Sylvia Pankhurst's East London Federation and suggested that the government felt the need to appease the working-class vote on this issue and perhaps, by so doing, to draw off some of Labour's growing support. However, while the demand for women's suffrage had been increasingly united with the call for wider democracy, and a major section of the suffrage movement was moving into an even deeper alliance with the Labour Party, it was the National Union that had played the major role in these developments. Such considerations, together with the national Union's past deep roots in the Liberal Party, would suggest that it would be the constitutional suffragists whom a Liberal government might most wish to placate, together with its own organised women's supporters in the Women's Liberal Federation and the Liberal Women's Suffrage Union. On the other hand, it is clear from the actions and statements of suffragist ministers like Grey, Simon, and Haldane, that they were becoming increasingly confident of the strength of their position within the cabinet. The main stumbling block in securing a government initiative on women's suffrage remained militancy. Even if, as the evidence suggests, Asquith himself was keen to find some solution to the problem, he would need to offer convincing grounds to his past associates among the antisuffragist ministers. The cessation of militancy would clearly have eased his position in this regard. It made sense, then, to negotiate first with leaders of the two major recent break-aways from the WSPU, the East London Federation and the United Suffragists.

There is one further possible explanation for the government's initiative to be drawn from Catherine Marshall's deliberations at this time. She had been disturbed by Asquith's agreeing to receive a deputation from the East London Federation of Suffragettes, and began to make explicit some major differences of outlook between leading constitutionalist democratic suffragists and dissident militants. Catherine Marshall, like Sylvia Pankhurst, was committed to radical social and political change, and understood her own participation in the suffrage movement to be an expression of this commitment. In a draft speech from this period she once again asserted the significance of the simultaneous emergence of the women's movement, the labour movement, and the movement for colonial freedom. But she also made it clear that she herself was dedicated to the peaceful achievement of social and political reconstruction. She saw as 'the great mission awaiting women to help to keep the great revolution which is coming on sane and humane lines. I believe women will have no small voice in determining the manner in which that revolution is brought about.'[50] In consequence, Catherine Marshall was disturbed by the growing links becoming apparent between sections of the suffrage movement and revolutionary socialist groups. She felt Asquith's reception of the East London Federation might only lend credibility to those prepared to pursue social change by violent means: 'It is going to matter to the whole future of civilisation *how* the suffrage is won in England. It is vitally important . . . that it should not even appear as a concession to militancy.'[51]

In taking such a stand, Catherine Marshall ignored Sylvia Pankhurst's advocacy of a militant practice quite distinct from that of the WSPU. This was one which rejected the furtive tactics of arson and bombing in favour of the continuation of open, large-scale, popular demonstrations, at whatever the cost to the participants. Sylvia Pankhurst had also developed the use of the hunger strike to good effect. She had continued her own recent hunger strike beyond the period of her imprisonment. It was the presence of her severely emaciated and weakened body on a stretcher outside the House of Commons that had prompted Asquith's offer to receive a deputation from the East London Suffragettes. However, her expulsion from the WSPU did coincide with other developments within her organisation that suggest the kind of realignment of militant forces Catherine Marshall feared. In contrast to the National Union's links with the Labour Party, the East London Federation was closely associated with the unofficial 'rebel' wing of the socialist movement. It had particularly close links with the Daily Herald League, whose members were critical of the mainstream political organisations of the labour and socialist movements and who looked to syndicalism rather than parliamentary politics as the most likely strategy for achieving socialism. One of the main reasons given for the East London Federation's expulsion from the WSPU had been Sylvia Pankhurst's association with the Daily Herald League and its leading figure, George Lansbury.

Similar developments were evident within the other recent breakaway from the WSPU, the United Suffragists. It contained many who had been at the centre of WSPU activity before October 1912, including the Pethick-Lawrences, Henry Nevinson, Evelyn Sharp, and others who had also been important financial supporters of the WSPU, like Mrs. Hertha Ayrton, the Pethick-Lawrences again, and Henry Harben.[52] The latter, together with Harold Laski and other socialist suffragists, had continued for some time after the 1912 split to try to convince Christabel of the error of her ways, but had received short shrift.[53] The United Suffragists represented more than a group of disgruntled former WSPU activists, squeezed out of the inner circle around Christabel and Mrs. Pankhurst after the expulsion of the Pethick-Lawrences. The existing evidence suggests that it was a further attempt to link the suffrage movement with the 'rebel' socialist politics then organising around the Daily Herald League.[54] George Lansbury became a leading member of the United Suffragists. Another important figure from the Daily Herald League, John Scurr, provided the bodyguard of dockers who protected United Suffragist speakers in Hyde Park.[55]

The East London Federation had been formed in mid-1913 and expelled from the WSPU early in 1914. The United Suffragists also formed early in 1914. By the outbreak of war it had held three large public demonstrations, but had as yet formed no real network of branches.[56] It did not officially take control of *Votes for Women*, the Pethick-Lawrences' paper, until mid-August 1914. However, there is evidence that this realignment of militants was not confined to London, and that other WSPU branches were following a similar line of development. For example by the summer of 1914 the Glasgow WSPU, led by Helen Crawfurd, was working closely with the Daily Herald League. Again when Mrs. Pethick-Lawrence undertook a speaking tour of the east of Scotland in the early summer of 1914, after the formation of the United Suffragists, she was accompanied by George Lansbury, and both were warmly received by local WSPU branches, in open opposition to central WSPU opinion.[57] Such evidence suggests that the militant forces, at both leadership and rank-and-file levels, were in the process of regrouping at the time of the outbreak of war, and that Sylvia Pankhurst's East London Federation was not the isolated breakaway from the WSPU it might appear. Instead it was part of a wider development in the militant wing of the suffrage movement which was bringing a significant part of it into close association with the 'rebel' socialist movement around the Daily Herald League.

George Lansbury later recalled the Albert Hall meeting in November 1913 demanding the release of the Irish strike leader James Larkin, at which militant suffragists had been much in evidence:

It is impossible to describe the red-hot enthusiasm which prevailed throughout the meeting, which was more like a religious revival than anything else. The women stewards all wore red caps, and the general feeling was such that some of the reporters really thought the social revolution had begun. The *Daily Sketch*, concluding a description of the meeting said: 'When next you tell your friends at the Club how you would manhandle the suffragettes if you were McKenna, just think of Miss Defarge, of Bow and Bromley. She has done a lot of knitting. Her little red cap is a danger lamp. Take heed.'[58]

Elsewhere he described the continuous close association between the
Daily Herald League and the militant suffragists, particularly in the matter of hiding 'mice' suffragettes who were avoiding rearrest under the
Cat and Mouse Act.[59] In the East End, Sylvia Pankhurst successfully
escaped rearrest under the protection of 'Kosher' Hunt, a noted prize-
fighter of the district. Militant demonstrations in this area now included
large numbers of men; many demonstrators carried sticks to parry police
truncheons, and others made use of a 'Saturday-Night' of knotted rope.
Sylvia Pankhurst recalled: 'I saw that the police now shrank from attacking us in the East End; I wanted that shrinking accentuated.' A 'People's
Army' began to drill, committed to full adult suffrage, and intended to
defend participants in a projected rent strike throughout this part of
London.[60]

It was undoubtedly this kind of alliance that Catherine Marshall particularly feared. In opposing the prime minister's reception of the East
London Suffragettes, she warned Francis Acland:

The present state of things is creating a revolutionary spirit in the women's
movement (quite apart from militancy) which will inevitably help to stimulate
and join hands with the revolutionary element in the Labour movement. If that
happens on a large scale the women, instead of having a steadying influence in
the social upheaval that is coming, will have the opposite effect, reinforcing all
that is most violent and uncontrolled and bitter. . . . I think the prospect is
rapidly becoming very serious. It affects not only this country but the whole of
Europe, because the Women's Movement, with the Socialist Movement, tends
to develop strongly on international lines.[61]

It is not improbable that the Liberal leadership, too, perceived this
new militant–'rebel' socialist alliance to be a far greater potential threat
to public order than the WSPU's periodic attacks on property. In opening his negotiations on the women's-suffrage issue with dissident militants, Lloyd George clearly aimed further to detach this section of opinion from that which remained loyal to Christabel Pankhurst. Moreover,
if he could secure an alliance of the dissident militants, the constitutional
suffragists, and the women Liberals behind the government's proposals, he might hope to undermine considerably the position of the antisuffragists in the cabinet. A new, more comprehensive government initiative on general franchise reform would then have become realisable.

Such evidence suggests, then, that by the late summer of 1914 the
varying pressures applied by democratic suffragists within the National
Union, by the Liberal Women's Suffrage Union, and by the new militant
groups were all effectively pushing the Liberal government towards some
commitment on women's suffrage in the near future. Pessimistic accounts of the position of the votes-for-women campaign that rest on the
increasing isolation and continuing organisational decline of the WSPU
in the period 1913–14 are inadequate, for they ignore the significant po-

litical advances other sections of the suffrage movement had secured for their cause. The Liberal government found itself being squeezed between the Labour Party's firm commitment to a wide extension of the franchise which included women, and the possibility of a limited Conservative measure of women's suffrage which would serve to strengthen the propertied vote. At the same time suffrage opinion within the Liberal Party was becoming increasingly forceful, and the position of suffragist ministers was strengthening within the cabinet. Moreover all sections of suffrage opinion, excluding the WSPU leadership, were now prepared to present the women's demand as part of a general call for a greater democracy. Campaigning by the National Union and by dissident militants in the East End and elsewhere had confirmed that the demand now had a significant degree of support among the working class.

It seems reasonable to argue, on such grounds, that British suffragists might fairly have expected to have gained the vote by 1918 if a Liberal government had been returned in the expected general election. It is even possible that there might have been a limited measure of women's suffrage under a Conservative government. All this must significantly modify those interpretations which stress the advent of war as the decisive factor in the eventual winning of the women's vote. It might even be that the war postponed such a victory. What can be confidently asserted is the importance of women's suffragists' own efforts, especially the efforts of the democratic suffragists, in securing the strong position enjoyed by their cause at the outbreak of war. Women's war work may have been important in converting some former opponents, or providing others with a face-saving excuse to alter their positions. But even before this, the political alliances the democratic suffragists had formed in support of their demand had ensured that women would have to be included in any future reform bill.

The continuing strength of the suffrage organisations (outside the WSPU) was further evidenced in their ability to rise above the inevitable social and political dislocation that followed the outbreak of war. This was especially true of the National Union. Shortly before the outbreak of war the constitutionalists participated in the planning of a demonstration in support of peace. In the event, this meeting, at the Kingsway Hall on 4 August, was overtaken by the declaration of war, and some among the National Union leadership began to show themselves anxious not to become publicly committed to a pacifist stand.[62] Mrs. Fawcett sought to deflect concern about the war into relief work. She advised National Union branches that the best way suffragists could help in the inevitable distress to come was 'by devising and carrying through some well-thought-out plan which can be worked continuously over many months to give aid and succour to women and children brought face to face with destitution in consequence of the war'.[63] It was decided, after hasty consultations with the branches by post, to suspend political activities for the time being and use the staff (by this time numbering almost 150) and organising capacities of the National Union for relief work. Mrs. Fawcett's most immediate concern was to avoid the danger of a split in the suffrage ranks over the issue of support for the war.[64] Relief work, with all its ambiguities, seemed to offer a solution to this quandary, and certainly the pacifists within the National Union played a full part in the National Union's relief schemes. Further, relief work provided the means for maintaining the National Union organisation in some sort of working order until the time when the fight for the vote could usefully be taken up again. The extensive nature of the National Union's relief activities may be found recorded in its annual reports for the war years and in the columns of *The Common Cause*. Only a brief account will be offered here, as evidence of the continuing vitality and organisational capacity of the suffrage movement.

One of the first acts of the typical National Union society was to establish a register of voluntary workers in its area, allocating them to suitable work among a wide variety of charitable and relief agencies. It also encouraged these bodies to locate voluntary workers in occupations where they would not be displacing other women from paid work. Unemployment among women was one of the most pressing problems for the first year or so of the war, and the National Union and its branches were responsible for the establishment of a number of workshops and cost-price canteens to help women in this situation. By the end of 1915 most of these had been closed down as the need receded. In some towns the National Union branch appears to have become the centre and organising force in the local relief committees; elsewhere National Union organisers and members were important in staffing the relevant agencies. National Union members were involved in a broad range of relief work – for example the Red Cross, the Belgian Relief Committee, the Soldiers' and Sailors' Families Association – and branches often took on the responsibility for the establishment of infant and maternity welfare centres in their areas.[65]

The most impressive achievement of the National Union's relief work was the equipping and staffing of a number of hospital units for soldiers at the front. The idea for such a unit was initiated by the Scottish Federation, which also administered the work throughout the war, though the funds were raised throughout the National Union. Five units had been established by the end of 1915, and were operating in Corsica, Salonika, France, and Serbia. By 1916 the cost of running the units was estimated at £6,999 per month, and £150,000 had been raised since the scheme began. The London Society set up similar units, and had raised nearly £25,000 by the end of 1916. Two further units, the Millicent Fawcett Hospital Units for Russian refugees, raised over £12,000 between November 1915 and August 1917.[66] There is no doubt that in a number of societies such work came to dominate suffrage activities, and that much of it was undertaken in a spirit that was assertively patriotic, sometimes jingoistic.

The London Society provides perhaps the most extreme example of undisguised involvement in the war effort itself. Their Women's Service Bureau was established specifically to release men needed at the front by providing women workers to replace them. Organisers were withdrawn from relief work for this purpose, and the bureau registered 15,000 women in 1918 alone. There was a special department for the recruitment of munition workers which selected the first eighty women to be employed in the Woolwich Arsenal. 'Training schools were also opened by the Society for various *war trades'* including one for oxy-acetylene welders. Ray Strachey proudly recorded that its ever-expanding offices were never requisitioned because of the 'national importance' of its work, testified to by the War Office, the Ministry of Munitions, and the Committee of Production, among others. Such efforts resembled the jingoistic participation of the WSPU leadership in government recruiting campaigns. But such an open involvement with the war effort was unique among National Union societies, and the essential difference between the mainstream of constitutionalist activities and that of the WSPU leadership should not be lost sight of.[67] The WSPU gave over its whole energies to support of the war effort, energies that Lloyd George was quick to harness to government campaigns. It declared itself 'Second to none in Patriotism', promoted xenophobic scares of German influence within the establishment, and handed out the white feather to those men who had not put on uniforms.[68]

In contrast, the National Union retained something of its prewar feminist perspectives. This was evidenced in the establishment by the National Union of a Women's Interest Committee to watch over the social, industrial, and economic concerns of women. In 1915 for example it took part in a Conference of Women's Organisations and Women's Trade Unions convened by the Board of Trade to discuss women's industrial problems. It also campaigned against the practice of employing women only in 'subordinate positions', selecting the civil service for particular censure. Further, it worked on the need for trade schools for women, and cooperated with the British Association to produce a report on the displacement of men by women. The work of this committee continued and developed throughout the war, and many National Union branches set up local committees for the same purpose.[69] The National Union regularly rejected assertions that it had abandoned the suffrage cause, and although it had suspended political work, the definition of what constituted 'political work' had by 1916 narrowed down to intervention in by-elections. Otherwise it continued to keep a careful watch on developments in parliament that might put an obstacle in the way of women's suffrage in the future.

Mrs. Fawcett's policy of using relief work to maintain the organisation of the National Union proved effective. There is no question that that body suffered some decline in membership during the first two years of the war. It would be extremely remarkable if it had not. The affiliation fees for 1915 were £612, only £10 less than those for 1914, indicating that the membership had held quite firm for the first year. The Manchester, Glasgow, and London Society records support this picture; indeed in organisational terms the Glasgow Society continued to expand for the first few months of the war.[70] The main loss at this point was clearly in financial resources for suffrage work – receipts for relief work, of course, continued to reach large figures – and in the number of staff the National Union and its societies could afford to employ. In 1916 affiliation fees dropped from £612 to £462. The executive estimated that the latter represented a membership of 33,334 – a drop of almost 10,000 from the prewar figure. However, these losses were not evenly spread. There was by now considerable variety in the situation of the various federations of societies which made up the National Union. The more vigorous included the Manchester, the North-Eastern, and the Scottish federations and the London Society. Others like the Central Counties, the North-Western, the South Wales, and the Kentish federations found it more difficult to keep their branches together. Similarly, while 145 societies reported a decrease in membership, 35 reported an increase. Moreover, new societies were still forming in 1916, and new members were being recruited.[71] However, though involvement with relief work had succeeded to a remarkable extent in maintaining the National Union's organisation, constitutionalists were becoming increasingly seriously divided over the issue of war, and significant realignments among them were beginning to emerge in 1916.

CHAPTER 7

WINNING THE VOTE

During the prewar period democratic suffragists had gradually been expelled from the WSPU and formed new militant groups like the Women's Freedom League, the East London Federation of Suffragettes, and the United Suffragists. Those in the National Union had found it possible to work from within that organisation, and had made a significant impact on both the political strategy and mode of campaigning of the constitutional wing. But with the outbreak of war a number of issues were raised which created irresolvable tensions between democratic suffragists and the mainstream of the movement. Democratic suffragists were generally internationalists by conviction, and many, like Catherine Marshall, had been involved with peace groups even before the war. They were quite out of sympathy with that brand of fierce nationalism which was to inform the attitude and actions of Mrs. Fawcett and her supporters. They could see no reason in pursuing the war to victory if some negotiated settlement might be reached by the two sides. They did not view the war as a struggle between the forces of enlightened democracy and autocratic militarism, but rather as the outcome of bungling on the part of politicians and greed among the warmongers already making fortunes from the tragedy. Their understanding of women's potential role in political life convinced them that an organisation like the National Union should be used to resist such resorts to physical force as a way of managing human affairs. Democratic suffragists wanted to see their organisation used at least to stimulate public discussion concerning the causes of war. Some among them even hoped that it might be used to promote a negotiated settlement between the two sides to secure a more rapid end to the bloodshed.

To the nationalists within the suffrage movement, in contrast, German aggression and brutality were self-evidently the causes of the war. There was no need for such discussion, and any talk of a negotiated settlement with such an enemy was seen as a cowardly retreat before the world's greatest bully. Mrs. Fawcett and other nationalists like her feared that even its suggestion by leading suffragists threatened the women's cause. It would associate votes for women with what was seen by themselves and others as pro-German, unpatriotic sentiment. As we have seen, Mrs. Fawcett's strategy of immersing the National Union in any number of relief schemes was generally successful in pre-empting immediate conflict between its members while at the same time keeping its organisational machinery intact. But the democratic suffragists, while participating fully in the National Union's relief work, refused to be fobbed off indefinitely in this way. They formed two peace groupings, each opposed to Mrs. Fawcett's increasingly emphatic commitment to Britain's participation in the war. The first, led by Helena Swanwick and Isabella Ford, wanted the National Union to lead an antiwar campaign. The other group, led by Catherine Marshall, Kathleen Courtney, and Margaret Ashton, suggested the compromise of an educational campaign by National Union societies on the causes and prevention of war.

The antiwar factions joined in a successful effort to delete Mrs. Fawcett's patriotic resolution from the agenda of the first council meeting to follow the outbreak of war. This had read: 'The British Empire is fighting the battle of representative government and progressive democracy all over the world and therefore the aim of the National Union as a part of the general democratic movement is involved in it.'[1] Instead the moderate antiwar suffragists successfully argued for an educational campaign 'to keep public opinion sane', building on a recent statement by Asquith which stressed the ultimate aim of the war as the securing of 'the enthronement of the idea of public right as the governing idea of European politics', a 'definite repudiation of militarism', 'the independent existence and free development of the smaller nationalities', and finally, 'the substitution for force . . . of a real European partnership based on the recognition of equal rights and established and enforced by a common will'. The council also passed resolutions that *The Common Cause* carry articles on the causes and prevention of war.[2]

A far stronger resolution from the Manchester Federation had called on the National Union to affirm its support for conciliation and arbitration and to demand the democratic control of all diplomacy. This had been withdrawn by Manchester under pressure from National Union head office, and on this occasion Mrs. Fawcett appears to have been supported by the Marshall–Courtney faction of the antiwar group, who feared precipitating a split in the National Union, and who hoped to see a compromise solution.[3] Catherine Marshall and Kathleen Courtney still believed that Mrs. Fawcett could be persuaded to support an educational campaign on the subject of war and peace in return for their own agreement to abstain from other more controversial antiwar activities. Throughout the last months of 1914 they continued to press for some such compromise, threatening their own resignations from the executive if it could not be achieved. In Catherine Marshall's words: 'This question is for some of us such an integral part of the whole question of women's political duties.'[4] The Manchester and North-Eastern federations also kept up pressure for some such development of National Union policy.[5]

A new antiwar group, the Union for Democratic Control (UDC), was forming at this time. It was to campaign for open diplomacy, national self-determination, and arms reduction. Its organisers saw the National Union as a possible foundation on which to build up their own network of branches.[6] Both antiwar factions within the National Union leadership were initially involved in negotiations with UDC leaders and were seen as being associated with it by pro-war opinion in the leadership.[7] As we have seen, the Manchester Society had already evidenced its adherence to the UDC's position on the war in its withdrawn council resolution. Eventually only the Swanwick group agreed to join the UDC. This included Isabella Ford, Margaret Robertson, now married and known from this time as Margaret Hills, Ethel Snowden, and Ethel Williams.[8] The Marshall–Courtney faction remained suspicious of this alliance, particularly as the UDC would not take up the principle of women's suffrage as one of its objects.[9] Instead Catherine Marshall and Kathleen Courtney began to think in terms of forming a new organisation.

A sort of Liberty–Equality–Fraternity League that would combine real feminism, real democracy, and real internationalism. . . . Of course, it may be said that the ILP combines all these objects, but it includes others as well which many National Union members would not, I think, be prepared to accept. And I think we ought to put women's suffrage absolutely first – as essential to the realisation of other things.[10]

Support for such an organisation grew as the antiwar factions in the National Union found themselves constantly baulked by Mrs. Fawcett and her supporters.

The antiwar groupings had gained their initial victory at a provincial council, which by the constitution could not determine National Union policy. It was necessary therefore to have those successful provincial council resolutions on an educational campaign ratified by the general council at the following Annual Meeting, in the spring of 1915. The antiwar contingent on the executive were encouraged by the fact that the platform at this meeting was to include the renowned internationalist Madame Vérone. In the event the conference proved a defeat for the antiwar suffragists. Whereas it declared its belief in arbitration as opposed to war and its support for the establishment of 'a real international partnership, based on the recognition of equal right and established and enforced by a common will', it did not agree to support the use of the National Union organisation for an educational campaign to support such principles. Madame Vérone's speech proved a further setback when she roundly declared her support for the war against Germany.[11] After this defeat Helena Swanwick, Catherine Marshall, and Kathleen Courtney resigned from the executive, and Maude Royden resigned from the editorship of *The Common Cause*.[12] These reverses for the antiwar suffragists were reinforced when Mrs. Fawcett succeeded in preventing the National Union from sending delegates to the International Women's Congress in the Hague, despite the general council's resolution that they should be sent. Mrs. Fawcett insisted that the congress was a peace conference and that the executive had no mandate to work in the peace movement. She believed attendance would damage 'the reputation of the National Union for common sense' and would indicate its 'total aloofness from national sentiment'. Her opponents asserted that attendance would be in line with the council's decision. A compromise was reached whereby members were allowed to attend the congress, but not as National Union representatives.[13]

But this decision did not prevent the threatened split in the National Union. Opposition continued to be expressed, largely by societies within the Manchester and North-Eastern federations, that is, among those branches that had already shown themselves to be dominated by democratic suffragists in the immediate prewar years. This body of opinion insisted that the executive decision was at variance with the spirit of the council resolutions. Many societies requested permission to send a representative to the congress, and at least one, Alice Clark's home branch, the Street Society, announced a firm decision to do so despite the executive's ruling. Margaret Ashton reported that the Manchester Federation felt the executive 'were over-straining their powers and over-riding the Societies. It had seriously considered leaving the Union.' The executive refused to reconsider, and the resignation of further democratic suffragists among the leadership followed, with accusations of a 'tide which is converting the Union into a de facto autocracy, under the cover of a de jure democratic constitution'.[14] Letters poured into the National Union offices, some regretting the decision not to attend the congress, others supporting Mrs. Fawcett. Many demanded a special council meeting to discuss the issue, and this was fixed for June. It was to consider the interpretation of the policy decided at the last council and an extension of societies' rights to separate action. It was also to fill the vacancies that had been created on the executive. The North-Eastern Federation and the Manchester Federation also made repeated demands for a general re-election of all the officers of the union.[15] The special council resulted in a victory for those who wanted to restrict National Union activity to relief work.[16] Moreover, the ground was laid for further controversy when Ray Strachey, of the London Society, was elected to the post of parliamentary secretary to replace Catherine Marshall. From this position she was to lead future attacks on the National Union's Election Fighting Fund policy and its alliance with the Labour Party, and in the process compound the increasing alienation of the democratic suffragists within the constitutionalists' ranks.

The internationalists in the National Union went on to provide inspiration and leadership for many of the peace organisations that developed during the war, notably the Women's International League for Peace and Freedom (WILPF). Plans for a new organisation had continued to be discussed among the antiwar suffragists and became the focus of their activity after the split. Helena Swanwick doubted the wisdom of Catherine Marshall's suggested Women's Independent Party. She wrote:

I would like to see a great humanist party rise, keen on equal suffrage, proportional representation, devolution, a reformed House of Commons and an abolished House of Lords, Free Trade and reformed diplomacy, and tremendous economic changes. What I fear is that each group of reformers will have its first objects to which it wishes to subordinate the others, and I fear women will have to put the vote first till they get it – it is so boring a prospect![17]

Eventually democratic suffragists from both wings of the suffrage movement joined in the formation of the British section of the WILPF, which grew out of the Hague conference. This organisation had the double object of working for the settlement of international disputes by the establishment of arbitration and conciliation machinery, and the enfranchisement of women. Its chairwoman was Helena Swanwick, and its executive included Catherine Marshall, Kathleen Courtney, and Margaret Hills (formerly Robertson); other leading members included Maude Royden, Isabella Ford, Margaret Ashton, and Ethel Snowden of the National Union, Emmeline Pethick-Lawrence and Mrs. Ayrton Gould of the United Suffragists, Sylvia Pankhurst of the East London Federation of Suffragettes, and Mrs. Despard of the Women's Freedom League.[18]

The WILPF represented a thorough realignment within the suffrage movement, with democratic suffragists from all sections at last coming together in their own organisation. The issue of war had provided the occasion for the associated conflict within the National Union, but this had already been threatening to emerge prior to August 1914. One Manchester suffragist offered the following interpretation of these events: 'It is really the progressive section against the "moderates" that is the dividing line, and unfortunately we have shed the ablest women in the N.U.'[19] This dividing line had first become evident in conflicting attitudes to the suffrage–labour alliance. Not surprisingly, then, the wartime disaffection among democratic suffragists within the National Union was soon further compounded by controversy over whether or not the EFF policy should be maintained. The seceding faction of the executive had also been the most dedicated supporters of this policy and of the National Union's alliance with Labour. They were replaced by women who did not share this commitment, and the new parliamentary secretary, Ray Strachey (more often known as Mrs. Oliver Strachey at this time), began an active campaign to have the policy rescinded. Catherine Marshall had remained as secretary of the Election Fighting Fund after her resignation as parliamentary secretary, but she was not able to stem this movement against the alliance. As early as November 1914 Mrs. Fawcett was arguing that it would be necessary for the National Union 'to throw over its present policy' if a general election occurred before the end of the war, in order to support the war government.[20] By the time of Catherine Marshall's resignation from the executive, EFF organisers were being paid out of National Union central funds, as most of their time was now spent in relief work.[21] Whereas in Lancashire former EFF organisers like Annot Robinson, Selina Cooper, and Mrs. Tozer kept in touch with Labour organisations alongside their other work, elsewhere, for example in Scotland, EFF work came to a complete standstill.[22]

In May 1915 moves against the EFF policy were consolidated when the executive interpreted the council's resolution to suspend political work as also suspending all EFF activity. Catherine Marshall's final resignation as EFF secretary, and Margaret Hills's as EFF organiser, followed.[23] Meanwhile Margaret Ashton and Alice Clark, on behalf of the EFF Committee, continued to insist that the National Union's obligation to Labour Party candidates in EFF constituencies must be maintained. At this time it would appear that Catherine Marshall hoped the National Union's organisation might be divided between the democratic suffragists and the rest. In her plan the EFF Committee was to form the nucleus of the new women's organisation she and Kathleen Courtney had already advocated. It would agitate around the general principles that underlay the claim for political equality, and would 'work for the general advancement of women's position, socially, industrially, economically and politically'. Under this scheme the funds of the National Union and the EFF were to be divided between the two sections in proportion to their relative membership immediately after the division.[24] There is no record that these proposals were even discussed by the National Union leadership.

At a meeting of the EFF Committee on 14 July 1915 the two sides argued their case for the continuance or suspension of the EFF policy. Mrs. Fawcett made clear her view of the EFF as simply a whip with which the National Union had sought to beat the Liberal government. It was no longer relevant in wartime conditions. She advised the suspension of the EFF organisation for the meantime, but the keeping on reserve of its funds for a possible revival of its work in the future. At this time EFF reserves stood at almost £2,000. Catherine Marshall argued from an altogether broader view of EFF policy. In her opinion the election work had been its least important aspect: 'The most vital side of the work was the whole question of bringing the Women's Suffrage Movement into friendly relations with the Democratic movement in the country; and this was more important now than ever.' It was the EFF's activity among the rank and file of the Labour Party that had proved most productive: 'If we let the threads go now, we could not expect to pick up the work after the war at the point at which we had left it in August

1914.'[25] Catherine Marshall argued that Mrs. Fawcett's interpretation of the policy implied that the National Union had simply been using the Labour Party as a tool. Moreover, she maintained, if it was expected that the policy might continue after the war, it was essential to maintain links with the Labour Party during the present.

Nonetheless Catherine Marshall recognised that whole-hearted supporters of this policy were now probably in a minority within the National Union. She advised that if the executive felt it likely the policy would be reversed by a future council meeting, it would be better to make a clean break with the Labour Party immediately. Above all she wanted to avoid any misunderstanding that might arise if the Labour Party continued to believe the National Union was committed to the support of twenty-two of its candidates, only to see this retracted at the time of an actual election. After these discussions it was agreed unanimously that any continuance of EFF activity would form an obligation to support the Labour candidate at the next contested election, and that any withdrawal at a later date by the National Union 'would probably be disastrous for Women's Suffrage'. At this time East Bristol and Accrington were the only constituencies where active support of the local Labour Party machinery was still being maintained.[26]

Catherine Marshall advised friendly and informal meetings with Labour leaders now, and again stressed: 'The policy of regarding the Labour Party simply as a tool would be very unfair to the Labour Party and exceedingly damaging to the National Union.' She argued that if such a view were allowed to dominate National Union actions, the result could be an unfriendly response from the Labour Party. She was confident that women's suffrage was now certain to come through a government measure. Labour Party support would be critical either in the case of a very limited Unionist bill, or the likely Liberal choice of a women's-suffrage clause to a more general reform bill, by amendment. Despite opposition from Ray Strachey, the executive decided to accept this advice, and arranged informal meetings with Labour leaders, who were to be advised that for the present EFF policy was only in suspension. Future councils might decide to alter the policy altogether, but the executive expressed the belief that there were no grounds for fearing this at present.[27]

Controversy over the EFF policy re-emerged in October 1915 when it appeared that one of the EFF candidates, Walter Ayles in East Bristol, might be about to adopt a no-conscription platform. The labour movement, too, had been seriously divided by issues raised during the war. Most socialists were internationalists and pacifists, and the support of a number of labour leaders for the war was unwelcome to many. They offered particularly strong resistance to the introduction of compulsory military service.[28] By-election campaigns provided a good opportunity to publicise their views. The National Union's commitment to support

Ayles in any election in East Bristol promised to be especially embarrassing to its nationalist leadership once he identified himself with the no-conscription movement. When the National Union's executive decided to suspend registration work there, a conference was arranged among Mrs. Fawcett, Ray Strachey, and Miss Atkinson for the executive and Miss Tothill, president of the East Bristol Society; Mrs. Townley, the EFF organiser there; and Ayles himself. The representatives from East Bristol were told of the executive's decision to suspend EFF work during the war.

Ayles argued strongly that to abandon the existing registration work in East Bristol would lose all the ground gained within the local labour movement:

There are still influences in the Labour Party which are hostile. This part of it was convinced that the National Union was not sincere, and would not keep its pledges. It is the attitude of the working classes generally to the middle classes; and in East Bristol there is now more animosity to the middle classes than there was at the outbreak of war.[29]

He explained how Mrs. Townley had succeeded in winning the confidence of local trade unionists, which was critical to maintaining Labour Party support for women's suffrage in the area. His candidature had only gone ahead because of the pledges made by the National Union. If EFF support was now withdrawn, it would be seen as a betrayal. Miss Tothill argued that the East Bristol Society had been built up on the basis of support for EFF policy: 'Our Committee [that is, the existence of the society] and the fortunes of the Labour candidate are closely intertwined.' The East Bristol deputation continued to argue that all parties were continuing registration work, despite the political truce, and that to suspend it in their constituency would effectively reverse the National Union's earlier pledges.

Little headway was made at this meeting, and the East Bristol Society considered withdrawing from the National Union.[30] The EFF had been particularly valuable to Labour candidates in the work of registering potential Labour voters. Catherine Marshall pressed the National Union leadership to reconsider its decision to suspend such aid. She argued that to do so was to break the pledge made to the ILP conference in 1914, at least in those constituencies where promises had been made to support a specific candidate in any future election. In consequence the National Union executive agreed to investigate each constituency concerned to see what pledges had been made to the local Labour organisations on behalf of the EFF – were they to one particular candidate only, did they cover only the eventuality of a by-election, or was there a commitment for general election support? Catherine Marshall believed the national Union would find itself irrevocably committed in Accrington and East Bristol, where the EFF was directly responsible for labour candidatures, and this could also be so in Rotherham, North Monmouth, Midlothian, and North-West Durham, and possibly Holmfirth if the earlier Labour candidate, Lunn, were retained. She felt it imperative that where the National Union did not find itself pledged 'we shall see to it that they do not think we are'. In these instances she believed work could be suspended, but elsewhere the National Union should not renege on its pledges. Eleanor Rathbone argued that the executive needed to ask the council if it felt bound by these pledges. The executive would also have to decide its own position on this, put it to the council, and resign if council decided not to heed it.[31]

Having investigated the situation in EFF constituencies, Ray Strachey reported as follows: She felt the EFF was pledged only in four constituencies, East Bristol, Accrington, North Monmouthshire, and Rotherham, as the National Union had caused Labour candidates to run in these four seats. National Union support was also expected in North-West Durham, Barnards Castle, Bishop Auckland, and West Bradford, but this represented the expectations of the local societies only, not formal EFF pledges. Conversely the EFF Committee had made pledges in Leith and Midlothian, but, according to the Edinburgh EFF committee, there was no local expectation that they would be kept. There were also ten other constituencies where the National Union had been supporting a sitting Labour MP, and Portsmouth, where National Union support was pledged but a candidature was now unlikely.[32] On the basis of this investigation Ray Strachey succeeded in persuading the council meeting in February 1916 to reaffirm the suspension of the EFF policy until the circumstances of the next general election were known. However, the National Union also undertook not to oppose any suffragist labour candidate, whatever the circumstances, in recognition of the undertaking given to the ILP conference in Glasgow in 1914. Further, in those constituencies where pledges had been made, registration work might continue and electoral support would be provided in the event of an election within the three-party system. In the event, the National Union did stand by its commitment to Ayles in East Bristol, even though it entailed providing election aid to a candidate who had opposed conscription. Otherwise, all such political work remained in suspension until the executive or council decided that changed conditions required its recommencement.[33]

Having thus accomplished the effective end of the EFF policy, Ray Strachey resigned from the position of National Union parliamentary secretary. Seven of the most committed of the EFF Committee also resigned: Margaret Ashton, Fred Shaw, Isabella Ford, Mrs. Stanbury, Muriel Countess de la Warr, Catherine Marshall, and Alice Clark.[34] Margaret Ashton wrote to Catherine Marshall expressing the view that the EFF was no longer run by an independent committee in touch with the Labour Party. It was now controlled by the National Union executive and therefore 'the middle class woman attitude of the National Union Executive is bound to prevail'.[35] Conciliatory letters were sent by the new EFF Committee to Arthur Henderson and W. A. C. Anderson explaining the council decision and adding, rather disingenuously: 'From this explanation you will see that practically no change was made by our Council with regard to the attitude of the National Union to the Labour Party.' Cordial replies were received from the two Labour leaders, though Anderson's contained a sting in the tail: 'You may be quite certain that whatever you decide to do in the future', he wrote 'there will be no change in our attitude on a question which is to us a matter of principle and not expediency.'[36]

Alongside these disputes regarding the future of the EFF policy there emerged further tensions between democratic suffragists and the National Union leadership. These centred on the former's desire to restate the women's-suffrage demand explicitly in terms of universal suffrage – votes for all adults, men and women. By late 1916 franchise reform was once again the subject of public and parliamentary debate. By this time, too, democratic suffragists had become convinced that full adult suffrage was both a realistic and a right demand for the women's-suffrage organisations to adopt. When Margaret Ashton resigned from the Manchester Society's executive, for example, she made it clear she was now committed to working for full adult suffrage. Similarly in June 1916 the Newcastle Society passed an adult-suffrage resolution which was endorsed at its Annual Meeting a few days later, with no dissenting votes. When the National Union's executive questioned this action, Ethel Williams replied that her society considered it quite in order and that 'the feeling of the society was entirely for Adult Suffrage'. The resolution had been sent to government ministers and MPs in the area but had not been published in the press. Most of the opponents of adult suffrage had apparently left the society, and Ethel Williams was anxious to remain within the National Union. The executive requested a promise that no future independent action at variance with National Union policy would be undertaken. (During its own discussion a number of the executive made clear their personal preparedness to be involved in a campaign for adult suffrage if such a measure seemed imminent.[37] Since the joint labour–suffrage campaigning of the prewar years, adult suffrage had lost the threatening aspect of former years.) The Newcastle Society then went further and, rather than circulating the National Union's women's-suffrage resolution to local trade union branches, circulated its own adult-suffrage resolution. There was evidently similar trouble with the Leicester Society, which demanded explicit permission from the executive allowing member societies to work along adult-suffrage lines. Newcastle requested that the council meeting be moved forward. In their view adult suffrage was 'the only practicable line', and they wished to put a resolution to this effect to the council.[38] The discussion seems to have been dropped temporarily at this point, most probably because of the publication of the report of the Speaker's conference on franchise reform which gave the National Union leadership a positive programme to work on, and which provided it with a case for moderating the increasing intransigence of the democratic suffragists.

The calling of this Speaker's conference had been a response to political problems created by the war. Though it had been agreed to suspend party-political conflicts at the beginning of hostilities, this truce was constantly an uneasy one. At any time the government might have found itself called upon to seek a new mandate at a general election. Even after the formation of an all-party government in May 1915 the dissolution of parliament continued an ever-present possibility. The life of the 1910 parliament was repeatedly extended with the agreement of the opposition, but only for short periods at a time. In the event of a general election being called, the voting registers themselves promised to become the focus of considerable dispute and unrest. With the dislocations that attended the war, these registers no longer recorded the possible electorate at all adequately. In particular, men overseas on active service would effectively have been disenfranchised. Moreover, many presently hazarding life and limb at the front had never been enfranchised at all. These issues became particularly contentious with the extension of compulsory military service in May 1916. Arthur Henderson, the Parliamentary Labour Party leader, who had joined the all-party government formed the previous year, used the occasion to raise once more the general issue of franchise reform, including women's suffrage, in cabinet. He was supported in this by another minister, Sir Robert Cecil, the leader of the Conservative women's suffragists in parliament. Meanwhile other Unionists like Sir Edward Carson were waging a vociferous campaign for the 'soldiers' vote'. Franchise reform, then, had again become a live issue in 1915, and a pressing one by early 1916. The government attempted a series of initiatives during this period to resolve the more immediate issue of the voting disqualification of men at the front, but all were rejected in the House of Commons. The setting up of an all-party Speaker's conference in the autumn of 1916 was intended to resolve this impasse by identifying a compromise programme of franchise reform that would be acceptable to all sides.[39]

While these debates had focused only on how to protect the rights of existing voters, especially the troops at the front, women's suffragists had kept merely a watching brief. But once it became clear that some more fundamental reform might come under consideration, campaigning for votes for women began anew. This campaigning was, of course, to take place in a quite different context to that of the prewar period. The war had brought significant changes to women's lives. The most central of these was the extension of work opportunities, temporary though most of it proved to be. Women had been given a prominent place in the war effort, first in keeping going existing services and industries, but perhaps even more significantly in the massive manufacture of munitions required in twentieth-century warfare. Many, like the women's suffragists' former arch-enemy, Asquith, used such developments to explain their change of heart on votes for women. It remains a matter of dispute whether such longstanding male prejudice was significantly undermined or only put aside for practical reasons during this time.[40] But certainly there were a number of well-publicised 'conversions' to women's suffrage among prominent public figures in the war years, while the rationale of many of the old antisuffragist arguments was effectively undermined by wartime requirements. Modern warfare needed the mass mobilisation of women as well as men for its execution. Ironically, the ideology of separate spheres lost much of its former legitimacy as women provided essential support in this way.

Democratic suffragists had successfully married their cause to that of general franchise reform in the prewar years. When this issue again came to the fore in 1916 it was clear that women's suffrage would have to form part of the agenda for debate, and it was one of the questions that the Speaker's conference was asked to address. Equally important for suffragists was the changed political context. The renewed campaign for votes for women was to be undertaken during a period when party antagonisms were muted and compromise was a genuinely sought goal. The Speaker's conference proposals were to be adopted by an all-party government. From the end of 1916 this government was to be under the leadership of Lloyd George, a politician with whom suffragists had cooperated, albeit with much vexation, in prewar years. Further, the suffragists' opponents among the Irish Nationalists, and within the House of Lords, found themselves in no position to challenge such a government's commitment to electoral reform.[41] During the eighteen months or so between the establishment of the Speaker's conference in 1916 and the final enactment of the Representation of the People Bill in 1918 the main problem for the National Union leadership was the creation of unity among the women's-suffrage forces. The central issue among suffragists by this time was adult suffrage, and the democratic suffragists continued their challenge to any more restricted form of franchise.

In the early weeks of 1916 the National Union had remained cautious about any immediate renewal of suffrage campaigning. It, together with the Women's Freedom League and the United Suffragists, had also resisted pressure from the WILPF and Sylvia Pankhurst's renamed Workers' Suffrage Federation to adopt the demand of full adult suffrage. It was advice from two prominent suffrage politicians that finally encouraged the National Union leadership to think that it was now 'highly desirable' for suffragists to resume active agitation.[42] In consequence the Organising Committee of the National Union was instructed to draw up a scheme of work for the spring of 1916, and a new membership drive was started. The Women's Interests Committee was told that suffrage work would now be stepped up and the National Union would require the return of two of its organisers. Mrs. Fawcett sought further elucidation from Asquith on the nature of a bill being put forward by the government: 'Not, of course, that any of us are in any degree hostile to the enfranchisement of men who have been suffering and working for our country, but it is feared that the suffrage may be dealt with in a manner prejudicial to the future prospects of the enfranchisement of women.' Asquith replied in a conciliatory tone that no actual changes in the franchise were at present planned, 'but if, and when, it should be necessary to undertake it you may be certain that the considerations set out in your letter will be fully and impartially weighed without any pre-judgement from the controversies of the past'.[43]

A joint committee of suffrage societies was established (not including the WSPU, which rejected this renewal of the women's demand).[44] Meanwhile National Union branches were prodded back into action to organise a postal lobby of cabinet ministers in support of women's suffrage. Organisers were instructed to be ready to return to full-time suffrage agitation by September, 'in view of the necessity of reviving suffrage work'.[45] As a result of all this, when Henry Nevinson returned from war reporting in July 1916 he found a 'suffrage crisis in full blaze, but really promising for the first time'.[46] He had attended a conference of suffragist MPs and women's-suffrage leaders where he had found 'feeling for Adult Suffrage almost without exception'.[47] Subsequently Nevinson and the other dissident militants in the United Suffragists joined the dissident democratic suffragists of the National Union in reformulating their demand in terms of adult suffrage. It was at this meeting, too, that United Suffragists pressed their idea of a Speaker's conference as a means of finding a compromise solution to the problem of franchise reform that would be acceptable to all parties. Sir John Simon was to the forefront in this revival of the suffrage issue and led a renewed campaign in the House of Commons 'with an enthusiasm uncommon in one of his cool temperament'.[48] When a Speaker's conference was finally announced later in 1916, democratic suffragists from various groups came together with labour and socialist leaders to form the National Council for Adult Suffrage. Henry Nevinson acted as chairman, with Mrs. Pethick-Lawrence as treasurer and Kathleen Courtney and James Middleton (of the ILP) as secretaries. The National Council's executive included Margaret Bondfield, Margaret Llewelyn Davies, George Lansbury, Mary MacArthur, Robert Smillie, Catherine Marshall, Maude Royden, Helena Swanwick, and Evelyn Sharp.[49] However, dissension soon developed in the National Council among three factions. Sylvia Pankhurst and her supporters wanted to work only for full adult suffrage and would accept no compromise short of it. The other women's suffragists on the National Council were also universalists, but were prepared to accept a compromise while wanting to press for as wide a measure as possible.

Most Labour leaders followed the more cautious position of the National Union and preferred to settle for whatever the Speaker's conference offered[50] (though it should be noted the National Union was also backing Sir John Simon's call for a 'wide and simple franchise', and did take part in an adult-suffrage conference in October).[51]

With the announcement of the Speaker's conference, National Union societies were at once advised to begin holding propaganda meetings, and a press campaign was planned with the help of a group of women journalists. A large women's demonstration in London was organised for the new year. Meanwhile deputations and memorials to MPs continued. Resolutions were still flowing in from trade union branches and were forwarded to the Speaker's conference.[52] In mid-December an informal conference was held at the home of Sir John Simon to discuss the position of the women's-suffrage issue at the Speaker's conference. Present were Sir John Simon, W. H. Dickinson, Henry Nevinson, Mary MacArthur, Kathleen Courtney, and Millicent Fawcett. Mrs. Fawcett's memorandum on the conversation recorded:

Sir John Simon and Mr. Dickinson both considered there was a good chance of the Conference recommending Women's Suffrage. The difficulty and danger would arise when concrete proposals for Women's Suffrage came to be discussed. The two Members of Parliament thought there was little or no chance of Adult Suffrage being recommended by the Conference, and that for the Adultists to press for it would risk the loss of even a general recommendation for Women's Suffrage in any form. Men like Sir F. Banbury would take alarm and might probably wreck the chance of any success at all. . . . A good deal of talk took place about various ways of dealing with the excess of women over men. Finally I think there was a general agreement that raising the voting age for women was the least objectionable way of reducing the number of women. . . . Finally the outcome to which I think we all agreed as the best course was first to secure, if possible, a recommendation from the conference of the principle of Women's Suffrage and then test the feeling of the conference by raising one after another definite schemes for carrying Women's Suffrage into effect.[53]

On Dickinson's advice Mrs. Fawcett later contacted Lady Selborne of the Conservative and Unionist Women's Franchise Association to urge Sir William Bull to bring forward a scheme for women's suffrage at the conference, since it would 'have a better chance of being carried than anything proposed by the Liberal members'.[54]

Thus though representatives of the suffrage organisations were not able to take part in the proceedings of the conference itself, they did not fail to bring pressure to bear on that conference and would appear to have put forward the idea of an age restriction on the women's vote as the most preferable form of limitation. This formula was to be part of the recommendations embodied in the conference report, and was not simply 'hit upon' by its members, as one writer has suggested.[55] Constitutional suffragists had recognised the possible need for some such compromise since the ill-fated Franchise Reform Bill of 1912–13. At that time Eleanor Rathbone had first investigated the effect of various age restrictions to the women's vote. During the course of the Speaker's conference Mrs. Fawcett took up Lord Northcliffe's suggestion of a deputation to the new prime minister, Lloyd George. None of this evidence supports the picture of a moribund or ineffectual suffrage movement drawn in some recent accounts of this period.[56] As the publication day of the Speaker's conference report approached, W. H. Dickinson hinted to Mrs. Fawcett: 'I think that you will have something very substantial upon which to build a demand which I have great hopes will be successful.' He advised that it would be 'bad tactics to fall foul of the Conference'. This could only provide the government with an excuse to shelve the issue once more. What was needed now was a united front among suffragists, and in particular some moderation of the dogmatic universalists' position, if the ground won were not to be endangered.[57] This advice was echoed by another member of the conference, the Unionist cabinet minister Walter Long.[58]

When the Speaker's conference report was published it advised full adult suffrage for men on a residential qualification. It then recommended a measure of women's suffrage based on age and property qualifications. Women over thirty or thirty-five should be qualified to vote if they or their husbands were on the local government register, then based on an occupier franchise. As we have seen, suffragists had themselves advised MPs on such a means of limiting the women's vote. Nonetheless it was to be a source of further discord among suffragists. It was pointed out that the young women munition workers, for example, would be excluded by such a franchise. Democratic suffragists in the North Riding and Manchester federations made use of their remaining EFF resources to begin a campaign against such limitation of votes for women. The National Union leadership subsequently agreed to run similar campaigns wherever there were munition works.[59] Yet all their parliamentary advisers stressed the danger of the full adultist demand. Consequently Mrs. Fawcett advised working to lower the age limitation but to take care not to upset the whole basis of the compromise that had been achieved. On these grounds the National Union executive resolved to welcome the Speaker's report, while expressing the hope that the House would improve on the recommendations.[60]

The democratic suffragists on the National Council for Adult Suffrage were split between those who wanted to hold out for complete adult suffrage and those prepared to accept some degree of compromise while working for a wider measure than that recommended by the Speaker's conference.[61] Its leadership felt harassed by the intransigence of those like Sylvia Pankhurst who rejected any compromise, and hampered by the refusal of most of the Labour leadership, along with that of the National Union, to raise an active campaign for full adult suffrage.[62] The National Union leadership experienced a mixed success in its efforts to achieve a measure of agreement with the uncompromising universalists among the democratic suffragists. When Mrs. Fawcett and Ray Strachey first discussed the question with Kathleen Courtney as secretary of the WILPF, she could not agree to their policy of avoiding hostile statements on the conference recommendations. She did not accept the need to avoid controversy for fear of losing all. Margaret Llewelyn Davies similarly held to her intention to work for full adult suffrage, at least until the bill was introduced. She was only prepared to work for a more limited demand once convinced there was no chance for full equality.[63]

In contrast the National Union leaders and the Labour Party leaders joined together to celebrate the Speaker's conference Report at a Women Workers' Demonstration held in the Queen's Hall in February 1917. Mrs. Fawcett's speech sounded a triumphant note:

The result of the Speaker's Conference was an illustration of the deathless energy and vitality of the Suffrage Movement. The Conference had been initiated by an anti-suffragist, presided over by an anti-suffragist, and consisted at first of fifty per cent anti-suffragists; yet though the brew seemed distinctly anti-suffrage, when the tap was turned – Suffrage came out.[64]

It was estimated that six million women would be enfranchised under these recommendations. Walter Runciman and J. H. Thomas also spoke and 'urged adult suffragists not to ruin the Electoral Reform Bill by pressing their own special desires too much'.[65] The National Union made a final attempt to reach an agreement with Kathleen Courtney and Sylvia Pankhurst, but at this point democratic suffragists remained firm in their intention to work for full adult suffrage, unless convinced that it would wreck any forthcoming bill.[66] Kathleen Courtney later modified this stance. She and George Lansbury put a resolution to the National Council for Adult Suffrage welcoming the Speaker's conference recommendation, but urging the additional enfranchisement of women industrial workers and war widows. After much discussion the resolution was passed, and Sylvia Pankhurst's resolution calling for nothing short of full adult suffrage was rejected. She and her followers then withdrew from the council.[67]

A National Labour Suffrage Conference called on 20 March 1917 upheld a similarly moderate position. It included representatives from the Trades Union Congress, the national Labour Party, the Parliamentary Labour Party, and women's industrial organisations. The conference voted to accept the resolutions of the Speaker's conference 'as a minimum . . . provided the enfranchisement of women, including women wage-earners and widows, is agreed to'. A resolution calling for full adult suffrage was put by Robert Smillie and Mary MacArthur, but was defeated.[68] *The Common Cause* commented:

It is very encouraging to see how truly the Labour Party are the friends of the enfranchisement of women. The fact that their only difficulty arose from the desire to enfranchise more women than the actual proposals of the Conference is very important, and still more so is the fact that, passionately though they believe in the principle of adult suffrage, they are prepared to accept a measure which falls short of it for the sake of breaking down the sex barrier.[69]

This compromise position was reinforced by the advice given to suffragists by Lloyd George during their deputation in March 1917,[70] and was upheld by the Labour Party's Annual Conference.[71] Though by now very much out of sympathy with such a cautious approach, democratic suffragists had been the promoters of the broadened conception of political emancipation within both the suffrage and labour movements which made such unity possible. The increasingly firm commitment of the Labour Party to women's suffrage in the two years prior to the war had been the direct outcome of democratic-suffragist political strategy. It had ensured that votes for women would have to be included in any future attempts at franchise reform. Such support was to stand the suffrage movement in equally good stead in the wartime political context. The Labour leadership proved a valuable ally both in maintaining pressure from within the government and in organising rank-and-file labour-movement support for the all-party compromise devised to resolve the issue. Though the democratic suffragists' desired goal of universal adult suffrage was not immediately secured, it was their earlier influence which had ensured that women of all classes were now to be enfranchised, and in greater numbers than would have been the case in the simple equal-suffrage bills of the prewar years.

With the successful passage of the Representation of the People Act in 1918 all women on the local government register, or who were wives of men on the local government register and were over the age of thirty were enfranchised.[72] For the remaining period of the war, suffragist bodies concentrated on the registration of women voters and the reorganisation of their own societies in the light of these advances.[73] Only three weeks before the general election at the end of 1918 women were also granted the right to stand for parliament. Eighteen came forward as candidates in that election. Only one, Christabel Pankhurst, received the endorsement of the coalition government. Only one, the Sinn Feiner Countess Markiewicz, was elected. Being imprisoned in Holloway for her Republican activities and refusing to take the oath, she never sat in the House of Commons. The first woman to do so was Nancy Astor, who successfully contested her husband's former seat in Plymouth for the Conservative Party the following year. It was to take another ten years before full universal suffrage was introduced in Britain. In 1928 the Conservative Party, with the support of both opposition parties, finally redeemed an earlier election pledge to equalise the franchise laws. With this legislation women in Britain were at last given equal political rights with men.[74]

POSTSCRIPT

The suffrage movement had, to a notable extent, remained intact under the impact of war. It had continued to exert significant pressure to ensure the inclusion of women in the eventual reform of the franchise. It was to provide the organisational leadership for continuing feminist campaigning in the postwar period. But the wartime distancing of many democratic suffragists from the rest of the movement was to prove permanent. Some, like Ada Nield Chew and Selina Cooper, had already been active socialists when they joined the suffrage movement. Others, like Catherine Marshall, Helena Swanwick, and Margaret Hills (Robertson), had become socialists in the course of suffrage and peace work. Many were unwilling to restrict themselves to nonpartisan campaigning around women's issues after the war. Such an approach was to dominate the work of feminist organisations in the 1920s and 30s, including that of the 'New Feminists' who now provided the leadership of the National Union of Societies for Equal Citizenship (NUSEC), the revised name of the National Union. Many former democratic suffragists, in contrast, chose increasingly to immerse themselves in movements for internationalism, for colonial freedom, and against fascism.

The exact character of the New Feminism still awaits detailed research, as does the extent of the influence of democratic suffragists within postwar feminist groups. But certain of its main features are evident.[1] To begin with, it offered a quite clearly articulated rejection of the attitudes and concerns of those sometimes identified at the time as 'individualistic' feminists. The New Feminists expressed a dissatisfaction with what they viewed as the narrow, formalistic, equal-rights conception of emancipation, one that in its focus on the problems of the independent woman, gave priority to assimilating women's social position to that of men.[2] They rejected, for example, the primacy claimed for the demand for equal wages and economic autonomy by those around *The Freewoman* in the years before the war, and the Women's Freedom League and the Six Point Group subsequently.

The Freewoman had promoted its programme as one addressed to an elite among women, those able and willing to act as a vanguard, to mark

151

out the path to emancipation for the rest of their sex.[3] In contrast the New Feminists sought to speak for the larger mass of dependent women, women whose well-being and security, they believed, could be improved far more immediately by achieving adequate family incomes; good, cheap housing; access to birth control; and maternity care. They took the problems of the wife and mother at home, living in or on the borderline of poverty, as the main measure of women's social disabilities. They believed such disabilities would be little affected by securing equal wages with men.[4] Instead they looked to providing for the special, particular needs of the family woman, especially the less wealthy among them. Hence from the mid-1920s NUSEC, under the leadership of the New Feminists, gave increasing priority to campaigns for family allowances, maternity and infant welfare services, housing reform, and birth-control clinics. Its most explicit rejection of the equal-rights approach came in 1929 when the Annual Conference modified the longstanding opposition to protective legislation for women workers.[5]

The dominance of this perspective in interwar feminist campaigning has often led it to be interpreted as a conservative phase in the history of feminism, though recently more complex assessments of similar developments in the United States have been put forward.[6] There is no doubt that the New Feminism represented a considerable moderation of the high optimism of the suffrage movement. Faith in women's ability to revolutionise political life for the benefit of all had been replaced by an anxiety simply to ameliorate the day-to-day problems of the most disadvantaged women. But the seeds for such a special-needs approach had first been sown by the democratic suffragists in their conviction of the need for the most broadly relevant formulation of feminist demands, one that could acknowledge class as well as sexual inequality. They had recognised that the disabilities of women from differing backgrounds in relation to the franchise laws, as in other matters, were not of the same order. It was that perception which was carried over into the interwar period and which informed the outlook of the New Feminists. In this respect, at least, the New Feminism was not as novel as its designation would indicate. There was a degree of continuity between pre- and postwar feminism which has not generally been acknowledged, largely because of the way suffragism has been characterised as an equal-rights movement dominated by the perspectives of middle-class women.

The organising concept for this study has been that of 'democratic suffragist'. It will be clear from the preceding pages that democratic suffragists were not a homogeneous body and democratic suffragism not a monolithic ideology. Originally, of course, the term was coined with rhetorical intent, rather than with a concern for analytic rigour. The main aim of Margaret Llewelyn Davies had been to find a unifying idea around which suffragists with different class and party-political loyalties might rally. The value of the term lay in its very vagueness and generality. In this account, too, it has been used to identify an impulse, an orientation, within the suffrage movement, not a clearly distinguished faction or grouping. Its value for this writer has lain not in its precision or exhortatory appeal, but in its identification of a significant cross-current within the votes-for-women campaigns. The notion of democratic suffragism suggests an alternative framework which orders material that was previously somewhat difficult to integrate into existing interpretations: how it was, for example, that the supposedly conservative wing of the movement was to be found making an alliance with the Labour Party in 1912; or that those identified as 'radical suffragists' by other writers were more closely identified with this same wing; or that the major new feminist organisation to be formed during the war years, the WILPF, combined former militants, constitutionalists, and 'radical suffragists'. This alternative framework also locates the suffrage agitation firmly within the party politics of the day, rather than leaving it on the periphery as a somewhat bizarre phenomenon unrelated to broader political movements. It highlights the not insignificant part played by the women's-suffrage agitation in the realignment of party politics that began in this period, most particularly in the movement of support away from the Liberal Party in favour of the Labour Party. Recovering the experience of the democratic suffragists dramatises the difficulties confronting local Labour organisations in mounting electoral challenges to the Liberal Party during this period. Such a framework reveals, too, the fluid nature of suffrage-movement politics, so that we may no longer think of terms like 'militant' and 'constitutionalist', 'radical' and 'conservative' as rigid, exclusive, or self-evident categories of suffragists.

The intention has not been to argue for the abandonment of existing terminology and the interpretations based upon it, but rather for further efforts towards the refinement of both. There was greater sympathy among different sections of the movement, greater tensions within them, and more complex relations with other political movements than the existing conventions of suffrage history have allowed.

NOTES

The National Union of Women's Suffrage Societies has been abbreviated to NUWSS when identifying the records of that organisation. All these are located in the Fawcett Library, City of London Polytechnic, unless otherwise stated.

Other abbreviations used in the notes:

CMP   Catherine Marshall Papers, Cumbria Record Office, Carlisle
FAC   Fawcett Autograph Collection, Fawcett Library, City of London Polytechnic
JRMP   James Ramsay MacDonald Papers, Public Record Office, Kew
LGP   Lloyd George Papers, House of Lords Record Office
LPA   Labour Party Archives, Labour Party Library, London
MGFP   Millicent Garrett Fawcett Papers, Fawcett Library, City of London Polytechnic
MPLA   Manchester Public Library Archives

Introduction

1 Sheila Rowbotham, *Hidden from History* (London: Pluto Press, 1973).
2 Renate Bridenthal and Claudia Koonz, *Becoming Visible: Women in European History* (Boston: Houghton Mifflin, 1977).
3 Sylvia Pankhurst, *The Suffragette Movement* (reprint London: Virago, 1977); Christabel Pankhurst, *Unshackled* (London: Hutchinson, 1959); Annie Kenney, *Memories of a Militant* (London: Arnold, 1924); Mary Richardson, *Laugh a Defiance* (London: Weidenfeld and Nicolson, 1953); Hannah Mitchell, *The Hard Way Up* (reprint London: Virago, 1977); Dora Montefiore, *From a Victorian to a Modern* (London: Archer, 1927); Helena Swanwick, *I Have Been Young* (London: Gollancz, 1935); Millicent Garrett Fawcett, *What I Remember* (London: Fisher and Unwin, 1924).
4 George Dangerfield, *The Strange Death of Liberal England* (London: Paladin, 1970); Ray Strachey, *The Cause* (1928) (reprint London: Virago, 1978); Roger Fulford, *Votes for Women* (London: Faber and Faber, 1957); Constance Rover, *Women's Suffrage and Party Politics in Britain, 1866–1914* (London: Routledge and Kegan Paul, 1967); Andrew Rosen, *Rise Up Women* (London: Routledge and Kegan Paul, 1974); Leslie Parker Hume, *The National Union of Women's Suffrage Societies 1897–1914* (New York: Garland Publishing, 1982).
5 David Mitchell, *The Fighting Pankhursts* (London: Jonathan Cape, 1967), *Women on the Warpath* (London: Jonathan Cape, 1966), and *Queen Christabel* (London: Macdonald and Jane, 1977); Ray Strachey, *Millicent Garrett Fawcett* (London: Murray, 1933); Andro Linklater, *An Unhusbanded Life: Charlotte Despard. Suffragette. Socialist. Sinn Feiner* (London: Hutchinson, 1980).
6 See for example Jill Roe, 'Modernisation and Sexism: Recent Writings on Victorian Women', *Victorian Studies*, 20 (1977): 179–192, and Patricia Hollis, 'Working Women', *History*, 62 (1977): 439–445.

7 Richard Evans, 'The History of European Women: A Critical Survey of Recent Research', *Journal of Modern History*, 52 (1980): 655–75, esp. p. 671.

8 The phrase is Carroll Smith Rosenberg's in 'The New Woman and the New History', *Feminist Studies*, 3 (1975): 185–198, esp. p. 189. Further discussion of both the limitations and value of suffrage history may be found in the symposium 'Politics and Culture in Women's History', *Feminist Studies*, 6 (1980): 26–64.

9 Smith Rosenberg, 'The New Woman', p. 185.

10 Ibid., p. 186.

11 See for example Kathryn Kish Sklar, *Catherine Beecher: A Study of American Domesticity* (New Haven: Yale U.P., 1973); Carroll Smith Rosenberg, 'The Female World of Love and Ritual: Relations between Women in Nineteenth Century America', *Signs*, 1 (1975): 1–29; Linda Gordon, *Woman's Body, Woman's Right* (Harmondsworth: Penguin Books, 1977). Much valuable recent work in British women's history shares similar foci. See for example Sara Delamont and Lorna Duffin (eds.), *The Nineteenth Century Woman: Her Cultural and Physical World* (London: Croom Helm, 1978); Leonore Davidoff, 'The Separation of Home and Work? Landladies and Lodgers in Nineteenth and Twentieth Century England', in Sandra Burman (ed.), *Fit Work for Women* (London: Croom Helm, 1979), pp. 64–97; Anna Davin, 'Imperialism and Motherhood', *History Workshop Journal*, no. 5 (1978): 9–65; Sheila Rowbotham, *A New World for Women: Stella Browne – Socialist Feminist* (London: Pluto Press, 1977). See also my 'Feminine Authority and Social Order: Florence Nightingale's Conception of Nursing and Health Care', *Social Analysis*, no. 15 (1984): 59–72.

12 A notable example is Barbara Epstein's *The Politics of Domesticity* (Middletown, Conn.: Wesleyan U.P., 1981). This point will be developed further in Chapter 1.

13 Smith Rosenberg, 'The New Woman', pp. 186–187.

14 Ibid., p. 195.

15 Jill Liddington and Jill Norris, *One Hand Tied behind Us* (London: Virago, 1978), and Ada Nield Chew, *The Life and Writings of a Working Woman* (London: Virago, 1982).

16 E. P. Thompson, *The Making of the English Working Class* (London: Gollancz, 1963), p. 12.

17 John Wallach Scott, 'Survey Articles. Women in History II. The Modern Period', *Past and Present*, no. 101 (1983): 141–157, esp. p. 156.

18 See for example Smith Rosenberg, 'The New Woman', p. 186.

19 Rover, *Women's Suffrage and Party Politics*, provides a very general outline of the political policies taken up by the larger suffrage groups, and the position taken on the issue by the various political parties. But neither Rover nor any of the accounts of the women's-suffrage campaigns cited in note 4 analyse in detail the debates within the movement concerning political strategy.

20 P. F. Clarke, *Lancashire and the New Liberalism* (Cambridge: Cambridge U.P., 1971).

21 David Morgan, *Suffragists and Liberals* (Oxford: Blackwell Publisher, 1975).

22 Ross McKibbin, *The Evolution of the Labour Party, 1910–1924* (London: Oxford U.P., 1974).

23 See for example the depiction in Strachey, *The Cause*, esp. pp. 302–310.

24 See for example Jane Marcus, 'Transatlantic Sisterhood', *Signs*, 3 (1978): 744–755, and Edith Hurwitz, 'Carrie C. Catt's "Suffrage Militancy" ' ibid., pp. 739–743, both of which embody unquestioned assumptions of the equation between militancy and 'radical' feminism.

25 Liddington and Norris, *One Hand*.

26 Fulford, *Votes for Women*, ch. 10, and Liddington and Norris, *One Hand*, pp. 231–251 and passim, both note the emergence of this issue at the level of local suffrage politics in Lancashire but do not discuss its impact on the suffrage movement nationally. Similarly, Hume, *National Union*, pp. 44–46, remarks the importance of this issue for the outcome of the suffrage campaigns, but does not explore constitutionalists' debates on how to relate their own cause to it. As a consequence she underestimates the

full significance of developments in National Union political strategy from 1912.

27   Margaret Llewelyn Davies, letter to *The Common Cause,* 21 October 1909.

28   For the application of the term 'progressive' to British politics in the early twentieth century see P. F. Clarke, 'The Progressive Movement in England', *Transactions of the Royal Historical Society,* 5th ser., 24 (1974): 159–181; Martin Petter, 'The Progressive Alliance', *History,* 58 (1973): 45–59; Rodney Barker, 'Socialism and Progressivism in the Political Thought of Ramsay MacDonald', in A. J. A. Morrison (ed.), *Edwardian Radicalism* (London: Routledge and Kegan Paul, 1974), pp. 114–130.

29   Socialist politics in Britain at this time represented a complex and constantly shifting pattern of diverse currents of thought. R. J. Holton, '*Daily Herald* versus *Daily Citizen,* 1912–15', *International Review of Social History,* 19 (1974): 347–376, suggests that one strand of extraparliamentary socialist politics might best be identified as the 'rebel' movement. See also his *British Syndicalism* (London: Pluto Press, 1976).

30   The Catherine Marshall Papers are held at the Cumbria Record Office, Carlisle. I must thank Bob Holton for drawing them to my attention. When I first saw this collection there were scores of boxes of completely unsorted material. Historical researchers owe an enormous debt to Jo Vellacott for undertaking their ordering. Jo Vellacott Newberry, 'Anti-War Suffragists', *History,* 62 (1977): 411–425, is, to my knowledge, the only other work on the suffrage movement that draws extensively on these papers. The Catherine Marshall Papers have been catalogued since the research for this study was completed.

31   See Olive Banks, *Faces of Feminism* (Oxford: Martin Robertson, 1981); Les Garner, *Stepping Stones to Women's Liberty* (London: Hutchinson, 1984). Brian Harrison, *Separate Spheres* (London: Croom Helm, 1978), offers a comprehensive study of the ideas of the antisuffragists.

32   This aspect of the British suffrage movement contrasts with the experience in Germany and America. On Germany see Richard Evans, 'Bourgeois Feminists and Women Socialists in Germany, 1894–1914: Lost Opportunity or Inevitable Conflict', *Women's Studies International Quarterly,* 3 (1980): 355–376. On the United States see Meredith Tax, *The Rising of the Women* (New York: Monthly Review Press, 1980), esp. pp. 164–201.

1. 'Feminising democracy'

1   Compare Aileen Kraditor, *The Ideas of the Woman's Suffrage Movement 1890–1918* (New York: Columbia U.P., 1965), and William O'Neill, 'Feminism as a Radical Ideology', in Alfred F. Young (ed.), *Dissent: Explorations in the History of American Radicalism* (Dekalb: Northern Illinois U.P., 1968), pp. 273–300, and his *Everyone Was Brave* (Chicago: Quadrangle Books, 1969), with Ellen DuBois, *Suffragism and Feminism* (Ithaca: Cornell U.P., 1980), and her 'The Radicalism of the Woman's Suffrage Movement: Notes towards a Reconstruction of Nineteenth Century Feminism', *Feminist Studies,* 2 (1976): 84–103, and Epstein, *The Politics of Domesticity,* esp. pp. 115–151.

2   See for example Dangerfield, *The Strange Death;* Strachey, *The Cause;* Fulford, *Votes for Women;* Rosen, *Rise Up Women;* Liddington and Norris, *One Hand;* Hume, *The National Union,* all of which focus almost exclusively on organisations, campaigns, and personalities.

3   A brief summary of the arguments used by British suffragists may be found in Rover, *Women's Suffrage and Party Politics.* Banks, *Faces of Feminism,* identifies three intellectual traditions – evangelical, equal rights, and socialist – within feminism, and offers a comparative account of the American and British movements from the late eighteenth century to the present day. This is based largely on secondary sources, however, and the discussion of suffragism follows the conventional understanding that votes-for-women campaigning in Britain rested upon the equal-rights tradition of feminism, a viewpoint which this chapter seeks to modify in the light of evidence drawn from

primary sources. Only recently has a book-length study of the ideas of British suffragists appeared, Garner's *Stepping Stones*. Much of the evidence presented by Garner could be used to support the argument offered here, although her more particular concern is to identify variations in ideology among the different suffrage organisations. See also Martha Vicinus, 'Male Space and Women's. Bodies: The Suffragette Movement', in her *Independent Women: Work and Community for Single Women, 1850–1920* (Chicago: Chicago U.P., 1985), pp. 247–280, for an illuminating discussion of the metaphorical content of militant ideas and action.

4   See for example Richard Evans, *The Feminists* (London: Croom Helm, 1977), pp. 1–23, 64–65; Banks, *Faces of Feminism*, p. 118.

5   Mary Wollstonecraft, *Vindication of the Rights of Woman* (1795) (Harmondsworth: Penguin Books, 1975), p. 139. See also Mrs. Hugo Reid's account of the case for women's suffrage in 'A Plea for Women', quoted in Patricia Hollis, *Women in Public: The Women's Movement 1850–1900* (London: Allen and Unwin, 1979), p. 293: 'The ground on which equality is claimed for all men is of equal force for all women. . . . It is the possession of the noble faculties of reason and conscience, which elevates man above the brutes, and invests him with this right of exercising supreme authority over himself.'

6   John Stuart Mill, *The Subjection of Women* (1869), reprinted in Alice Rossi (ed.), *Essays on Sex Equality* (Chicago: Chicago U.P., 1970), pp. 125–242.

7   William Thompson, *Appeal on Behalf of One Half the Human Race . . .* (1825) (New York: Source Book Press, 1970).

8   Wollstonecraft, *Vindication*, p. 15.

9   Mill, *Subjection of Women*, pp. 169, 178–179. See also his essay 'Marriage and Divorce', in Rossi (ed.), *Essays*, p. 15, where he argues of the woman's role in marriage that 'it will be for the happiness of both that her occupation should rather be to adorn and beautify'. Wendall Robert Carr, in his Introduction to *The Subjection of Women* (Cambridge, 1970), p. xxii, points to Mill's inconsistency concerning women's domestic specialisation. Barbara Caine, 'John Stuart Mill and the English Women's Movement', *Historical Studies* (Melbourne), 18 (1978): 52–67, analyses anomalies in Mill's relations with English feminists, particularly his dislike of 'strong-minded women'.

10 Thompson, *Appeal*, pp. x–xii.

11 Ibid., pp. 177, 182.

12 Barbara Taylor, 'The Feminist Theory and Practice of the Owenite Socialist Movement in Britain 1820–45' (unpublished D. Phil. dissertation, University of Sussex, 1980), p. 33, since published as *Eve and the New Jerusalem* (London: Virago, 1983). She makes a similar point in her 'The Woman-Power: Religious Heresy and Feminism in Early English Socialism', in Susan Lipshitz (ed.), *Tearing the Veil* (London: Croom Helm, 1978), pp. 117–144, esp. pp. 138–139. This aspect of utopian socialist thought is even more clearly revealed in Claire G. Moses, 'Saint Simonian Men/Saint Simonian Women: The Transformation of Feminist Thought in 1830s France', *Journal of Modern History*, 54 (1982): 240–267. Claire Moses describes the replacement of humanist by essentialist arguments in Saint Simonian theory concerning the role of women, though she does not formulate it in these terms.

13 I am adopting this term from Penelope Brown and L. J. Jordonova, 'Oppressive Dichotomies: The Nature/Culture Debate', in Cambridge Women's Studies Group, *Women in Society: Interdisciplinary Essays* (London: Virago, 1981), who use the term 'essentialist thinking' and comment: 'By this we mean the common conviction that sex differences in the sense of gender ultimately refer to concrete, biological distinctions between men and women' (p. 225).

14 Banks, *Faces of Feminism*, pp. 48–59, esp. p. 49.

15 Ibid., pp. 85–102.

16 Frances Power Cobbe, 'The Final Cause of Woman', in Josephine Butler (ed.), *Woman's Work and Woman's Culture* (London: Macmillan, 1869), p. 5.

17 Banks, *Faces of Feminism*, p. 95.

18   'The Enfranchisement of Women', *Westminster Review*, July 1851, pp. 289–311, also reproduced in Rossi (ed.), *Essays*, pp. 89–122. See Rossi's Introduction, pp. 41–45, for the debate on the authorship of the article and the evidence that Harriet Taylor wrote it.

19   Reported in *The Women's Suffrage Journal*, 9 (1878): 44.

20   In *Nineteenth Century*, 26 (1889): 96.

21   Mabel Atkinson, in Brougham Villiers (ed.), *The Case for Women's Suffrage* (London: Fisher and Unwin, 1907), pp. 126–127. See also Margaret Macmillan's and Constance Smedley's contributions to the same book, esp. pp. 115 and 99, and Mrs. Henry (Millicent Garrett) Fawcett, 'Home and Politics' (London Society for Women's Suffrage, n.d.), and 'Men Are Men and Women Are Women' (National Union of Women's Suffrage Societies, 1909, reprinted from *The Englishwoman*).

22   Butler (ed.), *Woman's Work*, pp. 1–25, for Frances Power Cobbe's essay 'The Final Cause of Woman'; see also Julia Wedgwood's essay 'Female Suffrage Considered Chiefly with Respect to Its Indirect Results', pp. 247–289, esp. pp. 274–275, 287–289. Both essays are resonant with the tensions within feminist thought at this time. For example Cobbe's stated aim is to dispute the Comtists' emphasis on the domestic role of women, and yet she feels unable to deny the domestic part of their natures. Her arguments turn full circle when she concludes that women's domesticity should properly be realised in the service of God, rather than in the service of man, for 'The woman who lives to God in the first place can, better than anyone else, serve Man in the second; or rather, live to God in the service of his creatures. It is she who may best rejoice to be a wife and mother, she who may best make her home a little heaven of love and peace' (p. 25).

23   See Janet Penrose Trevelyan, *The Life of Mrs. Humphry Ward* (London: Constable, 1923), esp. pp. 224–245. Harrison, *Separate Spheres*, concentrates largely on the ideas of the male leadership of the Anti-Suffrage League.

24   See Harrison, *Separate Spheres*, pp. 133–136.

25   In John Ruskin, *Sesame and Lilies*, in *The Works of John Ruskin* (12 vols., New York: Wiley, 1885), vol. 11, pp. 5–186. See the analysis of Ruskin's views on women in Kate Millett, 'The Debate over Women: Ruskin versus Mill', in Martha Vicinus (ed.), *Suffer and Be Still* (Bloomington: Indiana U.P., 1973), pp. 121–139.

26   Ruskin, *Sesame and Lilies*, p. 100.

27   Butler (ed.), *Woman's Work*, p. xxvii.

28   Ibid., p. xviii. See also Mrs. Henry Fawcett, 'Home and Politics', and Lady Groves's contribution to Olga Fenton Shafer and Emily Hill (eds.), *Great Suffragists and Why* (London: Henry Drane, 1909), pp. 79–84.

29   Butler (ed.), *Woman's Work*, p. xxxvii.

30   Mrs. Emmeline Pankhurst, 'The Importance of the Vote' (London, 1913).

31   Millicent Fawcett, speech reported in *The Women's Suffrage Journal*, 18 (1887): 136.

32   Constance Smedley in Villiers (ed.), *The Case for Women's Suffrage*, p. 99.

33   Fawcett, 'Home and Politics', p. 3.

34   Butler (ed.), *Woman's Work*, pp. xvii–xviii. See also Miss Abadam's contribution to Shafer and Hill (eds.), *Great Suffragists*, p. 222, and Catherine Marshall's draft speech, January 1913, Catherine Marshall Papers (henceforth CMP), Carlisle Record Office, which includes the notes 'Women's Suffrage = Power of Service to the State, power of women to protect their practical side of life in homes, family and children' and 'The children of the State, the weak, the sick, the oppressed are crying aloud for a mother's as well as a father's care.'

35   See for example J. Gibson, 'The Sphere of Women' (London, [1894]).

36   James Keir Hardie, in Villiers (ed.), *The Case for Women's Suffrage*, p. 83.

37   W. Lyon Blease, *The Emancipation of Women* (London: Constable, 1910), p. 219.

38   Mary Stocks, *My Commonplace Book* (London: Hart Davies, 1970), p. 63.

39   Introduction to Villiers (ed.), *The Case for Women's Suffrage*. See also Blease, *Emancipation*, pp. 219, 236.

40 Banks, *Faces of Feminism*, p. 52.
41 Sheila Rowbotham and Jeffrey Weeks, *Socialism and the New Life: The Personal and Sexual Politics of Edward Carpenter and Havelock Ellis* (London: Pluto Press, 1977), p. 19.
42 Ibid., p. 110.
43 Ibid., p. 112.
44 Angus McLaren, *Birth Control in Nineteenth Century England* (London: Croom Helm, 1978), p. 163.
45 Werner Thönnessen, *The Emancipation of Women: The Rise and Decline of the Women's Movement in German Social Democracy 1863–1933* (London: Pluto Press, 1973), pp. 97–106. For socialist women's resistance to these ideas see Jean H. Quataert, *Reluctant Feminists in German Social Democracy, 1885–1917* (Princeton: Princeton U.P., 1979), pp. 100–106.
46 See Garner, *Stepping Stones*, who stresses in particular differing attitudes to class politics and to sexual radicalism.
47 Helena Swanwick, *The Future of the Women's Movement* (London: G. Bell, 1913), pp. vii and 207, and *I Have Been Young*, p. 207.
48 Christabel Pankhurst, 'The Great Scourge, and How to End It' (London: E. Pankhurst, 1913); Cicely Hamilton, *Marriage as a Trade* (London: Chapman and Hall, 1909).
49 DuBois, 'The Radicalism'.
50 Compare this assessment with Vicinus, 'Male Space', esp. pp. 250–252, and Epstein's discussion of the WCTU in *Politics of Domesticity*, esp. pp. 125–137.
51 Gerda Lerner, 'Woman's Rights and American Feminism', *American Scholar*, 40 (1970–71): 235–248, reproduced in her *The Majority Finds Its Past* (New York: Oxford U.P., 1979), pp. 48–62, and her contribution in the symposium 'Politics and Culture'.
52 Lerner, in the symposium 'Politics and Culture', pp. 50–51.
53 Ibid., p. 50.
54 Carroll Smith Rosenberg, in ibid., pp. 55–64, esp. pp. 58, 62–63.
55 Ibid., pp. 61–62.
56 Temma Kaplan, 'Female Consciousness and Collective Action: The Case of Barcelona, 1910–1918', *Signs*, 7 (1982): 545–566.
57 Ibid., pp. 565–566.
58 Nancy Cott, *The Bonds of Womanhood* (New Haven: Yale U.P., 1977).
59 Eric Richards, 'Women in the British Economy since about 1700: An Interpretation', *History*, 59 (1974): 337–357; Sally Alexander, 'Woman's Work in Nineteenth Century London: A Study of the Years 1820–50', in Juliet Mitchell and Ann Oakley (eds.), *The Rights and Wrongs of Women* (Harmondsworth: Penguin Books, 1976), pp. 59–111. See also Louise A. Tilly and Joan W. Scott, *Women, Work and Family* (New York: Holt, Rinehart and Winston, 1978), pp. 63–77, which compares the impact of industrialisation on women's work in France and England, and Davidoff, 'The Separation of Home and Work?'
60 See for example Leonore Davidoff, Jean L'Esperance, and Howard Newby, 'Landscape with Figures: Home and Community in English Society', in Mitchell and Oakley (eds.), *Rights and Wrongs*, pp. 139–175; Delamont and Duffin (eds.), *The Nineteenth Century Woman*; Davin, 'Imperialism and Motherhood'; Carol Dyhouse, *Girls Growing Up in Late Victorian and Edwardian England* (London: Croom Helm, 1981); Catherine Hall, 'The Early Formation of the Victorian Domestic Ideology', in Burman (ed.), *Fit Work for Women*, pp. 15–32; S. Holton, 'Feminine Authority and Social Order'. For America see Smith Rosenberg, 'The Female World of Love and Ritual', and 'Beauty, the Beast and the Militant Woman: A Case Study in Sex Roles and Social Stress in Jacksonian America', *American Quarterly*, 24 (1971): 562–584; Mary P. Ryan, 'The Power of Women's Networks: A Case Study of Female Moral Reform in Antebellum America', *Feminist Studies*, 5 (1979): 66–85.
61 Jo Manton, *Elizabeth Garrett Anderson* (London: Methuen, 1965), and *Mary Carpenter and the Children of the Streets* (London: Heinemann 1976); F. K. Prochaska, *Women and Philanthropy in Nineteenth Century England* (Oxford: Oxford U.P. [Clarendon Press], 1980).

62   Liddington and Norris, *One Hand*, esp. pp. 112–142, and Jill Liddington, *The Life and Times of a Respectable Rebel: Seline Cooper 1864–1946* (London: Virago, 1984), esp. pp. 145–148. See also Ellen Ross, 'Women's Neighbourhood and Sharing in London before the First World War', *History Workshop Journal*, no. 15 (1983): 4–27.

63   See for example the context of Millicent Garrett Fawcett's apprenticeship in feminist politics, provided in Manton, *Elizabeth Garrett Anderson*. See also the evidence concerning the extensive links of one of the major British suffrage organisations, the National Union of Women's Suffrage Societies, with other women's groups in my 'Feminism and Democracy: The Women's Suffrage Movement in Britain . . . (unpublished Ph.D. dissertation, University of Stirling, 1980), esp. pp. 91, 96–98, 105, 112.

64   DuBois in the symposium 'Politcs and Culture', p. 30.

65   Lerner in ibid., p. 50.

66   *The Common Cause*, 14 April 1910.

67   Helena Swanwick, *The Future*, pp. 99–100.

68   See for example the correspondence on this issue in *The Freewoman*, 21 and 28 December 1911 and 11 January 1912. Nancy Cott, 'Passionlessness: An Interpretation of Victorian Sexual Ideology', *Signs*, 4 (1978): 219–236, discusses aspects of this issue. See also Rowbotham, *A New World for Women*, p. 11.

69   Swanwick, *The Future*, pp. 106–107.

70   See for example Wilma Meikle, *Towards a Sane Feminism* (London: Grant Richards, 1916), pp. 82–97.

71   See for example the article 'Motherhood' in *The Common Cause*, 18 July 1912. Gordon, *Woman's Body, Woman's Right*, ch. 5, discusses the concept of voluntary motherhood and American feminist involvement in its promotion.

72   For example Fulford, *Votes for Women*, pp. 285–287; Rosen, *Rise Up Women*, ch. 17; Dangerfield, *Strange Death*, p. 104.

73   Mitchell, *Queen Christabel*, pp. 227–230.

74   Judith Walkowitz, 'The Politics of Prostitution', *Signs*, 6 (1980): 123–135.

75   See for example Helen Wilson, 'The Moral Revolution', in Zoe Fairfield (ed.), *Some Aspects of the Women's Movement* (London: Student Christian Movement, 1915), esp. p. 126. Helena Swanwick, *The Future*, p. 103, went so far as to argue that many 'respectable' women's experience of marriage was equivalent to prostitution.

76   Great Britain, *Parliamentary Papers*, 1914, vol. 49, *Report of the Royal Commission on Venereal Diseases*, Appendix to the First Report 1914, Cd. 7475, esp. the evidence of Dr. Florence Willey, pp. 370–402. See also the discussion between Dr. Helen Wilson and Dr. Scharlieb, ibid., pp. 187–188 (the commissioners included three women: Mrs. Creighton, leading member of the National Council of Women; Dr. Scharlieb; and Mrs. Burgwin). See also Dr. Jane Walker's evidence in Great Britain, *Parliamentary Papers*, 1912–13, vol. 20, *Report of the Royal Commission on Divorce and Matrimonial Causes*, vol. 3, Cd. 6481, p. 25.

77   See for example Swanwick, *The Future*, pp. 17–18. Compare this aspect of suffrage agitation with the women's strikes in Barcelona in the early years of the twentieth century described in Kaplan, 'Female Consciousness'.

78   Mrs. Pankhurst, 'The Importance of the Vote', p. 7.

79   Cicely Hamilton, 'Women's Vote' (London: National Union of Women's Suffrage Societies, 1908), p. 2.

80   For example in the 1870s Millicent Fawcett and her husband had successfully opposed the extension of the Factory Acts to women working in private houses (Strachey, *Millicent Garrett Fawcett*, p. 90). For a discussion of the significance of this in the development of sweating see Barbara Hutchins, 'The Historical Development of the Factory Acts', in Beatrice Webb (ed.), *The Case for the Factory Acts*, 2nd ed. (London: Grant Richards, 1902), p. 92.

81   Clementina Black, 'Some Current Objections to Factory Legislation for Women', in Webb (ed.), *The Case for the Factory Acts*, pp. 193–223.

82   Clementina Black, 'Legislative Proposals', in Gertrude Tuckwell, Constance Smith,

Mary R. MacArthur, et al., *Woman in Industry from Seven Points of View* (London: Duckworth, 1908), pp. 186–202.

83 Mrs. Pankhurst, 'The Importance of the Vote', p. 9.

84 Ibid. For one married working woman's tenacious pursuit of her own economic in-dependence see Doris Nield Chew's memoir of her mother in Nield Chew, *Life and Writings*, pp. 3–72.

85 Mrs. Pankhurst, 'The Importance of the Vote,' p. 8.

86 Emilia Dilke, Preface to Amy Bulley and Margaret Whitley, *Women's Work* (London: Methuen, 1894), pp. xii–xiii. See also pp. 157–159.

87 In *The Common Cause*, 21 April 1910. See also Clementina Black, *Married Women's Work* (London: Women's Industrial Council, 1915), p. 5.

88 Great Britain. *Parliamentary Papers*, 1912–13, vol. 19, *Report of the Royal Commission on Divorce and Matrimonial Causes*, vol. 2, Cd. 6480, pp. 462–465. See also Nield Chew, *Life and Writings*, pp. 135–183, for astute commentaries on the political economy of working-class marriage at this time.

89 *R.C. Divorce*, vol. 2, p. 373.

90 'Motherhood', in *The Common Cause*, 1 July 1912.

91 *R.C. Divorce*, vol. 2, pp. 149–173.

92 E.g. Clementina Black, *Married Women's Work*. In a review of Dr. Elizabeth Sloan Chesser's *Women, Marriage and Motherhood* in the *Sociological Review*, 7 (1914): 165, Clementina Black commented: 'Housework as it is among the conditions ordinarily existing in wage-earning families ought to be recognised by enlightened eugenists as a trade unfit for mothers.' See also Swanwick, *The Future*, pp. 91–96; 'Why House-Keeping Women Want the Vote', *The Common Cause*, 16 May 1913; 'Cooperative Housekeeping', *The Common Cause*, 12 September 1912; and *The Common Cause*, 28 November 1913 and 13 March 1914, for attacks on the existing conditions of house-work.

93 Marion Holmes, 'The ABC of Votes for Women' (London: Women's Freedom League, 1913). See also Margaret MacMillan in Villiers (ed.), *The Case for Women's Suffrage*, pp. 116–118; *The Common Cause*, 9 November 1911, 16 May 1913, and 29 August 1913.

94 Jessie Craigen, 'On Women's Suffrage' (n.p., [1880], reprinted from *The Women's Suffrage Journal*, 14 February 1880).

95 Blease, *The Emancipation*, p. 167.

96 Swanwick, *The Future*, pp. 127, 160, 166.

97 See the manifesto 'Bondwomen and Freewomen' in *The Freewoman*, 23 November 1911.

98 See e.g. Hamilton, *Marriage as a Trade*.

99 Pankhurst, 'The Great Scourge', which also appeared as a series of articles in *The Suffragette* in August and September 1912. See also Sylvia Pankhurst's account of this campaign in *The Suffragette Movement*, pp. 521–523.

100 See Meikle, *Towards a Sane Feminism*, pp. 84–85.

101 Garner, *Stepping Stones*, esp. pp. 36–37, 42, notes that attitudes to class politics were significantly different among the various suffrage groups. This question will be pur-sued further in Chapter 3.

2. Militants and constitutionalists

1 Morgan, *Suffragists and Liberals*.

2 Ibid., esp. pp. 40–41, and Rover, *Women's Suffrage and Party Politics*, pp. 115–143.

3 Helen Blackburn provides a detailed account of late-nineteenth-century suffrage or-ganisations and campaigns in *Women's Suffrage: A Record of the Women's Suffrage Move-ment in the British Isles* (London: Williams and Norgate, 1902). For the formation and early organisational development of the National Union see also Hume, *The National Union*, pp. 1–7.

4 Quoted in Strachey, *Fawcett*, p. 18. This paragraph also draws on Fawcett, *What I Remember*, and Manton, *Elizabeth Garrett Anderson*.

5 For an analysis of the Liberal affiliations of the National Union leadership see Hume, *The National Union*, p. 36.

6 Rosen, *Rise Up Women*, p. 49; Rover, *Women's Suffrage and Party Politics*, p. 77.

7 *Annual Report of the North of England Society for Women's Suffrage*, 1898–9, 1899–1900, 1900–1, 1901–2, 1902–3, MPLA. The Glasgow Society was one that sought to emulate these successes. See the minutes of the Glasgow and West of Scotland Women's Franchise Association, 23 December 1903 and 27 January 1904, Mitchell Library, Glasgow (henceforth called the Glasgow Society minutes).

8 For first-hand accounts of early WSPU campaigning see Mitchell, *The Hard Way Up*, ch. 4, and Kenney, *Memories of a Militant*.

9 Liddington and Norris, *One Hand*, pp. 162–163, and Liddington, *Life and Times*, p. 140, both suggest the new body was formed to facilitate the pursuit of a new strategy, that of running suffrage candidates. It should be noted, nonetheless, that their campaigns on behalf of such candidates received considerable support from the National Union.

10 NUWSS minutes, 11 June and 9 July 1903, 4 February 1904, and 6 April 1905; *Annual Report of NUWSS*, 1903–4.

11 See Esther Roper to Mrs. Fawcett, n.d. [*c.* 24 October 1906], M50/21/1/230, MPLA.

12 This account is based on S. Pankhurst, *The Suffragette Movement*, esp. pp. 89–97, 116–163.

13 Ibid., pp. 164–166. See also C. Pankhurst, *Unshackled*, pp. 40–41.

14 See Henry Pelling, *A Short History of the Labour Party* (London: Macmillan, 1961).

15 S. Pankhurst, *The Suffragette Movement*, p. 168.

16 Ibid., pp. 189–191.

17 For example, Rosen, *Rise Up Women*, p. 36, contrasts the WSPU to 'that old-fashioned and official gang, the National Union of Women's Suffrage Societies'. Vicinus, 'Male Space and Women's Bodies', has recently offered a much more sophisticated interpretation of the symbolic significance of some better-known aspects of WSPU campaigning. Though her argument is convincing I would suggest that it could be applied equally to much constitutional activity; that is to say, she has revealed an aspect which is generic to suffragism at this time, not specific to militancy. Compare her account with the first-person testimonies concerning constitutionalists' experiences of suffrage agitation cited later in this chapter.

18 Notably in Dangerfield's *The Strange Death of Liberal England*.

19 Pelling, *Short History*, pp. 1–17.

20 S. Pankhurst, *The Suffragette Movement*, p. 169.

21 Mary Ward to Millicent Fawcett, 14 January 1906. See also K. Lyttelton to Millicent Fawcett, 12 January 1906, M50/2/1/216 and 217, MPLA.

22 London Society for Women's Suffrage minutes, 18 and 25 October 1905. See also a letter from a Liberal Party worker, Beatrice Brookshanks, to Edith Palliser, 12 January 1906, FAC.

23 London Society for Women's Suffrage minutes, 15 November and 20 December 1905.

24 Members of the Social Democratic Federation were to lead the opposition in the Labour Party to equal votes for women, and it soon became evident that Dora Montefiore herself supported women's suffrage only as part of a broader demand for adult suffrage. She soon left the suffrage movement and helped organise the Adult Suffrage Society. See Montefiore, *From a Victorian to a Modern*, pp. 119–123.

25 S. Pankhurst, *The Suffragette Movement*, pp. 197–200, 228–240.

26 Ibid., p. 220.

27 See for example Christabel Pankhurst to A. J. Balfour, 26 September and 28 October 1907, British Library Add. Mss. 49793.

28 Continuing WSPU–Labour movement links were evident in the activities of Adela Pankhurst. See Mitchell, *The Fighting Pankhursts*, p. 46. A fuller understanding of this

aspect of WSPU organisation will require more local studies of the suffrage movement. The Manchester WSPU, for example, was still advertising its meetings in the socialist press as late as 1908; see *The Labour Leader*, 25 February and 5 June 1908.

29   C. Pankhurst, *Unshackled*, pp. 66–67.

30   Ibid., p. 69.

31   S. Pankhurst, *The Suffragette Movement*, pp. 241–251.

32   *The Labour Leader*, 27 September 1908.

33   *The Woman Worker*, 25 September 1908.

34   Quoted in M. Rendel, 'The Contribution of the Women's Labour League to the Winning of the Franchise', in Lucy Middleton (ed.), *Women in the Labour Movement* (London: Croom Helm, 1977), p. 63.

35   Quoted in *British Journal of Nursing* cutting, 20 January 1906. See also *Manchester Guardian* cutting, 15 January 1906, M50/2/1/20, MPLA.

36   W. T. Stead to Millicent Fawcett, 13 January 1906, M50/2/1/219, MPLA.

37   *Votes for Women*, July 1908.

38   *Jus Suffragii*, 15 November 1906.

39   Millicent Fawcett–J. Cobden Sanderson correspondence between 28 October and 11 November 1906, M50/2/1/231, 233, 237, 238, 239, 241, MPLA.

40   Elizabeth Robins to Millicent Fawcett, 27 October 1906, M50/2/1/232, MPLA.

41   *Glasgow Herald*, 7 October 1907; *Labour Leader*, 13 March and 12 June 1908; NUWSS minutes, 2 April and 7 May 1908.

42   NUWSS minutes, 18 October 1907.

43   Ibid., 23 July 1908. See the leaflet 'By-Election Policies Compared' [October 1908], CMP.

44   Isabella Ford to Millicent Fawcett, 14 February 1908, MGFP.

45   For example, Rosen, *Rise Up Women*, esp. p. 245; Dangerfield, *Strange Death*, esp. pp. 137–141.

46   See for example Glasgow Society minutes, 17 October and 11 December 1906, Mitchell Library, Glasgow, and *Glasgow Herald*, 8 November 1906, for a report of a discussion on militancy within the society.

47   Louisa Garrett Anderson to Millicent Fawcett, 22, 24, and 25 June 1908, M50/2/1/246–248, MPLA. At this time, too, the Men's League for Women's Suffrage was pressing for a union between the National Union and the Women's Freedom League (Lady Frances Balfour to Millicent Fawcett, 6 November 1908, FAC). The previous year had also seen considerable cooperation between the WFL and the National Union: see Linklater, *An Unhusbanded Life*, p. 129.

48   Beatrice Harraden in *The Women's Franchise*, 23 July 1908.

49   Mrs. Fawcett, reported by Mrs. Hylton Dale in a letter to Edith Palliser, 8 March 1907, FAC, and Fawcett, *What I Remember*, p. 185.

50   For a while even the issuing of an annual report from the central office appears to have been suspended, the local societies preferring to issue their own (NUWSS executive minutes, 6 November 1902 and 4 December 1902).

51   See E. M. Gardner to Catherine Marshall, 22 March [1910], CMP; Maude Royden to Catherine Marshall, 23 March 1910, CMP.

52   See *NUWSS Annual Report*, 1909 and 1910; *The Common Cause*, 24 March and 21 and 28 April 1910. The federations that had been formed by 1912 were the Eastern Counties; the Kentish; the Manchester and District; the Midlands East; the Midlands West; the North and East Ridings; the Northern; the North-Western; the Oxford, Beds., and Bucks.; the South Wales; the Surrey, Sussex, and Herts.; the West Riding; the West of England; the West Leicester, West Cheshire, and North Wales; and the Scottish.

53   This point will be elaborated in later chapters, particularly those concerning the Election Fighting Fund policy.

54   For an account of the construction and purpose of the various National Union councils, see *The Common Cause*, 24 March and 21 and 28 April 1910.

55   See the editorial in *The Labour Leader*, 20 September 1907.

56	C. Pankhurst, *Unshackled*, p. 81; S. Pankhurst, *The Suffragette Movement*, pp. 261–274.
57	The WFL leadership were all active socialists: Charlotte Despard, Teresa Billington Greig, Marian Coates Hanson, Annie Cobden Sanderson, Mrs. Morrissey. The organisers' reports in *The Vote* indicate the close links the WFL maintained with labour and socialist organisations in each branch locality.
58	See for example the report of a Birmingham WSPU member to the Women's Labour League conference in *The Labour Leader*, 24 January 1908.
59	This is particularly clear in the records of the Glasgow Society concerning a by-election campaign in 1909; see Glasgow Society minutes, 10 and 31 March and 11 April 1909, Mitchell Library, Glasgow.
60	See *NUWSS Annual Report*, 1913, and Catherine Marshall's 'Notes for Exeter Council', 23 May 1913, CMP.
61	See e.g. *The Common Cause*, 11 April and 18 July 1912 for accounts of one such summer school.
62	This account is based on a biographical sketch provided by Jo Vellacott. For Catherine Marshall's later career see also Vellacott Newberry, 'Anti-War Suffragists', and Fenner Brockway, *Inside the Left* (London: Allen and Unwin, 1942), pp. 68–77.
63	*NUWSS Annual Reports*, 1911, 1912, and 1913.
64	Ibid.
65	See ibid., 1909; NUWSS minutes, 3 and 17 December 1908 and 7 and 21 January 1909; Swanwick, *I Have Been Young*, p. 207.
66	This account is based on Swanwick, *I Have Been Young*.
67	Ibid., p. 228. Swanwick resigned the editorship in 1911 because of controversy over her strong attacks on the increased use of violence during WSPU demonstrations. Clementina Black and Maude Royden were subsequent editors of the paper.
68	See e.g. C. P. Scott to Catherine Marshall, 28 July 1913, CMP.
69	Strachey, *The Cause*, p. 306.
70	Swanwick, *I Have Been Young*, pp. 199–201.
71	Agnes Maude Royden, 'Bid Me Discourse', typescript, Fawcett Library, City of London Polytechnic.
72	See biographical sketch 'Miss Agnes Maude Royden', NUWSS Information Bureau, n.d., M50/2/10/30, MPLA. For an account of her later life see Maude Royden, *A Threefold Cord* (London: Gollancz, 1948).
73	Royden, 'Bid Me Discourse', pp. 43–45.
74	*NUWSS Annual Report*, 1911, 1912, and 1913.
75	S. Pankhurst, *The Suffragette Movement*, p. 289.
76	Ibid., p. 309; C. Pankhurst, *Unshackled*, p. 131.
77	C. Pankhurst, *Unshackled*, pp. 143f.
78	Quoted in Strachey, *Fawcett*, p. 223.
79	Millicent Garrett Fawcett to Alice Blackwell, 22 February 1909, M50/2/1/270, MPLA.
80	Millicent Garrett Fawcett to Philippa Strachey, 12 October 1908, FAC.
81	Quoted in Strachey, *Fawcett*, p. 224.
82	*The Women's Franchise*, 19 November 1908; and the report of the NUWSS quarterly council in *The Common Cause*, 7 October 1909. For the text of the statement see *Jus Suffragii*, 15 November 1909.
83	NUWSS minutes, 23 July and 17 and 20 November 1908.
84	Ibid., 3 and 17 December 1908 and 7 January 1909.
85	*The Common Cause*, 4 November 1909; see also ibid., 16 September 1909, 'Violence and Reaction: The Two Forces of Disorder'.
86	Helena Dowson to Millicent Fawcett, 10 October 1909, M50/2/1/284, MPLA.
87	Millicent Fawcett to Helena Dowson, 15 October 1909, M50/2/1/286, MPLA.
88	See NUWSS executive's circular letter on special general meeting of the London Society, MGFP, and Clara Collett to Millicent Fawcett, 3 December 1909, M50/2/1/289, MPLA. There were similar attempts by militant sympathisers in the Newcastle and Scarborough societies to win over constitutionalists to a militant political policy.

89 Millicent Garrett Fawcett's notes on the circular letter and copy of her letter to Lady Frances Balfour, 18 December 1909, MGFP.
90 These included founding members Mrs. David Grieg, Janie Allan, Helen Waddell, Margaret Irwin, Grace Paterson, and Dr. Marion Gilchrist. Mrs. Grieg and Helen Waddell had also been active in the Women's Liberal Federation prior to this time. See Glasgow Society minutes, 11 and 25 April, 30 May, and 30 November 1907, Mitchell Library, Glasgow; reports in *The Glasgow Herald,* 16 December 1907 and 21 October 1908. After these resignations the society fell under the domination of committed Liberals, notably Andrew Ballantyne and Mrs. Hunter, chairman and secretary respectively.
91 *London Society for Women's Suffrage Annual Report,* 1907 and 1908, Fawcett Library. Flora Murray was supported by Louisa Garrett Anderson, Evelyn Sharp, Margaret Nevinson, and Mrs. Hylton Dale.
92 Winifred Ball–Millicent Fawcett correspondence, 14–16 November 1908, M50/2/1/254–256, MPLA.
93 Ethel Snowden to Millicent Fawcett, 18 September 1909, M50/2/1/283, MPLA.
94 NUWSS minutes, 27 February 1911, CMP.
95 See for example *The Common Cause,* 7 October 1909, 4 August 1910, and 27 April 1911.
96 See Fulford, *Votes for Women,* p. 164, for Wimbledon; Liddington and Norris, *One Hand,* pp. 197–200, 243–246, for Wigan and Rossendale.
97 Fulford, *Votes for Women,* p. 233.
98 See Catherine Marshall's account of the South Salford campaign (possibly a draft of an article for publication), [November 1910], CMP.
99 *The Common Cause,* 15 September 1910.

3. Adult suffrage or women's suffrage?

1 See Neil Blewett, 'The Franchise in the United Kingdom, 1885–1918', *Past and Present,* no. 32 (1965): 27–56.
2 See Pelling, *A Short History of the Labour Party,* pp. 1–17.
3 Rowbotham and Weeks, *Socialism and the New Life,* p. 19.
4 Charlotte Despard, 'The Next Step to Adult Suffrage', in *The Reformer's Year Book 1907* (London: Clarion Co., 1907), p. 153.
5 Lady Frances Balfour of the National Union was a case in point. See Edith Palliser to Lady Frances Balfour, 21 January 1907, FAC. See also the manifesto of the Conservative and Unionist Women's Franchise Association, which declared its opposition to full adult suffrage, quoted in Rover, *Women's Suffrage and Party Politics,* pp. 23–24.
6 Quoted from Bruce Glasier's diary in Laurence Thompson, *The Enthusiasts* (London: Gollancz, 1971), p. 136.
7 For one example of this kind of thought see F. F. Mills, 'The Great Divorce: The Mother and the Home', in the ILP's journal, *The Labour Leader,* 19 March 1909, one of a series seeking to show that the number of married working women was increasing in order to provide a cheap source of labour for capitalism, and arguing that this trend was linked to high infant-mortality rates.
8 Katharine Bruce Glasier–James Ramsay MacDonald correspondence, 13 March and 1 and 2 April 1914, James Ramsay MacDonald papers, PRO 30/69/1158/35–43.
9 S. Pankhurst, *The Suffragette Movement,* p. 244.
10 *Labour Party Annual Conference Report,* 1907.
11 James Ramsay MacDonald, *Margaret Ethel MacDonald* (London: Hodder and Stoughton, 1912), pp. 204, 200. Adultists at Labour Party conferences often appealed to the antipathy within the labour movement to militant tactics. See for example SDFer Harry Quelch's speech in *Labour Party Annual Conference Report,* 1908, where he referred to the 'Merry Andrew tactics' of suffragists 'who thought that the best way to advance a cause was to suppress the right of public meeting'.
12 Esther Roper to Mrs. Fawcett, n.d. [*c.* 24 October 1906], M50/2/1/230, MPLA.

13 E. Belfort Bax, *The Fraud of Feminism* (London: Grant Richards, 1913).
14 See Sir Almroth Wright, *The Unexpurgated Case against Woman Suffrage* (London: Constable, 1913).
15 Malcolm Muggeridge, Introduction to Anna Raeburn, *The Suffragette View* (Newton Abbot: David and Charles, 1976), p. 6.
16 Harry Quelch's speeches in *Labour Party Annual Conference Report*, 1906 and 1907.
17 *Labour Party Annual Conference Report*, 1907.
18 *The Labour Leader*, 16 August 1907.
19 See for example Tom Johnston's articles on women's suffrage in the Glasgow ILP paper *The Forward*, 5, 12, and 19 November 1910.
20 *Labour Party Annual Conference Report*, 1908.
21 Published in pamphlet form as 'Sex Equality versus Adult Suffrage' (Manchester: Women's Freedom League, 1908). Significantly, the pro–women's-suffrage resolution was passed in terms of votes for women as 'the speediest and most practical way to real democracy'.
22 Ibid., p. 18.
23 Ibid., p. 17.
24 Ibid., p. 25.
25 Ibid., p. 14.
26 Ibid., pp. 27–28.
27 James Keir Hardie, 'The Citizenship of Women' (London: ILP, 1906).
28 Rowbotham, *Hidden from History*, pp. 82–83.
29 Eva Gore Booth, in Villiers (ed.), *The Case for Women's Suffrage*, pp. 54–55.
30 See the report in *The Women's Franchise*, 17 October 1907.
31 Letter to *The Common Cause*, 16 February 1911. Compare Liddington, *Life and Times*, p. 181, for a discussion of Selina Cooper's involvement with the National Union.
32 See Doris Nield Chew's account of her mother's experience as a suffrage organiser in Nield Chew, *Life and Writings*, pp. 46–47.
33 Rowbotham and Weeks, *Socialism and the New Life*, p. 20.
34 Quoted in Gillian Scott, 'The Politics of the Women's Cooperative Guild: Working Women and Feminism during the First World War' (unpublished M.A. dissertation, University of Sussex, 1980).
35 Ibid., p. 8.
36 Catherine Webb, *The Woman with the Basket* (Manchester: WCG, 1927), p. 99.
37 *Women's Cooperative Guild Annual Report*, 1906–7.
38 *Labour Representation Committee Annual Conference Report*, 1904. The WCG's case for the revised bill is set out in 'The Franchise and Married Working Women' (Manchester, WCG, 1908).
39 See for example Christabel Pankhurst's speech reported in *The Independent Labour Party Annual Conference Report*, 1905, and the report of Dora Montefiore's speech to the International Women's Suffrage Alliance on behalf of the WSPU in *Jus Suffragii*, 15 October 1906, both of which presented the women's-suffrage demand as part of the adult-suffrage cause.
40 *The Women's Franchise*, 8 January 1907.
41 Ibid., 12 September 1907, in the correspondence column.
42 Letter from A. B. Wallis Chapman, ibid., 19 September 1907. See also Lilian Harris's rebuttal, ibid., 26 September 1907.
43 Ibid., 12 December 1907.
44 In Villiers (ed.), *The Case for Women's Suffrage*, pp. 67–68.
45 *The Women's Franchise*, 7 November 1907.
46 *The Labour Leader*, 24 January 1908.
47 See *Votes for Women*, 11 and 26 February and 12 and 26 March, 1909; *The Common Cause*, 15 April 1909.
48 *The Suffrage Annual and Who's Who* (London, 1913). Reports of the activities of the

Adult Suffrage Society continued to appear in the SDF's paper *Justice* (on the women's page) and made no mention of the new organisation. See also Rendel, 'The Contribution of the Women's Labour League', pp. 63–68.

49 *Women's Cooperative Guild Annual Report*, 1909–10.
50 Ibid., 1907–8 and 1908–9.
51 Ibid., 1909–10.
52 The 294 women's-suffrage meetings held in 1905–6 had fallen to 134 in 1908–9, by which time the Guild's Special Women's Suffrage Fund had also become very low. See ibid., 1905–6 and 1908–9.
53 *Votes for Women*, 22 October 1909.
54 *The Common Cause*, 25 November 1909. The editor, Helena Swanwick, was also a close friend of one of the leading members of the WCG, Rosalind Vaughan Nash.
55 Millicent Garrett Fawcett to Marion Phillips, 12 September 1909, MGFP.
56 Mrs. Fawcett's papers include notes entitled 'My Counts against Miss Phillips' with the item 'continually trying to push us in the direction of Adult Suffrage'. Marion Phillips's political affiliations no doubt played some part in the issue (she went on to become secretary of the Women's Labour League and then chief women's officer to the Labour Party). One of her firmest opponents on the National Union executive was Mrs. Broadley Reid, a leading member of the Women's Liberal Federation. Ethel Bentham of the Newcastle Society considered resigning her place on the National Union executive over this controversy; see her letter to Walter McLaren, 8 March 1910, MPLA. For an account of Marion Phillips's later career see Beverley Kingston, 'Yours Very Truly, Marion Phillips', in Ann Curthoys, Susan Eade, and Peter Spearritt (eds.), *Women at Work* (Canberra: Australian Society for the Study of Labour History, 1975), pp. 123–131.
57 *The Common Cause*, 9 December 1909. Conversely the socialist suffragist Ethel Snowden resigned from the ILP to protest at Mary Macarthur's involvement in the PSF, for Mary Macarthur was the only woman on the ILP's National Administrative Council.
58 *The Common Cause*, 21 October 1909.
59 Ibid., 11 November 1909.
60 Swanwick, *The Future of the Women's Movement*, p. vii.
61 Swanwick, *I Have Been Young*, p. 207.
62 London Society minutes, 11 June 1907, and typewritten duplicated NUWSS quarterly council reports, 9 July 1907; *The Labour Leader*, 5 July 1907. See also *The Women's Franchise*, 25 July, 5 September, and 17 October 1907, for further reports of the campaign.
63 *The Women's Franchise*, 2 April 1908.
64 Ibid., 17 and 24 September and 8 and 15 October 1908.
65 See for example the Newcastle Society's report to *The Common Cause*, 23 June 1910.
66 NUWSS quarterly council reports, 9 July 1907.
67 Ibid., 25 October 1907.
68 Ibid., 29 January, 1 May, and 14 July 1908, and Newcastle Society reports in *The Women's Franchise*, 2 April, 17 September, and 8 and 15 October 1908.
69 *North of England Society for Women's Suffrage Annual Report*, 1908. (The society was generally referred to as the Manchester Society, and later adopted that name formally.)
70 Swanwick, *I Have Been Young*, p. 204.
71 *The Common Cause*, 1 September 1910; *North of England Society for Women's Suffrage Annual Report*, 1910.
72 *The Common Cause*, 21 and 28 July 1910 and 27 July 1911, for reports of the Kirkdale and Middleton by-elections respectively.
73 Ibid., 14 and 28 September and 5 October 1911.
74 Morgan, *Suffragists and Liberals*, pp. 77–78. See also Rover, *Women's Suffrage*, pp. 97–98. Briefly, in 1910 and 1911 the Liberal governments' energies were absorbed by the constitutional crisis that followed the House of Lords' rejection of Lloyd George's

'People's Budget' and precipitated two general elections in 1910. With its resolution in the passage of the Parliament Act in 1911 the government's attention returned to its longstanding programme of Irish home rule, Welsh disestablishment, and the National Insurance Bill. The women's-suffrage demand remained confronted by a hostile prime minister, a divided cabinet, and a crowded parliamentary programme.

75   See the pamphlet 'Conciliation Committee for Woman Suffrage' (London, [1910]), M50/2/1/304, MPLA.

76   Rosen, *Rise Up Women*, p. 125.

77   H. N. Brailsford letters to Mrs. Fawcett between January and March 1910, M50/2/291/300–303, MPLA.

78   See 'One Man, One Vote: One Woman, One Vote' (London: People's Suffrage Federation [*c.* 1909]).

79   'Conciliation Committee for Woman Suffrage'. See also 'The Conciliation Bill Explained', a Conciliation Committee leaflet reproduced in *The Common Cause*, 11 August 1910. Both contain the full text of the bill.

80   The PSF accepted that the large majority of voters enfranchised under such a bill would be working-class women, though it did not necessarily accept the 82 per cent claimed by the women's suffragists; see 'Could Women Vote on the Same Terms as Men?' (London: People's Suffrage Federation [*c.* 1909]).

81   J. A. Pease diaries, 15 June 1910, Gainford Papers 38, Nuffield College Library, Oxford. Asquith also agreed to receive a deputation on this 'most repulsive subject'. The bill, also known as Shackleton's Bill, had passed its second reading by a majority of 110.

82   Ibid., 23 June 1910.

83   See for example R. D. Denman to Catherine Marshall, 3, 7, and 21 November 1910, and Beatrix Morton to Catherine Marshall, 10 and 13 November 1910, CMP.

84   *People's Suffrage Federation Annual Report*, 1909–10. The PSF continued to insist it was a women's-suffrage organisation, though *The Common Cause* disputed this on the grounds that it gave priority to changing the basis of the franchise rather than to sexual equality for itself. See the editor's response to Rosalind Nash's letter, *The Common Cause*, 16 June 1910.

85   In all a total of 4,220 meetings were organised by the National Union in support of the Conciliation Bill during 1910 alone. See *NUWSS Annual Report*, 1910; *The Common Cause*, 7 July 1910, for full details of the various platforms and speeches at the major Trafalgar Square demonstration. For other National Union demonstrations see *The Common Cause*, 8 June 1910 and 27 April 1911.

86   Kathleen Courtney's 'A Democratic Measure' in *The Common Cause*, 7 July 1910, argued against such reservations.

87   The title was changed from 'A Bill to Extend the Parliamentary Franchise to Women Occupiers', to 'A Bill to Confer the Parliamentary Franchise on Women'. See *The Common Cause*, 27 April 1911, for the text of the Conciliation Committee's leaflet on what was also known as Kemp's Bill. See also 'Votes for Women: The Conciliation Bill Explained' (London: NUWSS, 1911).

88   The definition of 'working-class' employed in the survey was based, in Dundee, on the number of rooms occupied, and in Bangor and Carnarvon on the lack of a servant: *The Common Cause*, 23 February 1911.

89   'All or Some or Some or None?' (London: NUWSS [1911]). See also 'What Working People Say' (London: NUWSS, 1911), a leaflet originally issued by the LCTOWRC. Unlike the WCG, the textile workers actively campaigned on behalf of the bill.

90   See Philip Snowden, 'Speech on the Parliamentary Franchise (Women) Bill 1910' (London: NUWSS [1910]) and 'In Defence of the Conciliation Bill' (London: WFL, n.d.). Snowden had been one of the opponents of the women's-suffrage resolution at the 1905 Labour Party conference, but had since married a committed socialist suffragist and prominent National Union speaker, Ethel Snowden.

91 J. L. Hammond, *C. P. Scott of the Manchester Guardian* (London: Bell, 1934), p. 98.

92 Lloyd George to Elibank, 5 September 1911, MSS Elibank 8802, National Library of Scotland, Edinburgh. See also Swanwick, *I Have Been Young*, p. 211, for Lloyd George's view on the Conciliation Bills as he expressed them to her.

93 C. P. Scott memos., 15 June 1911, British Library, Add. Mss. 50901.

94 Ibid.

95 Ibid., 26 October 1911.

96 Ibid.

97 Ibid.

98 Pease diaries, 13 December 1911 and 25 April 1912. Scott memos., 22–3 January 1912. Asquith to King, 25 April 1912, Asquith Papers 6, Bodleian Library, Oxford. See also a report of the discussion in the cabinet at this time in Lady Frances Balfour's letter to Mrs. Fawcett, 7 March 1912, FAC.

99 *NUWSS Annual Report*, 1910 and 1911. Joint militant–constitutional campaigning was evident in numerous localities in this period. See for example *The Common Cause*, 29 June 1911. But such cooperation was no longer uncontroversial among constitutionalists. At one point the Leicester National Union society had been refused permission to cooperate with the local WSPU (NUWSS minutes, 5 January 1911), and the National Union's decision to join the WSPU's coronation procession brought a protest from the London Society (NUWSS minutes, 27 April 1911). In the event, constitutionalists formed the largest contingent in this procession.

100 Henry Woodd Nevinson diaries, Bodleian Library, Oxford, 1 December 1910. In this period Nevinson first noticed Christabel Pankhurst's growing antipathy to male involvement in the suffrage movement.

101 Ibid., 3, 7, 8, and 29 November; 2 and 20 January 1911; 8 February 1911. See also Lord Lytton to Mrs. Fawcett, 17 November 1910, FAC.

102 Nevinson diaries, 21 January, 16 February, and 7 and 16 March 1911. See also Richardson, *Laugh a Defiance*, p. 10.

103 Nevinson diaries, 9, 10, 14, 16, 20, 25, 26, and 30 November; 4, 6, 7, and 21 December 1911; 3 January 1912. Nevinson himself shared in this confusion. He accepted the sense of Brailsford's pragmatic approach as opposed to Jane Brailsford's and other leading WSPU activists' insistence on a stand on the principle of equality. 'My reason in practice agrees with him. My spirit is all on the other side.' The tensions in his own mind are clear in a description he wrote of the WSPU meeting at this time, referring to Christabel's 'strong lapses into cheap gallery appeal', and Pethick-Lawrence's presentation of a £1,000 donation 'in rather a theatrical style'. Other supporters were worried about the new turn to large-scale violence in WSPU demonstrations, including Joseph Clayton, who himself was prepared to use violence on occasion. He asked Nevinson 'if a certain woman took drugs and a horrible suspicion came over me' (Nevinson diaries, 19 November 1911). By this time WSPU leaders were discouraging male involvement in violent demonstrations. Nevinson reported, however, that by early March feeling was very high among the male suffragists. He found Joseph Clayton 'was suddenly cantankerous and insane, accusing me of having no feeling for the women because I have seen so many horrors [Nevinson was one of the leading war correspondents of the time]. He wanted to get together a party of men to threaten to thrash McKenna if forcible feeding begins again.' Disruption in the Men's Political Union was also evident, both over the use of violence and Nevinson's attempts to introduce a democratic constitution to the organisation (this was opposed by WSPU leaders). Alongside all this there was developing a discussion on how far men could usefully be involved in militant suffrage activities. For example, Nevinson's involvement with the production of *Votes for Women* and later *The Suffragette* while the leaders and editors were in prison became suspect. There had been considerable anger when Jessie Kenney had found Scott present at a discussion among some leading WSPU activists on November 1911. Mrs. Pethick-Lawrence went

so far as to say: 'Men in prison only embarrass us.' See Nevinson's diaries for January to April 1912. He also records the increasing retaliatory violence being suffered by WSPU workers; see his diaries, 4, 7, and 10 March 1912. The anger with Brailsford gradually extended to all male supporters. Nevinson and Pethick-Lawrence both believed their friendship with Brailsford was at the root of their eventual exclusion from the WSPU.

104   Linklater, *An Unhusbanded Life*, pp. 151–155.
105   See for example the furore which surrounded Lloyd George's public assertion that he had 'torpedoed' the Conciliation Bills, expressed in Brailsford's telegrams to Scott (25, 26, and 27 November 1911; Scott's reply, 25 November 1911, Kathleen Courtney Papers, Fawcett Library, City of London Polytechnic – as yet unsorted and uncatalogued). See also Henry Brailsford to Mrs. Fawcett, 26 November 1911, M50/2/1/341, MPLA.
106   Morgan, *Suffragists and Liberals*, p. 99. See also Margaret Ward, ' "Suffrage First – Above All Else!" ': An Account of the Irish Suffrage Movement', *Feminist Review*, 10 (1982): 21–36.
107   When miners' leader Robert Smillie had announced that the miners' 600,000 votes would go against the women's-suffrage resolution, Mary MacArthur had responded: 'We have often been told that we women adult suffragists were being misled. We have replied that we trusted our labour men, and yet the miners now say they will take manhood suffrage and leave the women out' (*Labour Leader*, 2 February 1912). Women universalists and women suffragists could only be pushed closer together by such pockets of labour-movement resistance to issues of sexual equality on the one hand, and official party policy sympathetic to women's suffrage on the other hand.
108   Mrs. Fawcett to J. R. MacDonald, 28 January 1912, JRMP, PRO 30/69/1156/62–64.
109   Eleanor Acland to Catherine Marshall, postmark 1 April 1912, CMP.
110   *The Common Cause*, 27 June 1912. See also ibid., 11 July and 1 August 1912, for further attacks along these lines.
111   Ibid., 11 April 1912.
112   Ibid., 25 April and 20 June 1912.
113   Ibid., 4 July 1912. The impact of increasing numbers of working-class organisers on the political allegiances of the National Union's largely middle-class membership is at present not clear, but there is some suggestive evidence presented in Liddington, *Life and Times*, pp. 194–196.
114   M. Norma Smith to Catherine Marshall, n.d. [March 1912]; Beatrice Kemp to Catherine Marshall, 9 March 1912; Lucy A. Stirling to Catherine Marshall, 10 March 1912, CMP; and Theobald C. Taylor to Mrs. Fawcett, 9 March 1912, MGFP, for protests concerning militancy. See M. G. Fawcett to Lloyd George, 2 December 1911, and to Alfred Lyttelton, 12 March 1912, MGFP, for the constitutionalists' response.
115   McKibbin, *The Evolution of the Labour Party*, pp. 48f.

4. A suffrage–labour alliance

1   NUWSS minutes, 29 March 1912.
2   Kathleen Courtney to Arthur Henderson, 23 April 1912, Labour Party Archives (henceforth LPA), LP/WOM/12/4 i–iv. The idea had been floated in *The Common Cause*, 18 April 1912. See also 'Mr. Brailsford on a Practical Policy', *The Common Cause*, 9 May 1912.
3   Letter from the Newcastle Society headed 'Proposed Cooperation with the Labour Party', n.d. [c. 23 April 1912], CMP.
4   Ibid.
5   Kathleen Courtney to Arthur Henderson, 23 April 1912, LPA, LP/WOM/12/4 i–iv.
6   Maude Royden to Kathleen Courtney, 22 April 1912. See also Margaret Ashton to

Kathleen Courtney, 23 April 1912, and letters from the secretaries of the Sheffield and Huddersfield branches to Catherine Marshall, n.d. [May 1912], CMP.

7 Eleanor Rathbone to Mrs. Fawcett, 27 April 1912, CMP. Brailsford was also pushing for some such move from the Labour Party. See his letter to Henderson, LPA, LP/WOM/12/13: 'I feel that unless we can show Redmond that there are dangers in the course he has followed the disaster of March 28th [the defeat of the Conciliation Bill] will be repeated when the Reform Bill comes up.'

8 Henry Brailsford to James Ramsay MacDonald, 23 April 1912, JRMP, PRO/30/69/1156/25–32.

9 Arthur Henderson to Kathleen Courtney, 25 April 1912, LPA, LP/WOM/12/5.

10 'Suggested Questions for Tuesday', n.d. [c. 30 April 1912], CMP.

11 Circular report of NUWSS meeting with the Labour Party signed by M. G. Fawcett, Mrs. Auerbach, Edith Palliser, Kathleen Courtney, n.d. [c. 1 May 1912], CMP.

12 Arthur Henderson to Edith Palliser, 3 May 1912, LPA, LP/WOM/12/11.

13 Henry Brailsford to Arthur Henderson, 4 May 1912, LPA, LP/WOM/12/14 i–ii.

14 Ibid.

15 Edith Palliser and Kathleen Courtney to Arthur Henderson, 6 May 1912, CMP.

16 Report of the interview between Mrs. Fawcett and Kathleen Courtney and J. R. MacDonald, 13 May 1912, CMP.

17 Memorandum, n.d. [c. 1 May 1912], CMP.

18 Circular letter to NUWSS societies on the new policy, 2 May 1912, CMP.

19 Eleanor Rathbone to Mrs. Fawcett, 10 May 1912, CMP.

20 Circular letter signed by Mrs. Fawcett, Kathleen Courtney, Edith Palliser, Mrs. Auerbach, 10 May 1912, CMP.

21 National Union press release, 16 May 1912, LPA, LP/WOM/12/19 i–ii. See also NUWSS leaflet 'Our Policy', May 1912, CMP. For report of the special council meeting see *The Common Cause*, 23 May 1912.

22 Arthur Henderson to Kathleen Courtney, 15 May 1912, CMP.

23 Kathleen Courtney to Arthur Henderson, 16 May 1912, LPA, LP/WOM/12/18.

24 Cutting from the *Standard*, 31 May 1912, LPA, LP/WOM/12/22.

25 J. Malcolm Mitchell to Arthur Henderson, LPA, LP/WOM/12/9.

26 The early EFF Committee consisted of Mrs. Anstruther, Margaret Ashton, Mrs. Auerbach, Mrs. Cavendish Bentinck, Mrs. Stanton Coit, H. N. Brailsford, Kathleen Courtney, Lady de la Warr, Mrs. Fawcett, Isabella Ford, Mrs. Homan, Laurence Housman, Miss M. Lees, Lord Lytton, Catherine Marshall, Lady Meyer, Edith Palliser, Julia Reckitt, Ethel Snowden, Mrs. Stanbury, and Mr. G. E. S. Streatfield. There were further additions and some resignations over the next two years (report to provincial council, 11 July 1912, CMP). Brailsford, Laurence Housman, and Lady de la Warr had been previously more closely associated with the WSPU.

27 See Brockway, *Inside the Left*, p. 33, and *Towards Tomorrow* (London: Hart Davis, 1977), p. 31.

28 Catherine Marshall's other notable achievements were as secretary of the No Conscription Fellowship. See Brockway, *Inside the Left*, p. 68, and Vellacott Newberry, 'Anti-War Suffragists'.

29 Kathleen Courtney became a prominent figure in the League of Nations movement after the war; see her papers in the Fawcett Library.

30 See Alice Clark, *Working Life of Women in the Seventeenth Century* (reprint New York: Kelley, 1968), and the privately published *Alice Clark of C. & J. Clark Ltd., Street, Somerset* (n.d.) in the Fawcett Library.

31 EFF minutes, 19 July 1912.

32 Ibid., 20 September 1912.

33 Arthur Henderson to Edith Palliser, LPA, LP/WOM/12/21. The constituencies were Newton, Lancs.; Jarrow; Wigan; W. Wolverhampton; St. Helens; Leigh.

34 See Nield Chew, *Life and Writings*; Liddington and Norris, *One Hand*; Liddington, *Life*

and Times; The Reformers' Year Book 1907, p. 151, for more biographical details concerning Ada Nield Chew and Selina Cooper. Mitchell, *The Hard Way Up,* esp. pp. 128–157, provides a further account of socialist–suffrage campaigning in the Manchester area in these years.

35 *The Common Cause,* 13, 20, and 27 June 1912. For background on this election see McKibbin, *The Evolution of the Labour Party,* p. 26.

36 *The Common Cause,* 18 July 1912. For further discussion of this election see McKibbin, *The Evolution of the Labour Party,* pp. 54–56.

37 *The Common Cause,* 1 August 1912.

38 Correspondence between Catherine Marshall and Arthur Henderson, 6 August 1912, LPA, LP/WOM/12/33, and CMP; EFF minutes, 20 September, 18 October and 8 and 12 November 1912. For further discussion of this election see McKibbin, *The Evolution of the Labour Party,* pp. 55–56.

39 EFF minutes, 14 and 20 August and 20 September 1912; NUWSS minutes, 19 September 1912; *The Common Cause,* 15 August and 19 September 1912; Catherine Marshall's draft article on the EFF, n.d. [*c.* 26 November 1913], CMP. For an assessment of this result see McKibbin, *The Evolution of the Labour Party,* pp. 83–84.

40 Catherine Marshall's circular letter to the EFF Committee, 1 July 1912, CMP.

41 EFF minutes, 14 and 20 June 1912; Labour Party executive minutes, 11 June 1912, LPA; EFF circular, 18 June 1912; Frank Marshall to Catherine Marshall, 19 June 1912; Mrs. Cowmeadow to Catherine Marshall, 23 June 1912; Catherine Marshall telegram to Mrs. Cowmeadow, 24 June 1912; Catherine Marshall to Arthur Henderson, 25 June 1912 (all correspondence, CMP).

42 Catherine Marshall's notes for the provincial council meeting, 5 and 19 July 1912, CMP; Catherine Marshall to Arthur Henderson, 5 July 1912, LPA, LP/WOM/12/31. At this time MacDonald told Bruce Glasier that he no longer felt committed to oppose a third reading of the Reform Bill that excluded women, because of the WSPU's 'foolish game' (Thompson, *The Enthusiasts,* p. 175).

43 See the *Daily Herald,* 19 October 1912, for Mrs. Pankhurst's explanation of this decision.

44 Henry Brailsford to J. R. MacDonald, 14 October 1912, JRMP, PRO 30/69/1156/25–32.

45 *Daily Herald* cutting, 17 October 1912, LPA, LP/WOM/12/43.

46 NUWSS minutes, 17 October 1912.

47 See for example *Manchester Guardian* cutting, 21 October 1912, LPA, LP/WOM/12/43.

48 Catherine Marshall to J. R. MacDonald, 19 October 1912, JRMP, PRO 30/69/1156/124–127.

49 Ibid. (her emphasis). See also Catherine Marshall's notes headed 'Entente Cordiale between the Labour Party and the Women's Suffrage Movement' where she insisted on the common goals of both (n.d. [*c.* January 1913], CMP).

50 Katharine Bruce Glasier/J. R. MacDonald correspondence, 13 March and 1 April 1914, JRMP, PRO 30/69/1158/35–43 (her emphasis).

51 Ibid.

52 EFF minutes, 9 and 14 August 1912; Catherine Marshall to W. C. Anderson, 14 August 1912; Catherine Marshall's notes on the selection conference, n.d. [August 1912]; L. F. Waring to Catherine Marshall, 4 August 1912 (all CMP); *The Common Cause,* 29 August 1912.

53 EFF minutes, 18 October and 20 December 1912; M. McKenzie to J. Middleton, 9 December 1912, LPA, LP/WOM/12/46.

54 EFF minutes, 9 July, 2 August, and 20 December 1912; NUWSS minutes, 31 October and 7 November 1912.

55 EFF minutes, 2 August and 2 and 19 September 1912; NUWSS minutes, 29 September 1912.

56 Catherine Marshall to Arthur Henderson, 5 October 1912, LPA, LP/WOM/12/39.

57 Ibid., 14 October 1912, LPA, LP/WOM/12/42.

58 Ibid.
59 NUWSS minutes, 17 October 1912.
60 For more details see Chapter 5. The National Union ensured that Liberal politicians
    became aware of the success of such activity by arranging for them to meet some of
    their leading organisers for the EFF, like Margaret Robertson, at informal dinners
    given by sympathetic Liberal hostesses. See for example Catherine Marshall draft let-
    ter to Lloyd George, 22 February 1912, CMP.
61 *The Labour Leader*, 31 October 1912.
62 *The Common Cause*, 14 November 1912.
63 Ibid., 31 October and 14 November 1912, and 7 February 1913.
64 Ibid., 14 February 1913.
65 James Mylles to Catherine Marshall, 8 February 1912, CMP.
66 Kathleen Courtney to Annot Robinson, 22 May 1912, CMP.
67 EFF minutes, 22 November 1912.
68 Ibid., 20 December 1912.
69 See report of his speech at the women's-suffrage demonstration, 6 December 1912, in
    The Common Cause, 13 December, 1912.
70 NUWSS minutes, 20 November and 7 December 1911.
71 Ibid., 7 December 1911.
72 Ibid., 4 January 1912.
73 See the file 'Joint Board', 1912, CMP.
74 NUWSS minutes, 18 April and 16 May 1912. Joint Campaign Committee work was
    suspended at the time of the final reading of the Conciliation Bill. When it was reac-
    tivated it included representatives from a range of Labour and Liberal organisations:
    the Fabian Society, the Women's Labour League, the People's Suffrage Federation,
    the Scottish Women's Liberation Federation, the Women's Liberal Federation, and the
    Women's Cooperative Guild (ibid., 7 and 12 March 1912; Joint Committee file, May
    1912, CMP).
75 James Mylles to Catherine Marshall, 8 February 1912, CMP.
76 Elsie Inglis to Kathleen Courtney, 27 May and 13 June 1912, CMP.
77 Henry Brailsford to Kathleen Courtney, 5 October 1912, CMP.
78 NUWSS minutes, 19 December 1912.
79 Scott memos., British Library, 15–16 and 20 January 1913; Pease diaries, Gainford Pa-
    pers, Nuffield College Library, Oxford, 20, 21, and 27 November 1912. See also Pease's
    memorandum on a meeting with Whitley and Thring, 28 November 1912, on the
    order in which the bill was to be read (Gainford Papers [65(1)]); memorandum on
    Franchise and Registration Bill, first draft, n.d. third and final draft, 18 December 1912
    (Gainford Papers [67]); Kathleen Courtney's notes on her meeting with Birrell, 1 No-
    vember 1912; Kathleen Courtney to Florence Balgarnie, 29 November 1912; C. P. Scott
    to Kathleen Courtney, 22 December 1912 (all CMP); NUWSS minutes, 19 December
    1912. See also Hammond, *C. P. Scott*, pp. 113–115.
80 Franchise and Registration Bill, 2 December 1912, Gainford Papers [67].
81 See *Daily Telegraph* cutting, 20 January 1913, Gainford Papers [68], and Eleanor Rath-
    bone's 'Memorandum on the Approximate Number of Women who would be Enfran-
    chised by various amendments to the Reform Bill, Their Advantages and Disadvan-
    tages', n.d. [1912], CMP. The NUWSS had been worried that the Norway amendment,
    as first formulated, would be felt to enfranchise too many women – approximately
    seven to eight million. This is presumably why a higher age limitation was attached
    to the amendment in its final form.
82 'Points for Parliamentary Interviews', July 1912, CMP.
83 NUWSS minutes, 17 January 1913.
84 Nevinson diaries, Bodleian Library, 13 January 1913.
85 *Manchester Guardian* cutting, 23 January 1913, Gainford Papers [68].
86 A. Thring to Pease, 8 January 1913. See also the somewhat ambiguous memorandum

on the Franchise and Registration Bill amendments on a similar point, both n.d., Gainford Papers [65 (1)].

87   Letter to Arthur Steel-Maitland, signed 'Bal' (Lord Balcarres), 24 January 1913, GD193/159/2, Steel-Maitland Papers, Scottish Record Office.
88   Pease diaries, 24 and 27 January 1913.
89   Cutting from the *Times*, 28 January 1913, Gainford Papers [68].
90   Edward David (ed.), *Inside Asquith's Cabinet: From the Diaries of Charles Hobhouse* (London: Murray, 1977), p. 132.
91   J. Wilson to Arthur Steel-Maitland, 30 January 1913, GD193/159/3, Steel-Maitland Papers.
92   Philip Snowden to Mrs. Fawcett, 26 January 1913, MGFP; NUWSS minutes, 27 and 28 January 1913.
93   Catherine Marshall draft circular, February 1913, CMP.
94   NUWSS minutes, 6 February 1913.
95   Ibid., 2 January and 6 February 1913.
96   Ibid., 19 December 1912 and 17 January 1913.
97   *The Common Cause*, 7 February 1913.
98   Philip Snowden to Mrs. Fawcett, 26 January 1913, MGFP.
99   *The Common Cause*, 7 February 1913.
100 NUWSS minutes, 28 January 1913.
101 Nevinson diaries, 28 January 1913.
102 Scott memos., 3 February 1913.
103 Pease diaries, 11 February and 6 March 1912; Asquith to King, 13 March 1913, Asquith Papers, Bodleian Library.
104 Morgan, *Suffragists and Liberals*, p. 124.
105 Reported in NUWSS minutes, 6 February 1913.
106 See Rosen, *Rise Up Women*, pp. 242–245, for his assessment of WSPU decline over this period. One of the WSPU's most loyal and self-sacrificing members recalled her own sense of 'fierce rebellion' against its policies by this time (Richardson, *Laugh a Defiance*, p. 178).

5. Suffrage–labour campaigning

1   *The Common Cause*, 7 March 1913; 'Circular on Policy' following the February council, 1913, MGFP.
2   NUWSS minutes, 13 March, 5 June, and 2 October 1913.
3   Catherine Marshall's notes, 14 April 1913, CMP.
4   Report of the provincial council meeting of the NUWSS, 23 May 1913, MGFP; Catherine Marshall's notes for her reports to this meeting, 23 May 1913, CMP.
5   NUWSS minutes, 3 July 1913.
6   Catherine Marshall's notes, n.d. [c. April 1913], CMP.
7   NUWSS minutes, 1 and 15 May and 31 July 1913; Jessie Beavan to Catherine Marshall [c. May 1913], and C. M. Gordon to Kathleen Courtney, 3 June 1913, both CMP.
8   Margaret Robertson to Catherine Marshall, 29 May 1913, CMP. Margaret Bondfield's participation in this aspect of National Union activity is an indication of the shift in views on women's suffrage among many women universal suffragists in the Labour movement. See also NUWSS minutes, 15 May 1913.
9   Arthur Peters to Catherine Marshall, 2 September 1913, CMP.
10 Margaret Robertson to Catherine Marshall, 18 September 1913; and see also G. W. Evans to Catherine Marshall, 8 September 1913, CMP.
11 Report of the TUC conference, *The Common Cause*, 12 September 1913.
12 Margaret Robertson to Catherine Marshall, 1 September 1913, CMP. Margaret Robertson saw this as part of a concerted and ongoing campaign to persuade Asquith of the strength of working-class support for the women's vote.
13 *The Common Cause*, 17 October 1913; NUWSS council meeting EFF report, n.d. [c.

October/November 1913; filed July 1913], CMP. For an account of Selina Cooper's organising among the miner during this period see Liddington, *Life and Times*, pp. 235–243.

14　*The Common Cause*, 17 October 1913.
15　*The Common Cause*, 20 February 1914; see also ibid., 27 February 1914, for the list of official delegates.
16　*The Common Cause*, 17 January 1913.
17　This analysis is based upon Henry Pelling, *The Social Geography of British Elections, 1885–1910* (London: Macmillan, 1967), esp. pp. 243–246, 304, 342–345, 392–393, 397.
18　Ibid., pp. 405–406, 410.
19　NUWSS minutes, 15 May 1913.
20　K. O. Morgan, *Wales in British Politics, 1869–1922* (Cardiff: University of Wales Press, 1963), esp. pp. 254–255.
21　Henry Pelling, *Popular Politics and Society in Late Victorian Britain* (London: Macmillan, 1968), pp. 130–132.
22　*Manchester Society for Women's Suffrage Annual Report*, 1913, MPLA.
23　Ibid.
24　*The Common Cause*, 10 March 1914.
25　NUWSS minutes, 5 June 1913. Ada Nield Chew contributed a series of articles on women's suffrage to the *Accrington Observer* in the autumn of 1913 to promote the issue and the constitutionalists' campaign in the constituency. See Nield Chew, *Life and Writings*, pp. 209–226.
26　Arthur Peters to Catherine Marshall, 22 June 1913, CMP; *Manchester Society for Women's Suffrage Annual Report*, 1913, and minutes, 31 March 1914, MPLA.
27　Manchester Society minutes, 31 March 1914. See Betty D. Vernon, *Ellen Wilkinson 1891–1947* (London: Croom Helm, 1982), for details of Ellen Wilkinson's involvement in university socialist politics (in Manchester) prior to her appointment as an EFF organiser.
28　Ada Nield Chew to Margaret Robertson, 28 May 1913; Margaret Robertson to Catherine Marshall, 29 May 1913, CMP.
29　G. W. Evans to Catherine Marshall, 28 August and 8 September 1913; Arthur Peters to Alice Clark, 15 September 1913, CMP.
30　Manchester Society minutes, 31 March 1914, MPLA.
31　McKibbin, *The Evolution of the Labour Party*, pp. 73–75.
32　NUWSS council meeting EFF report, n.d. [July 1913], CMP.
33　C. Gordon to Kathleen Courtney, 3 June 1913, CMP; NUWSS minutes, 20 February 1913.
34　NUWSS minutes, 6 March 1913.
35　Ibid., 13 March 1913. Joseph Storey to Catherine Marshall, 18 April 1913; Catherine Marshall draft article 'EFF By-Elections' [c. 26 November 1913], CMP. The election result was J. E. Wing, Liberal, 6,930; R. Richardson, Unionist, 4,807; W. House, Labour, 4,165. See McKibbin, *The Evolution of the Labour Party*, pp. 83–84, for an assessment of this result.
36　NUWSS council EFF report, n.d. [July 1913]; Catherine Marshall's notes on EFF, 26 May 1913, both CMP.
37　Labour Party executive minutes, 8 October 1913; Organisation and Electoral Subcommittee, 6 May 1914, LPA.
38　Catherine Marshall's notes on EFF, 26 May 1913, CMP.
39　NUWSS minutes, 6 February 1913.
40　Ibid., 4 July 1914.
41　C. M. Gordon to G. W. Evans, 12 June 1913; C. M. Gordon to Catherine Marshall, 4 August 1913, CMP. The EFF had also had to insist to Clementina Gordon that she should not send independent reports of her work to *The Labour Leader* (EFF minutes, 23 June 1912).
42　Helena Renton to Catherine Marshall, 2 and 4 April and 6 May 1913, CMP.

43   Helena Renton to M. MacKenzie, 2 and 9 April 1913, CMP.
44   See Mrs. Oldham's 'Scheme for work in Rotherham', n.d. [c. December 1913], CMP.
     Tom Richardson, Labour MP for Whitehaven, was reported to have spoken 'with real
     enthusiasm of Mrs. Oldham. Her evident capacity seems to have made a great
     impression on him, and he is delighted that she is going to Cumberland. He has
     enthused about Rotherham to the other Labour men' (Margaret Robertson to Cather-
     ine Marshall, 29 May 1913, CMP).
45   Helena Renton to Catherine Marshall, 10 June 1914, CMP.
46   Mrs. Oldham to Catherine Marshall, 24 June 1914, CMP.
47   Catherine Marshall to Mrs. Oldham, 14 July 1914, CMP.
48   Ibid., and H. Oldham to Catherine Marshall, 15 July 1914; Catherine Marshall tele-
     gram to H. Oldham, 16 July 1914, CMP.
49   H. Oldham to Catherine Marshall and Helena Renton to Catherine Marshall, 31 July
     1914, CMP.
50   Helena Renton to Catherine Marshall, 27 July 1914, CMP.
51   NUWSS minutes, 2 January and 6 February 1913.
52   Ibid., 20 February, 17 April, and 5 June 1913; Mrs. Townley to Catherine Marshall, 28
     April 1913, CMP.
53   NUWSS minutes, 3 July 1913; G. Evans to Catherine Marshall, 12 September 1913,
     CMP.
54   See R. J. Holton, 'Daily Herald versus Daily Citizen, 1912–15'.
55   Alice Clark to Catherine Marshall, 17 November 1913, CMP.
56   East Bristol appears on Arthur Peters's list as a 'selected' constituency. McKibbin, The
     Evolution of the Labour Party, pp. 73–75, notes this indicated only 'formal sanction had
     yet to be given'.
57   Alice Low to Catherine Marshall, 25 November 1913, CMP. Earlier in the year she had
     to write about the organiser Miss Pressley-Smith, 'If the Scottish Federation insist on
     taking her away for ordinary work she has asked me to say that she will resign from
     the Federation if the EFF Committee will retain her' (Alice Low to Catherine Marshall,
     29 July 1913, CMP).
58   Catherine Marshall's annotated notes of a conversation, 'Edinburgh Society Miss Lisa
     Gordon', n.d. [1913], CMP.
59   Catherine Marshall to W. C. Anderson, 8 June 1914, CMP. A short extract that sur-
     vives from the Scottish Federation executive minutes, 30 May 1914, almost certainly
     pertains to this. It seems that the Scottish Federation executive hoped to put a leading
     member of the Glasgow Society, Andrew Ballantyne, onto the Scottish EFF commit-
     tee, despite the fact that he was very active in the local Liberal Party. A resolution was
     passed 'that the Scottish Federation agrees that it is bound to carry out the policy of
     the NUWSS as interpreted by the NUWSS Executive but cannot agree that "policy"
     includes the appointment of committees, but claim the right under the NUWSS con-
     stitution to appoint its own committees and carry out electoral work in its own area'
     (Muirhead Collection, Baillie's Library, Glasgow).
60   Scottish Federation list of constituencies, n.d. [c. Summer 1913]; M. MacKenzie to
     Catherine Marshall, 20 April 1913, CMP.
61   Alice Low to Catherine Marshall, 29 July 1913, CMP.
62   Ibid., 20 May and 29 July 1913; M. A. Pressley-Smith to Catherine Marshall, 1 August
     1914, CMP; The Forward, 21 and 28 February and 7 March 1914. The result of the Leith
     by-election was: Provost Malcolm Smith, Liberal, 5,143; G. W. Currie, Unionist, 5,159;
     J. N. Bell, Labour, 3,346.
63   NUWSS minutes, 6 and 20 February 1913.
64   Miss Hilston to M. MacKenzie, 20 April 1913, CMP.
65   Catherine Marshall's notes for Miss Price, 6 June 1913; Ethel Williams to Catherine
     Marshall, 11 June 1914, CMP.
66   Miss Hilston to Catherine Marshall, 21 June 1913; Arthur Peters to Catherine Mar-
     shall, 1913, CMP.

67 EFF report to NUWSS council, n.d. [July 1913], CMP.
68 Margaret Robertson to Catherine Marshall, 10 December 1913; C. M. Gordon to Catherine Marshall, 10 December 1913, CMP. The NUWSS's South Lanark Election Address, CMP, provides another interesting example of the kind of issues the suffragists took up – in this case an emphasis on housing and industrial safety.
69 NUWSS minutes, 5 June 1913.
70 Labour Party head office had not wanted to contest the seat. See McKibbin, *The Evolution of the Labour Party*, pp. 68–70, 83–84. The strength of the Conservative Party in this constituency may have affected the National Union's decision not to run an EFF campaign; see Pelling, *Social Geography*, p. 301.
71 Kathleen Courtney to Catherine Marshall, 17 November 1913; see also Alice Clark to Catherine Marshall, 17 and 18 November 1913, CMP.
72 Margaret Robertson and C. Gordon to Catherine Marshall, 25 November 1913, CMP.
73 Ethel Williams to Catherine Marshall, 26 November 1913, CMP.
74 Margaret Ashton to Catherine Marshall, 26 November 1913, CMP.
75 Alice Clark to Catherine Marshall, 28 November 1913, CMP. Her views on the Labour Party echoed Philip Snowden: 'He is sure that the Labour Party won't do anything for us against the Liberals either before or after the election. He agrees that the EFF may nevertheless be useful to us as causing the Liberals uneasiness in the country. He thinks the miners friendly only because they want our help. I think that even such friendliness is of great value to us' (Alice Clark to Catherine Marshall, n.d. [c. November–December 1913], CMP).
76 Mrs. Fawcett to Kathleen Courtney, 6 January 1913 (should read 1914). See also Helen Aneurin Williams to Mrs. Fawcett, 5 January 1913 (should read 1914); Mrs. Fawcett to Mrs. Williams, 7 January 1914, MGFP.
77 Alice Clark to Mrs. Williams, 7 January 1914, MGFP. The strength of the Liberal vote in this constituency may also have affected the National Union decision to support Labour. There was little danger of losing the seat to the Conservatives; see Pelling, *Social Geography*, p. 337.
78 Dr. Dunn to Mrs. Fawcett, 8 and 16 January 1914, MGFP. See also Mrs. Fawcett's circular letter, n.d. [c. December 1913], MPLA, M50/2/9/7, and Margaret Temperley to Mrs. Fawcett, 15 and 17 January 1914, MGFP.
79 Ethel Williams to Mrs. Fawcett, 15 January 1914, MGFP.
80 Statement made by a NUWSS deputation to the ILP National Administrative Council at Glasgow, 26 January 1914, CMP. It was felt necessary to make this statement because, at a conference of the North-West Division of the ILP, it had been claimed the National Union intended opposing Labour candidates at the general election (*The Common Cause*, 23 and 30 January 1914).
81 Chrystal Macmillan to Catherine Marshall, 8 April 1914; Catherine Marshall circular to executive, 17 April 1914; extract from NUWSS minutes, 5 February 1914, all CMP.
82 Catherine Marshall to Chrystal Macmillan, 20 April 1914. See also Catherine Marshall circular to executive, 17 April 1914; Chrystal Macmillan circular to executive 20 April 1914, all CMP.
83 Mrs. Fawcett to Eleanor Rathbone, 8 March 1914, MGFP. See also additions to résumé of executive minutes, 5 and 19 March 1914; NUWSS circular letter, 21 March 1914; NUWSS executive's circular to 'Members of the NUWSS Committee and Delegates to the Half Yearly Council'; 'Memorandum on Resolutions concerning General Election Policy on the Agenda of the Half Yearly Council by the Committee for the Discussion of General Election Policy', all in Manchester Society minutes, 1912–14, MPLA.
84 Committee for Discussion of General Election Policy memorandum, pp. 3–4, Manchester Society minutes, 1912–14, MPLA. Evidence in Catherine Marshall's papers that the NUWSS was organising suffrage support within the Unionist Party at this time confirms the reality of these fears, and indicates that at least some part of the executive already were preparing for an anti-Liberal campaign during the general election.

85 M. A. Marshall to Catherine Marshall, 5 June 1914; Agnes Gill to Helena Renton, 11 June 1914; Maude Dowson, Hon. Sec., East Midland Federation, to Mable Crooken-den, 13 June 1913, CMP.

86 Catherine Marshall to Miss Gunter, 24 April 1914, CMP.

87 For membership claims see *The Common Cause*, 21 March 1913, and Catherine Marshall to Lord Lansdowne, 9 August 1913, CMP.

88 *NUWSS Annual Report*, 1913–15, shows 1912 membership of 42,438; 1913, 52,366; and 1914, 54,592.

89 NUWSS minutes, 2 April 1914.

90 *The Common Cause*, 21 November 1913.

91 Ibid., 22 May and 5 June 1914.

92 Martha Garnett, Augusta Harrington, and Ethelwynne Bowman to Catherine Marshall, n.d. [*c*. July 1914], CMP.

93 *The Common Cause*, 4 July 1912.

6. The women's-suffrage movement and the impact of war

1 See for example Morgan, *Suffragists and Liberals*, pp. 77–78; Rover, *Women's Suffrage and Party Politics*, p. 195.

2 See for example Martin Pugh, 'Politicians and the Women's Vote 1914–18', *History*, 59 (1974): 358–374, esp. pp. 358–359.

3 NUWSS minutes, 3 July 1913.

4 Ibid., for an account of Reginald McKenna's (antisuffragist home secretary) favourable reaction.

5 Millicent Fawcett to Asquith, 26 July 1913, MGFP.

6 Asquith to Mrs. Fawcett, 31 July 1913, MGFP.

7 Quoted in Morgan, *Suffragists and Liberals*, p. 125.

8 NUWSS minutes, 18 September 1913; *The Common Cause*, 15 August 1913.

9 NUWSS minutes, 31 July 1913; Catherine Marshall draft letter to Lloyd George, 5 August 1913, CMP; Catherine Marshall to Lloyd George, 6, 10, and 11 August 1913, C/9/5/8, C/9/5/11–12, Lloyd George Papers (henceforth LGP), House of Lords Record Office.

10 Catherine Marshall to Lloyd George, 29 August 1913, C/9/5/20, LGP.

11 Typescript record of the deputation to Sir John Simon, 12 November 1913. See also Catherine Marshall's summary of notes for Sir John Simon, 12 November 1913, to-gether with more detailed arguments, both CMP.

12 Sir Edward Grey to Catherine Marshall, 4 December 1913; her notes for the meeting, 15 December 1913, CMP.

13 Mrs. E. Nuttall to Lloyd George, 24 October 1913, C/10/1/67, LGP.

14 Mrs. R. Bulley to Mrs. Lloyd George, for Lloyd George's attention, October 1913, C/10/1/68, LGP.

15 See for example the letter from Mrs. Egerton Stewart-Brown, president of the Lanca-shire and Cheshire Union of Women's Liberal Associations, to the *Manchester Guard-ian*, 18 June 1913, CMP. See also Mrs. Cunliffe, president of the North West Federa-tion, to Mrs. Fawcett, 9 March 1913, CMP. She had been disappointed at the WLF conference's failure to pass strong suffrage resolutions. She blamed Lady Carlisle's opposition for the defeat of Dickinson's private-member bill in March 1913 and asked whether she should resign as president of the Ambleside Women's Liberal Associa-tion as a protest at the attitude of both the government and the WLF. She estimated she could probably take seven others of its officers with her, adding that she had originally taken on the position only 'to stiffen the Association up on the Suffrage'.

16 *Women's Liberal Federation Annual Report*, 1903–4, 1911–12, 1913–14, 1914–15, Bristol University Library.

17 Eleanor Acland to Catherine Marshall, 7 May 1913, CMP.

18 NUWSS minutes, 15 May and 5 June 1913, for Catherine Marshall's reports on the formation of the Liberal Women's Suffrage Union. The officers of the new body were Mrs. Eva McLaren, Lady Aberconway, Lady Cowdray, the Hon. Lady Norman, Eleanor Acland, Mrs. Heron-Maxwell, Mrs. Alderton, Lady Bamford-Slack, Mrs. Bonwick, Mrs. Conybeare, Miss Crosfield, Mrs. Corbett Ashby, Mrs. Dowson, the Hon. Mrs. Fordham, the Hon. Mrs. Franklin, Alison Garland, the Hon. Mrs. Guest, Mrs. Hancock, Mrs. Hawksley, Mrs. Holman, Lady Horsley, Bertha Mason, Lucy Morland, Miss Salt, Lady Fisher-Smith, Mrs. Handley Spicer, Mrs. Stewart-Brown, Winifred Stephens, Miss Swankie Cameron, Lady Yoxall, Mrs. Hill, Helen Waddell; see the *Liberal Women's Review*, July 1914, F/DCK/2(1914 pt. 2), W. H. Dickinson Papers, Greater London Record Office. Mrs. Corbett Ashby and Mrs. Dowson were among the prominent members of the National Union who attempted to prevent the extension of the EFF policy in 1914. The papers of Eleanor and Francis Acland exist and may throw more light on this movement in the Liberal Party in the year or so before the war, but unfortunately they were not available at the time of this research.

19 Eleanor Acland to Lloyd George, 3 November 1913, C/10/2/12, LGP.

20 Mildred Ransom to Lloyd George, C/10/2/45, together with undated statement, C/10/2/45a, LGP.

21 *Manchester Guardian* cutting, 10 December 1913, CMP.

22 List of Liberal MPs and candidates, December 1913 and January 1914, C/17/3/26 and C/17/3/27; John N. Barran to Lloyd George, 1 January 1914, enclosing an issue of the Scottish women Liberals' magazine, December 1913, which reported the progress of the LWSU, C/10/3/1, LGP.

23 Eleanor Acland to Lloyd George, 4 April 1914, C/11/1/25; Lloyd George to Rhys Williams, 21 April 1914, C/11/1/33; Dorothea Jordan to Frances Stevenson, C/11/1/26, LGP.

24 Dorothea Jordan to Frances Stevenson, 26 May 1914, and her reply, 29 May 1914, C/11/1/50, LGP.

25 *The Common Cause*, 13 March 1914. Liberal men's suffrage unions had also been formed in London and Manchester.

26 *WLF Annual Report*, 1913–14, British Library of Political and Economic Science, London School of Economics; NUWSS minutes, 18 June 1914.

27 Eleanor Acland to Catherine Marshall, 20 November 1913 and 20 December 1913, CMP.

28 Proceedings of the conference of the executive committees of the NUWSS and LWSU, 27 July 1914, CMP. The disaffection which the National Union's policy indicated among some women Liberals was also evident among male Liberals. H. G. Barclay, a Liberal and a National Union member, was anxious that the National Union should commit itself to a firm antigovernment policy at the general election, and felt the EFF policy to be insufficiently aggressive, as it did not affect enough constituencies. 'Personally, I feel we are too much afraid of offending Liberal members of our societies. Better to have fewer members who will do something than many who want us to do nothing' (CMP). He also wrote to *The Common Cause*, 9 June 1914, declaring: 'I am a Liberal and an elector whose vote is already pledged to suffrage first.'

29 Catherine Marshall to Lady Selborne, 13 November 1913, CMP. The letter referred to was from Francis Acland.

30 Lord Robert Cecil to Catherine Marshall, 19 November 1913; Catherine Marshall to Lord Robert Cecil, 24 November 1913; memorandum headed 'Absolutely Confidential. Lord Lytton's Proposal for an Initiative on Women's Suffrage', 7 May 1914, and 'Private and Confidential. Various Proposals for getting a Conservative Government to legislate on the Women's Suffrage Question'; extract from NUWSS minutes, 21 May 1914, marked 'Political Situation. Absolutely Confidential, please destroy when read' (issued separately to the main body of the minutes, which went out to all National Union branches); NUWSS minutes, 25 May 1914; Catherine Marshall to Charles Ponsonby, 4 June 1914, all CMP. See also NUWSS minutes, 18 June 1914. Interestingly,

there is evidence that MPs were now beginning to seek National Union help in the House of Commons on issues outside the suffrage. Catherine Marshall wrote to W. H. Dickinson on the British Nationality Bill: 'I do not think we can send out yet a third whip about your amendment to the British Nationality Bill. We have already stretched our powers rather far, as it is not a question which *directly* affects the question of women's suffrage, though of course it is one on which all women must feel very strongly and be grateful to you for the stand you are making on their behalf.' Nonetheless she had reminded the Labour Party of their promise of support, and let Lord Robert Cecil know that the bill was on again that night (Catherine Marshall to W. H. Dickinson, 29 July 1914, CMP).

31 Catherine Marshall to Arthur Steel-Maitland, 11 July 1914, GD/193/163/3, Steel-Maitland Papers, Scottish Record Office; NUWSS minutes, 18 June 1914.

32 NUWSS minutes, 18 June 1914.

33 Catherine Marshall draft speech for the London Society, 19 June 1914, CMP.

34 NUWSS leaflet, April 1914, CMP.

35 See e.g. Catherine Marshall to Sir John Simon, 5 February 1914, and his reply, 6 February 1914, CMP. She complained that the Newcastle Society had been prevented by the local Liberal association from contacting him during his visit there to present evidence of working-class support for the suffragist demand.

36 Catherine Marshall's 'Notes for the Labour Party', 23 July 1914, CMP.

37 NUWSS minutes, 18 June 1914, and Catherine Marshall's 'Mr. Henderson, Labour Vote. General Election', n.d. [c. July 1914], CMP.

38 Catherine Marshall, miscellaneous parliamentary notes, July 1914, CMP.

39 Catherine Marshall to Francis Acland, 23 June 1914. See also a similar letter to Lady Betty Balfour, 22 June 1914, directed at Arthur Balfour, CMP.

40 See for example Catherine Marshall's taunting suggestion to Lloyd George that he and Asquith attend the Durham Miner's Gala in disguise to see the strength of suffrage feeling among the miners. Though Lloyd George declined the invitation, he did consider sending his secretary, Frances Stevenson, to report back to him (Catherine Marshall to Lloyd George, 11, 15, 17, and 22 July 1914, C/11/1/68, C/11/1/71, C/11/1/72, LGP). Her note of assertive self-confidence was echoed by Margaret Ashton. She wrote to give Catherine Marshall details of the formation of the Men's Liberal Suffrage Union, on the lines of existing women's organisation. The new body was to ask Asquith to receive a deputation at the time of the National Liberal Federation conference in November, and planned also to address an agents' meeting on women's suffrage. The Manchester Society was organising its own demonstration to coincide with the conference. 'I shall also propose that we have a Deputation to Asquith ourselves – to *tell* him not to ask him anything' (31 July 1914, CMP).

41 Lloyd George to Reginald McKenna, 6 July 1914, C/5/12/9, LGP.

42 Dangerfield, *Strange Death*, p. 336; William O'Neill, *The Woman Movement* (London: Allen and Unwin, 1969), p. 87. See also Morgan, *Suffragists and Liberals*, pp. 131–132.

43 Quoted in Morgan, *Suffragists and Liberals*, p. 131.

44 See n. 7, this chapter, and Chapter 3, n. 92.

45 Morgan, *Suffragists and Liberals*, pp. 132–133.

46 Sylvia Pankhurst to Lloyd George, 21 July 1914, C/11/1/74, LGP.

47 See Dangerfield's account in *The Strange Death*, p. 339, when he quotes *The Suffragette*: 'The WSPU desires to receive no private communication from the Government or any of its members.' By this account Christabel had also made it clear she had no wish to see Sylvia to discuss the matter. Compare Rosen, *Rise Up Women*, p. 240.

48 F. Blackett to 'Dear Emily', 2 June 1914, CMP.

49 See Rosen, *Rise Up Women*, pp. 242–245, for an assessment of the WSPU in the last two years before the war. He describes the WSPU at the outbreak of war as but 'a harried rump of the large and superbly organised movement it had once been'.

50 Catherine Marshall's draft speech to the London Society, 19 June 1914, CMP.

51 Catherine Marshall to Francis Acland, 23 June 1914, CMP.

52 The formation of the United Suffragists was first announced in *Votes for Women*, 13 February 1914. Its committee consisted of Lena Ashwell, Gerald Gould (an editor of the *Daily Herald*), Henry Nevinson, John Scurr, Evelyn Sharp, Mrs. Fred Whelan, J. Gillespie, Mrs. Ayrton Gould, Charles Grey, and Agnes Harben, wife of Henry Harben, an important financial supporter of both the WSPU and the *Daily Herald*. Vice presidents included Mrs. Bernard Shaw, Mrs. B. A. Thomas, Mrs. Arncliffe Sennet, and Israel Zangwill. It was open to men and women, militants and nonmilitants. Dangerfield, *The Strange Death*, pp. 327–330, notes the emergence of the United Suffragists alongside the East London Federation of Suffragettes as highly significant. Rosen, *Rise Up Women*, pp. 223–236, also records its appearance and traces some of the links with the *Daily Herald*, though he does not develop the point. David Mitchell has explored in greater depth the links between the United Suffragists and the *Daily Herald* in *Queen Christabel*, pp. 231–233, 237. For a discussion of the *Daily Herald* and its leagues see R. J. Holton, '*Daily Herald* versus *Daily Citizen*'; for an account of the syndicalist movement at this time see R. J. Holton, *British Syndicalism*.

53 See Mitchell, *Queen Christabel*, pp. 231–233, and Rosen, *Rise Up Women*, pp. 225–226, for Harben's correspondence with Christabel Pankhurst. See also Teresa Billington Greig, *The Militant Suffragette Movement* (London: Frank Palmer, 1911) for another contemporary critique of militancy.

54 See Nevinson diaries, Bodleian Library, 1 and 16 October, 24, 27, 28, and 30 November, 1 December 1913 and 8 and 14 January 1914.

55 For details of the Suffrage Speakers Defence Corps see *Votes for Women*, 19 June 1914. George Lansbury addressed some of the earliest United Suffragist branches in Stroud and Amersham (*Votes for Women*, 22 May 1914). Henry Harben was one of the leading speakers at the United Suffragists' demonstration, 7 July 1914 (*Votes for Women*, 5 July 1914). The United Suffragists and EFLS worked together during the Poplar by-election (*Votes for Women*, 20 February 1914), and Nevinson was very close to Sylvia Pankhurst at this time, being one of the bearers of her stretcher during the vigil outside Westminster that eventually persuaded Asquith to receive the East End deputation. See also Mitchell, *Queen Christabel*, p. 239.

56 The United Suffragists' centres of support by the outbreak of war were London, Edinburgh, Stroud, and Amersham, and possibly the Liverpool area (*Votes for Women*, 22 and 29 May, 26 June, and 3 July 1914). It is interesting that some Liverpool suffragists appear to have joined forces with local syndicalists and abandoned the demand for the vote; see R. J. Holton, 'Syndicalism, and its Impact in Britain, with Particular Reference to Merseyside 1900–1914' (unpublished D.Phil. dissertation, Sussex University, 1973), p. 423. Former WSPU organisers Mary Gawthorpe and Dora Marsden also left suffrage campaigning to set up a new journal, *The Freewoman*, which promoted economic independence and sexual liberation as the only effective paths to women's emancipation; see Jane Lidderdale and Mary Nicholson, *Dear Miss Weaver: Harriet Shaw Weaver 1876–1961* (London: Faber and Faber, 1970), pp. 46–108. This programme was described by one contemporary commentator as 'Sex Syndicalism'.

57 *Votes for Women*, 22 May and 5 June 1914, and James Logan, 'The East of Scotland Suffragist/Suffragette Movement 1900–1914' (unpublished Open University essay, 1977). The United Suffragists' first London public meeting in May required an overflow meeting, and was followed by a rally in Trafalgar Square in June and another London demonstration in July (*Votes for Women*, 29 May and 19 and 26 June 1914).

58 George Lansbury, *Miracle of Fleet Street* (London: Labour Publishing Co., 1925), p. 53.

59 Ibid., pp. 75–85. Mitchell, *Queen Christabel*, p. 232, describes how G. R. S. Taylor, a contributor to the *Daily Herald* and the *Clarion*, visited Christabel and suggested she join 'an alliance between militant suffragism and militant industrialism', but was rejected. Mitchell further quotes a letter to Harben from Christabel which declared: 'Between the WSPU and Daily Herald League and Movement there can be no connec-

tion. . . . It comes to this "the men must paddle their canoes and we must paddle ours".'

60 S. Pankhurst, *The Suffragette Movement*, esp. pp. 498–513.
61 Catherine Marshall to Francis Acland, 23 June 1914, CMP.
62 NUWSS minutes, 3 August 1914, M50/2/7/6, MPLA. For an account of the Kingsway Hall demonstration, see the *NUWSS Annual Report*, 1915, and Swanwick, *I Have Been Young*, p. 241.
63 *The Common Cause*, 7 August 1914.
64 Mrs. Fawcett to National Union members, 23 April 1915, MGFP. See also *NUWSS Annual Report*, 1915.
65 NUWSS minutes, 27 August 1914, CMP. See Peter Cahalan, 'The Treatment of Belgian Refugees in England during the Great War' (unpublished Ph.D. dissertation, McMaster University, 1977), pp. 29, 174, 133, for one aspect of suffragist involvement in relief work.
66 *NUWSS Annual Report*, 1915–18.
67 Ray Strachey, *Women's Suffrage and Women's Service* (London: London and National Society for Women's Suffrage, 1927), pp. 26–29; *London Society for Women's Suffrage Annual Report*, 1915 (my emphasis). The account in Pugh, 'Politicians and the Women's Vote', is distorted by its heavy reliance on evidence from the London Society.
68 Quoted in Garner, *Stepping Stones*, p. 55.
69 *NUWSS Annual Report*, 1915–18, and NUWSS, 'Weekly Notes' (typewritten, duplicated news sheets).
70 *NUWSS Annual Report*, 1915; *Manchester Society for Women's Suffrage Annual Report*, 1915, MPLA; Glasgow Society minutes, August–December 1914, Mitchell Library, Glasgow.
71 *NUWSS Annual Report*, 1916; NUWSS minutes, 21 September, 16 February, 2 March, and 3 November 1916; *London Society for Women's Suffrage Annual Report*, 1916.

7. Winning the vote

1   NUWSS minutes, 4 November 1914, CMP.
2   Annotated agenda for the provincial council, 12 November 1914, and report of the debate, CMP.
3   NUWSS minutes, 4 November 1914, and agenda for provincial council, CMP.
4   Catherine Marshall draft letter to Mrs. Fawcett, 28 November 1914, CMP.
5   See Manchester and District Federation circular, 23 November 1914, and leaflet advertising a North-East Federation meeting, 26 January 1915, CMP.
6   Marvin Swartz, *The Union for Democratic Control in British Politics during the First World War* (Oxford: Oxford University Press [Clarendon Press], 1971), p. 46. See also Helena Swanwick, *Builders of Peace* (London: Swarthmore Press, 1924), pp. 39, 55–56.
7   Mrs. Auerbach to Mrs. Fawcett, 9 November 1914, FAC.
8   See Swartz, *The Union for Democratic Control*, Appendix B, and Swanwick, *I Have Been Young*, pp. 244–266.
9   I. O. Ford to Catherine Marshall, 25 October 1914; Kathleen Courtney to Catherine Marshall, 31 December 1914; Catherine Marshall to Ethel Williams, 2 February 1915, CMP. The NUWSS was still resisting the influence of the UDC within its branches in 1915; see circular letter from NUWSS executive, 24 August 1915, M50/2/9/51, MPLA.
10 Catherine Marshall to Ethel Williams, 2 February 1915, CMP.
11 *NUWSS Annual Report*, 1915; NUWSS minutes, 18 February and 4 March 1915.
12 Helena Swanwick to Catherine Marshall, 22 March 1915; Catherine Marshall draft letter to Mrs. Fawcett, 3 March 1915, CMP; C. D. Rackham to Kathleen Courtney, 28 February 1915, Kathleen Courtney Papers, Fawcett Library, City of London Polytechnic; NUWSS minutes, 18 March 1915.

13 NUWSS minutes, 18 March 1915.

14 Those who resigned were Alice Clark, Isabella Ford, Emily Leaf, Cary Schuster, Mrs. Stanbury, Miss Tanner, Mrs. Harley, Maude Royden (NUWSS minutes, 15 April 1915). See also Mrs. Fawcett's letter to the membership, 23 April 1915, MGFP.

15 NUWSS minutes, 30 April, 6 and 20 May, 14 June, and 15 July 1915. Meanwhile the executive refused to participate in a petition for a negotiated peace settlement being organised by the Fellowship of Reconciliation, the Christian pacifist group in which Maude Royden was prominent.

16 NUWSS minutes, 14 June 1915.

17 Helena Swanwick to Catherine Marshall, June 1915, CMP.

18 See Vellacott Newberry, 'Anti-War Suffragists'. The WILPF issued monthly news sheets from April 1916 which give a full account of its activities. Copies are held in the Manchester Public Library. For similar conflicts within the WSPU see Rosen, *Rise Up Women*, pp. 252–253.

19 Quoted in Liddington, *Life and Times*, p. 264.

20 See NUWSS minutes, 4 November 1914, M50/2/7/8, MPLA. The section dealing with election policy is marked 'delete' and does not occur in the copy in Catherine Marshall's papers.

21 NUWSS minutes, 4 March 1915.

22 EFF minutes, 29 January and 5 March 1915, CMP; *Manchester Society for Women's Suffrage Annual Report*, 1915, and *Manchester Federation of Women's Suffrage Societies Annual Report*, 1915.

23 NUWSS minutes, 1 July 1915.

24 'Draft Resolution Proposed by Miss Marshall as a Basis for Discussion', n.d. [May 1915], CMP.

25 NUWSS minutes, 15 July 1915.

26 Ibid.

27 Mrs. Fawcett to Catherine Marshall, 11 October 1915, MGFP. There would seem to have been some disagreement as to what was actually said at these meetings. See 'Report of Meetings' with W. A. C. Anderson, John Hodge, and Fred Jowett, 3 August and 12 October 1915, CMP.

28 For a detailed analysis of the various views on the war within the labour movement, and of the successful strategies pursued to maintain a significant degree of united action, see Royden Harrison, 'The War Emergency Workers' National Committee, 1914–1920', in Asa Briggs and John Saville (eds.), *Essays in Labour History 1886–1923* (London: Macmillan, 1971), pp. 211–259, esp. pp. 217–224, 238–254.

29 'Interview with Representatives from East Bristol re EFF Work', n.d. [25 October 1915], CMP.

30 Mrs. Townley to Catherine Marshall, 1 November 1915, CMP.

31 Catherine Marshall to Mrs. Strachey, 4 November 1915, CMP.

32 Joint meeting of the EFF Committee and the NUWSS executive, 18 November 1915; NUWSS minutes, 18 November 1915. Here it is recorded that the East Bristol Society had written to say it was prepared to resign from the National Union if support for the Labour candidate did not continue. Ray Strachey hoped the situation in Accrington would be resolved by the candidate not standing. He had supported the recruiting campaign, whereas the local Labour committee was antiwar. Ray Strachey included the information that on National Union urging the Accrington ILP had built a club and had a debt of £50 on account of it.

33 NUWSS minutes, 20 January 1916. Compare with Catherine Marshall's assessment of National Union EFF commitments in EFF minutes, 14 July 1915, CMP. Walter Ayles to Mrs. Fawcett, 25 February 1917, FAC. It was also agreed that help would have to be given to labour candidates in Leith and Midlothian if it were sought.

34 NUWSS minutes, 3 February and 2 and 16 March 1916. For the executive's exposition of its understanding of the problems surrounding the EFF policy, see its circular letter

to NUWSS branches and delegates to council, n.d. [February 1916], MGFP. Catherine Marshall was granted ten minutes to address the council on points of fact in this letter (NUWSS minutes, 16 February 1916).

35 Margaret Ashton to Catherine Marshall, 12 March 1916, CMP.

36 Copy of letter from NUWSS executive to Arthur Henderson and W. A. C. Anderson, 6 April 1916, and their replies of 17 and 14 April respectively, MGFP. In November 1917, with women's suffrage safely on its way and Labour support secured, the EFF Committee wound itself up, passing the balance of its funds to the National Union. Support for Ayles's candidature still continued even after this formal ending of the fund (NUWSS minutes, 22 December 1917 and 14 February 1918).

37 NUWSS minutes, 20 July and 17 August 1916.

38 Ibid., 16 November and 7 December 1916. The Manchester Society had also passed an adult-suffrage resolution in November (ibid., 3 November 1916).

39 In this paragraph I have drawn heavily on Martin Pugh, *Electoral Reform in War and Peace, 1906–1918* (London: Routledge and Kegan Paul, 1978), esp. pp. 49–63, 137–154, and Morgan, *Suffragists and Liberals*, esp. pp. 134–149.

40 Compare Pugh, *Electoral Reform*, pp. 143–145, with Arthur Marwick, *Women at War 1914–1918* (London: Fontana, 1977), pp. 8, 12, 157. There is useful discussion of this and related issues in Garner, *Stepping Stones*, pp. 94–103.

41 Again, here I have drawn on Pugh, *Electoral Reform*, esp. p. 154, and Morgan, *Suffragists and Liberals*, esp. p. 149.

42 NUWSS minutes, 20 January, 3 and 16 February, and 2 March 1916.

43 Mrs. Fawcett to Asquith, 4 May 1916, with cutting of Asquith's published reply from *The Times*, n.d., MGFP.

44 This first met on 16 May 1916, and included representatives from the Catholic Women's Suffrage Society, the Church League for Women's Suffrage, the Conservative and Unionist Women's Franchise Association, the Free Church League for Women's Suffrage, the Liberal Women's Suffrage Union, the London Graduates Union for Women's Suffrage, the National and Professional Women's Suffrage Society, the New Constitutional Society, the Scottish Church League for Women's Suffrage, and the Women Writers Suffrage Union. Eleanor Rathbone also wanted to include representatives from other organisations with an interest in women's suffrage, most particularly the WILPF. She was defeated, and several societies wrote to regret the exclusion of the WILPF in particular (NUWSS minutes, 6 April, 18 May, 15 June, and 3 August 1916).

45 Ibid., 15 June and 20 July 1916. A few societies opposed the revival of suffrage agitation, and the North and East Riding Federation reported that financial difficulties made any such work impossible at present. Meanwhile Henderson continued to press from within the cabinet for women's suffrage (Cabinet papers, 1 August 1916, CAB/37/154/37, Public Record Office).

46 Nevinson diaries, Bodleian Library, 19 August 1916.

47 Ibid., 21 August 1916.

48 Henry Woodd Nevinson, *More Changes, More Chances* (London: Nisbet, 1925), p. 337.

49 Manifesto of the National Council for Adult Suffrage, 6 October 1916, CMP.

50 Nevinson diaries, 22 and 24 September and 15 December 1916; 1, 3, and 8 January 1917.

51 NUWSS minutes, 5 October 1916.

52 Ibid., 3 November and 7 December 1916.

53 Mrs. Fawcett's memorandum on the conversation at 36 Eccleston Square, 15 December 1916, MGFP.

54 NUWSS minutes, 4 January 1917.

55 See Pugh, 'Politicians and the Vote', p. 364. In early cabinet discussions Arthur Henderson had advised that an age qualification for women was acceptable to the suffragists (Cabinet Papers, 12 May 1916, CAB/37/147/31, Public Record Office). An age restriction of twenty-five had also been part of Dickinson's last private-member women's-

suffrage bill in 1913. See also Catherine Marshall's note on a discussion on means of limiting the women's franchise (18 January 1917, CMP).

56 See Pugh, *Electoral Reform*, p. 142; and 'Politicians and the Vote', p. 365, and compare with NUWSS minutes, 4 January 1917; correspondence among Lady Betty Balfour, Mrs. Fawcett, and Lord Northcliffe, 20–6 December 1916; Mrs. Fawcett to NUWSS secretary, Miss Atkinson, 26 December 1916; all letters FAC. None of this material supports Martin Pugh's assertion that Northcliffe was 'frostily rebuffed'.

57 W. H. Dickinson to Mrs. Fawcett, 19 January 1917, MGFP. See also NUWSS minutes, 17 and 18 January 1917, for the context in which this letter was written. There had been rumours that the conference was not to recommend votes for women. Dickinson's letter reads, then, like a message of reassurance, not the apology Pugh has suggested in his 'Politicians and the Vote', pp. 364–365.

58 NUWSS minutes, 19 January 1916. Walter Long had previously been one of the most committed antisuffragists. His change of view is explained by David Close, 'The Collapse of Resistance to Democracy: Conservatives, Adult Suffrage, and Second Chamber Reform, 1911–1928', *Historical Journal*, 20 (1977): 893–918, in these terms; Long's 'experience of the intractability of franchise problems at the local government board since 1915 . . . had led him to view franchise reform no longer as a Liberal nostrum but instead as a public necessity, which would obstruct the solution of post-war problems if allowed to persist' (p. 900). Compare Pugh's explanation of Long's change of attitude in 'Politicians and the Vote', p. 367.

59 See Liddington, *Life and Times*, p. 271.

60 NUWSS minutes, 1 February 1917. J. H. Thomas, Lord Robert Cecil, and Francis Acland had provided the advice on which this decision was taken.

61 Nevinson diaries, 6, 10, 13, 14, and 16 February 1917.

62 NUWSS minutes, 18 January and 1 February, 1917. One member of the National Union executive, Mrs. Thoday, appeared to support the democratic-suffragist viewpoint.

63 Ibid., 12 February 1917.

64 *The Common Cause*, 2 March 1917.

65 Ibid. Sir John Simon made a similar plea at another adult-suffrage rally and received a great ovation (NUWSS minutes, 12 February 1917).

66 NUWSS minutes, 12 February 1917.

67 Agenda for National Council for Adult Suffrage meeting, 27 February 1917, CMP.

68 *The Common Cause*, 23 March 1917. The Scottish Miners seem to have taken the lead in demanding full adult suffrage; see *Glasgow Herald*, 6 March 1917, for a report on their conference.

69 *The Common Cause*, 23 March 1917.

70 See a record of this deputation in F/229/3, LGP. Despite his warning of the danger in the use of government whips, they were eventually brought in to secure the passage of the bill; see Close, 'The Collapse of Resistance to Democracy', p. 901. Nor was Lloyd George averse to bringing his own influence to bear on previous antisuffragists to support the whole bill; see Sir Joseph Compton-Rickett to Lloyd George, 2 April 1917, F/43/6/2, LGP.

71 Mrs. Fawcett to Arthur Henderson, 23 August 1917; Arthur Henderson to Mrs. Fawcett, 30 August 1917, FAC. For Henderson's part in getting the Speaker's conference recommendation through cabinet see Frances Stevenson, *Lloyd George: A Diary*, ed. A. J. P. Taylor (London: Hutchinson, 1971), p. 148. The importance of the presence of two committed suffragists in the cabinet, Lord Robert Cecil and Henderson, has sometimes been underestimated. Both appear to have been more resolute than previous suffragist ministers. On the other hand it should be remembered that the Labour Party's position was equally determined by self-interest. It was generally recognised that no bill should be introduced unless it was on the lines of the Speaker's conference, and even such a measure, with its limitations, was very much in their interests as a party; see discussion in H. C. G. Matthew, R. I. McKibbin, and J. A.

Kay, 'The Franchise Factor in the Rise of the Labour Party', *English Historical Review*, 91 (1976): 723–752, esp. pp. 736ff.

72 D. E. Butler, *The Electoral System in Britain since 1918* (Oxford: Oxford University Press [Clarendon Press], 1953), pp. 8, 15–16. The usual National Union machinery had been set in motion to secure votes for the women's-suffrage clause. See e.g. *Manchester Society for Women's Suffrage Annual Report*, 1917, MPLA; Glasgow Society minutes, 1917, Mitchell Library, Glasgow. At one point the government put on its whips to oppose a suffragist amendment intended to extend the existing women's franchise for the local government registers. The National Union was able to organise such 'a remarkable outburst of support' that the government backed down and allowed a free vote (*NUWSS Annual Report*, 1917).

73 *NUWSS Annual Report*, 1918. Membership and organisational strength now began to show clear signs of fast decline. Whereas affiliation fees had indicated the membership of 447 societies in 1915, this had fallen to about 333 by October 1917 and to only about 234 by October 1918. To this extent it was the winning of the vote for a considerable number of women that precipitated the most rapid decline in suffrage organisations, not simply the conditions of war.

74 Strachey, *The Cause*, pp. 368–384.

Postscript

1 See the outlines provided in Mary Stocks, *Eleanor Rathbone* (London: Gollancz, 1949), pp. 105–126; Jane Lewis, 'Beyond Suffrage: English Feminism in the 1920s', *Maryland Historian*, 6 (1975): 1–17; and Banks, *Faces of Feminism*, pp. 163–179.

2 See for example Barbara Hutchins, *Conflicting Ideals* (London: Murby, 1913), esp. pp. 35, 68, 77, and the essays in Victor Gollancz (ed.), *The Making of Women: Oxford Essays in Feminism* (London: Allen and Unwin, 1917), esp. the contributions of Victor Gollancz and Maude Royden. See also Eleanor Rathbone's presidential address to the NUSEC Annual Conference in 1925, quoted in Stocks, *Eleanor Rathbone*, p. 116.

3 See for example the manifesto 'Bondwomen and Freewomen' in *The Freewoman*, 23 November 1911.

4 Some at least among the prewar democratic suffragists had also emphasised equal wages and had opposed the endowment of motherhood. It was the latter policy, reformulated in terms of the family allowance, that came to dominate the approach of the New Feminists. However, other democratic suffragists became closely involved with the demand for family allowances. See Nield Chew, *Life and Writings*, esp. pp. 239, 255, and compare Liddington, *Life and Times*, pp. 309–313.

5 Banks, *Faces of Feminism*, p. 170.

6 Compare for example Banks, *Faces of Feminism*, esp. pp. 159, 163, 175–179, and Rowbotham, *Hidden from History*, p. 162, with Nancy Cott, 'A Re-Evaluation of the National Women's Party, 1919–1930', *The Journal of American History*, 71 (1984): 43–68, and Kathryn Kish Sklar, 'The Debate between Florence Kelley and Alice Paul over ERA, 1921–1923', paper delivered to the Sixth Berkshire Conference on the History of Women, Smith College, Northampton, Mass., 1984.

SELECT BIBLIOGRAPHY

PRIVATE PAPERS

Janie Allan Papers, National Library of Scotland, Edinburgh
Asquith Papers, Bodleian Library, Oxford
Papers of Arthur, 1st Earl of Balfour, British Library
Kathleen Courtney Papers, Fawcett Library, City of London Polytechnic
W. H. Dickinson Papers, Greater London Record Office
Elibank Papers, National Library of Scotland, Edinburgh
Millicent Garrett Fawcett Papers, Fawcett Library, City of London Polytechnic
Gainford Papers, Nuffield College Library, Oxford
Haldane Papers, National Library of Scotland, Edinburgh
Lloyd George Papers, Beaverbrook Foundation, House of Lords Record Office
James Ramsay MacDonald Papers, Public Record Office, Kew
Catherine Marshall Papers, Cumbria Record Office, Carlisle
W. H. Nevinson Papers, Bodleian Library, Oxford
Agnes Maude Royden Papers, Fawcett Library, City of London Polytechnic
C. P. Scott Papers, British Library
Evelyn Sharp Papers, Bodleian Library, Oxford
Arthur Steel-Maitland Papers, Scottish Record Office, Edinburgh

RECORDS OF SUFFRAGE ORGANISATIONS

At the Fawcett Library, City of London Polytechnic

The NUWSS Annual Report, 1897–1918 (incomplete)
The NUWSS executive minutes, 1897–1918 (incomplete)
The Election Fighting Fund Committee minutes, June–December 1912
The NUWSS quarterly council reports, 1907–9 (incomplete)
The NUWSS weekly notes, 1914–18
Miscellaneous letters pertaining to women's suffrage (in the Fawcett Autograph Collection)
The London Society for Women's Suffrage Annual Reports (incomplete)
The London Society executive minutes (incomplete)

In the Manchester Public Library Archives

The North of England Society for Women's Suffrage (later *The Manchester Society) Annual Report*, 1892–1918
The Manchester Federation of Women's Suffrage Societies Annual Reports

The Manchester Society minute book, 1912–14
Miscellaneous letters pertaining to women's suffrage

In the Mitchell Library, Glasgow

The Glasgow and West of Scotland Women's Franchise Association minute books, 1902–18

In Baillies Library, Glasgow

A fragment from the minutes of the Scottish Federation of Women's Suffrage Societies minutes (Muirhead Collection)

RECORDS OF OTHER WOMEN'S ORGANISATIONS

The Women's Liberal Federation Annual Report, 1900–18, Bristol University Library Archives and British Library of Political and Economic Science, London School of Economics
The Women's Liberal Federation executive minutes, 1910–12, Bristol University Library Archives
The Scottish Women's Liberal Federation executive minutes, 1898–1910, Edinburgh University Library
The Women's Cooperative Guild Annual Reports
The Scottish Cooperative Women's Guild Annual Reports, and executive minutes, Scottish Co-operative Women's Guild headquarters, Glasgow

RECORDS OF OTHER ORGANISATIONS

Labour Party Archives, Labour Party Library, London
The Annual Conference of the Labour Party, 1900–14
The Annual Conference of the Independent Labour Party, 1900–14
The People's Suffrage Federation Annual Report, 1910–12, British Library of Political and Economic Science, London School of Economics

FEMINIST AND SUFFRAGIST JOURNALS

The Common Cause
The Freewoman
Jus Suffragii
The Liberal Women's Suffrage Review
The Suffragette
The Vote
Votes for Women
The Women's Franchise
The Women's Suffrage Journal
The Women's Suffrage Record

SUFFRAGIST PAMPHLETS

(A selection from the holdings of the Fawcett Library, City of London Polytechnic, and Glasgow University Library's Special Collections)
'All or Some or Some or None?' London: NUWSS, [1911].
Black, Rev. James. 'Address to a Women's Suffrage Service', 1914.
Campbell, Rev. R. J. 'Women's suffrage and the Social Evil'. Men's League for Women's Suffrage, 1907.

Catt, Mrs. Chapman. 'Address to the International Women's Suffrage Alliance'. London: NUWSS, 1909.

'Conciliation Committee for Woman Suffrage'. London, [1910].

'Could Women Vote on the Same Terms as Men?' London: PSF, [c. 1909].

Craigen, Jessie. 'On Women's Suffrage'. N.p., [1880], reprinted from *The Women's Suffrage Journal*, 14 February 1880.

Despard, Charlotte. 'Women's Franchise and Industry'. N.p., n.d.
'Woman and the Nation'. London: WFL, n.d.

Fawcett, Mrs. Henry (Millicent Garrett Fawcett). 'Home and Politics'. London: London Society for Women's Suffrage, n.d.
'Men Are Men and Women Are Women'. London: NUWSS, 1909.
'Wanted, a Statesman'. N.p., n.d.

'The Franchise and Married Working Women'. Manchester: WCG, 1908.

'Gentles Let Us Rest'. N.p., n.d.

Gibson, J. 'The Sphere of Women'. London, [1894].

Hamilton, Cicely. 'Women's Vote'. London: NUWSS, 1908.

Hardie, James Kier. 'The Citizenship of Women'. London: ILP, 1906.

Hodgson, Geraldine. 'The Parliamentary Vote and Wages'. London: NUWSS, 1909.

Holmes, Marion. 'The ABC of Votes for Women'. London: Women's Freedom League, 1913.

Homo Sum. 'A Letter from an Anthropologist to an Anti-Suffragist'. N.p., n.d.

McLaren, Walter. 'The Equality of Women before the Law'. N.p., 1909.

'One Man, One Vote: One Woman, One Vote'. London: PSF, [c. 1909].

Pankhurst, Christabel. 'The Great Scourge and How to End It'. London: E. Pankhurst, 1913.

Pankhurst, Mrs. Emmeline. 'The Importance of the Vote'. London, 1913.

Pethick-Lawrence, Frederick. 'Women's Vote and Wages'. N.p., n.d.

'Sex Equality versus Adult Suffrage'. Manchester: WFL, 1908.

Shillington, Violet. 'Women Wage Earners and the Vote'. London: NUWSS, n.d.

Snowden, Philip. 'In Defence of the Conciliation Bill'. London: WFL, n.d.
'Speech on the Parliamentary Franchise (Women) Bill 1910'. London: NUWSS, [1910].

'Some Reasons Why Working Women Want the Vote'. London: NUWSS, n.d.

Taylor, Mrs. 'To Women Who Are Well Off'. London: NUWSS, 1905.

'Votes for Women: The Conciliation Bill Explained'. London: NUWSS, 1911.

Wood, George H. 'The Woman Wage-Earner'. N.p., n.d.

OTHER CONTEMPORARY SOURCES

Books, memoirs, autobiographies, diaries

Balfour, Lady Frances. *Ne Obliviscaris*. London: Hodder and Stoughton, 1930.

Bax, E. Belfort. *The Fraud of Feminism*. London: Grant Richards, 1913.

Black, Clementina. 'Some Current Objections to Factory Legislation for Women'. In Beatrice Webb (ed.), *The Case for the Factory Acts*, 2nd ed., pp. 193–223. London: Grant Richards, 1902.
'Legislative Proposals'. In Gertrude Tuckwell, Constance Smith, Mary R. MacArthur, et al., *Woman in Industry from Seven Points of View*, pp. 186–202. London: Duckworth, 1908.
Review of Dr. Elizabeth Sloan Chesser, 'Women, Marriage and Motherhood'. *Sociological Review*, 7 (1914): 165.
Married Women's Work. London: Women's Industrial Council, 1915.

Blackburn, Helen. *Women's Suffrage: A Record of the Women's Suffrage Movement in the British Isles*. London: Williams and Norgate, 1902.

Blease, W. Lyon. *The Emancipation of Women*. London: Constable, 1910.
Brockway, Fenner. *Inside the Left*. London: Allen and Unwin, 1942.
  Towards Tomorrow. London: Hart Davis, 1977.
Bulley, Amy and Whitley, Margaret. *Women's Work*. London: Methuen, 1894.
Butler, Josephine (ed.). *Woman's Work and Woman's Culture*. London: Macmillan, 1869.
Fawcett, Millicent Garrett. *What I Remember*. London: Fisher and Unwin, 1924.
Gollancz, Victor (ed.). *The Making of Women: Oxford Essays in Feminism*. London: Allen and Unwin, 1917.
Greig, Teresa Billington. *The Militant Suffragette Movement*. London: Frank Palmer, 1911.
Hamilton, Cicely. *Marriage as a Trade*. London: Chapman and Hall, 1909.
Hutchins, Barbara. 'The Historical Development of the Factory Acts'. In Beatrice Webb (ed.), *The Case for the Factory Acts*, 2nd ed., pp. 75–123. London: Grant Richards, 1902.
  Conflicting Ideals. London: Murby, 1913.
Kenney, Annie. *Memories of a Militant*. London: Arnold, 1924.
Lansbury, George. *Miracle of Fleet Street*. London: Labour Publishing Co., 1925.
Meikle, Wilma. *Towards a Sane Feminism*. London: Grant Richards, 1916.
Mitchell, Hannah. *The Hard Way Up*. Reprint. London: Virago, 1977.
Montefiore, Dora. *From a Victorian to a Modern*. London: Archer, 1927.
Nevinson, Henry Woodd. *More Changes, More Chances*. London: Nisbet, 1925.
Nield Chew, Ada. *The Life and Writings of a Working Woman*. London: Virago, 1982.
Pankhurst, Christabel. *Unshackled*. London: Hutchinson, 1959.
Pankhurst, Sylvia. *The Suffragette Movement*. Reprint. London: Virago, 1977.
The Reformers' Year Book 1907. London: Clarion, 1907.
Richardson, Mary. *Laugh a Defiance*. London: Weidenfeld and Nicholson, 1953.
Royden, Maude, *A Threefold Card*. London: Gollancz, 1948.
Ruskin, John. *Sesame and Lilies*. In *The Works of John Ruskin*, vol. 11, pp. 5–186. 12 vols. New York: Wiley, 1885.
Shafer, Olga Fenton and Hill, Emily (eds.). *Great Suffragists and Why*. London: Drane, 1909.
Stevenson, Frances. *Lloyd George: A Diary*, ed. A. J. P. Taylor. London: Hutchinson, 1971.
Stocks, Mary. *My Commonplace Book*. London: Hart Davies, 1970.
The Suffrage Annual and Who's Who. London, 1913.
Swanwick, Helena. *The Future of the Women's Movement*. London: Bell, 1913.
  Builders of Peace. London: Swarthmore Press, 1924.
  I Have Been Young. London: Gollancz, 1935.
Villiers, Brougham (ed.). *The Case for Women's Suffrage*. London: Fisher and Unwin, 1907.
Wilson, Helen. 'The Moral Revolution'. In Zoe Fairfield (ed.), *Some Aspects of the Woman's Movement*, pp. 112–127. London: Student Christian Movement, 1915.
Wright, Sir Almroth. *The Unexpurgated Case against Woman Suffrage*. London: Constable, 1913.

National and local press

The Daily News
The Glasgow Herald
The Manchester Guardian
The Morning Post
The Standard
The Times

Labour and socialist press

The Daily Herald
The Forward (Glasgow)
The Labour Leader
The Woman Worker

Government papers

Report of the Royal Commission on Divorce and Matrimonial Causes, P.P. 1912–13, vols. 18–20. 3 vols., 1912–13. Cd. 6479–81.
Report of the Royal Commission on Venereal Diseases, P.P. 1914, vol. 49. Appendix to First Report, 1914. Cd. 7475.
Cabinet Papers, Public Record Office, Kew.

SECONDARY SOURCES

Books and articles

Alexander, Sally. 'Women's Work in Nineteenth Century London: A Study of the Years 1820–50'. In Juliet Mitchell and Ann Oakley (eds.), *The Rights and Wrongs of Women,* pp. 59–111. Harmondsworth: Penguin Books, 1976.
Alice Clark of C. & J. Clark Ltd., Street, Somerset. Privately published, n.d.
Banks, Olive. *Faces of Feminism.* Oxford: Martin Robertson, 1981.
Barker, Rodney. 'Socialism and Progressivism in the Political Thought of Ramsay Mac-Donald'. In A. J. A. Morrison (ed.), *Edwardian Radicalism,* pp. 114–130. London: Routledge and Kegan Paul, 1974.
Blewett, Neil. 'The Franchise in the United Kingdom, 1885–1918'. *Past and Present,* no. 32 (1965): 27–56.
Bridenthal, Renate and Koonz, Claudia. *Becoming Visible: Women in European History.* Boston: Houghton Mifflin, 1977.
Brown, Penelope and Jordonova, L. J. 'Oppressive Dichotomies: The Nature/Culture Debate'. In Cambridge Women's Studies Group, *Women in Society: Interdisciplinary Essays,* pp. 224–241. London: Virago, 1981.
Butler, D. E. *The Electoral System in Britain since 1918.* Oxford: Oxford U.P. (Clarendon Press), 1953.
Caine, Barbara. 'John Stuart Mill and the English Women's Movement'. *Historical Studies* (Melbourne), 18 (1978): 52–67.
Clark, Alice. *Working Life of Women in the Seventeenth Century* (1917). Reprint. New York: Kelley, 1968.
Clarke, P. F. *Lancashire and the New Liberalism.* Cambridge: Cambridge U.P., 1971.
  'The Progressive Movement in England'. *Transactions of the Royal Historical Society,* 5th ser., 24 (1974): 159–181.
Close, David. 'The Collapse of Resistance to Democracy: Conservatives, Adult Suffrage, and Second Chamber Reform, 1911–1928'. *Historical Journal,* 20 (1977): 893–918.
Cott, Nancy. *The Bonds of Womanhood.* New Haven: Yale U.P., 1977.
  'Passionlessness: An Interpretation of Victorian Sexual Ideology'. *Signs,* 4 (1978): 219–236.
  'A Re-Evaluation of the National Women's Party, 1919–1930'. *Journal of American History,* 71 (1984): 43–68.
Dangerfield, George. *The Strange Death of Liberal England.* London: Paladin, 1970.
David, Edward (ed.). *Inside Asquith's Cabinet: From the Diaries of Charles Hobhouse.* London: Murray, 1977.
Davidoff, Leonore. 'The Separation of Home and Work? Landladies and Lodgers in Nineteenth and Twentieth Century England'. In Sandra Burman (ed.), *Fit Work for Women,* pp. 64–97. London: Croom Helm, 1979.
Davidoff, Leonore, L'Esperance, Jean and Newby, Howard. 'Landscape with Figures: Home and Community in English Society'. In Juliet Mitchell and Ann Oakley (eds.), *The Rights and Wrongs of Women,* pp. 139–175. Harmondsworth, Penguin Books, 1976.
Davin, Anna. 'Imperialism and Motherhood'. *History Workshop Journal,* No. 5 (1978): 9–65.
Delamont, Sara and Duffin, Lorna (eds.). *The Nineteenth Century Woman: Her Cultural and Physical World.* London: Croom Helm, 1978.

DuBois, Ellen. 'The Radicalism of the Woman's Suffrage Movement: Notes towards a Reconstruction of Nineteenth Century Feminism'. *Feminist Studies*, 2 (1976): 84–103.
    Suffragism and Feminism. Ithaca: Cornell U.P., 1980.
Dyhouse, Carol. *Girls Growing Up in Late Victorian and Edwardian England*. London: Croom Helm, 1981.
Epstein, Barbara. *The Politics of Domesticity*. Middletown, Conn.: Wesleyan U.P., 1981.
Evans, Richard. *The Feminists*. London: Croom Helm, 1977.
    'The History of European Women: A Critical Survey of Recent Research'. *Journal of Modern History*, 52 (1980): 655–675.
    'Bourgeois Feminists and Women Socialists in Germany, 1894–1914: Lost Opportunity or Inevitable Conflict'. *Women's Studies International Quarterly*, 3 (1980): 355–376.
Fulford, Roger. *Votes for Women*. London: Faber and Faber, 1957.
Garner, Les. *Stepping Stones to Women's Liberty: Feminist Ideas in the Women's Suffrage Movement 1900–1918*. London: Hutchinson, 1984.
Gordon, Linda. *Woman's Body, Woman's Right*. Harmondsworth: Penguin Books, 1977.
Hall, Catherine. 'The Early Formation of the Victorian Domestic Ideology'. In Sandra Burman (ed.), *Fit Work for Women*, pp. 15–32. London: Croom Helm, 1979.
Hammond, J. L. *C. P. Scott of the Manchester Guardian*. London: Bell, 1934.
Harrison, Brian. *Separate Spheres*. London: Croom Helm, 1978.
Harrison, Royden. 'The War Emergency Workers' National Committee, 1914–1920'. In Asa Briggs and John Saville (eds.), *Essays in Labour History 1886–1923*, pp. 211–259. London: Macmillan, 1971.
Hollis, Patricia. 'Working Women'. *History*, 62 (1977): 439–455.
    Women in Public: The Women's Movement 1850–1900. London: Allen and Unwin, 1979.
Holton, R. J. '*Daily Herald* versus *Daily Citizen*, 1912–15'. *International Review of Social History*, 19 (1974): 347–376.
    British Syndicalism. London: Pluto Press, 1976.
Holton, Sandra. 'Feminine Authority and Social Order: Florence Nightingale's Conception of Nursing and Health Care'. *Social Analysis*, no. 15 (1984): 59–72.
Hume, Leslie Parker. *The National Union of Women's Suffrage Societies 1897–1914*. New York: Garland Publishing, 1982.
Hurwitz, Edith. 'Carrie C. Catt's "Suffrage Militancy" '. *Signs*, 3 (1977–8): 739–743.
Kaplan, Temma. 'Female Consciousness and Collective Action: The Case of Barcelona, 1910–1918'. *Signs*, 7 (1982): 545–566.
Kingston, Beverley. 'Yours Very Truly, Marion Phillips'. In Anna Curthoys, Susan Eade, and Peter Spearritt (eds.), *Women at Work*, pp. 123–131. Canberra: Australian Society for the Study of Labour History, 1975.
Kraditor, Aileen. *The Ideas of the Woman's Suffrage Movement 1890–1918*. New York: Columbia U.P., 1965.
Lerner, Gerda. 'Woman's Rights and American Feminism'. *American Scholar*, 40 (1970–71): 235–248, reprinted in her *The Majority Finds Its Past*. New York: Oxford U.P., 1979.
Lewis, Jane. 'Beyond Suffrage: English Feminism in the 1920s'. *Maryland Historian*, 6 (1975): 1–17.
Lidderdale, Jane and Nicholson, Mary. *Dear Miss Weaver: Harriet Shaw Weaver 1876–1961*. London: Faber and Faber, 1970.
Liddington, Jill. *The Life and Times of a Respectable Rebel: Selina Cooper 1864–1946*. London: Virago, 1984.
Liddington, Jill and Norris, Jill. *One Hand Tied behind Us*. London: Virago, 1978.
Linklater, Andro. *An Unhusbanded Life: Charlotte Despard. Suffragette. Socialist. Sinn Feiner*. London: Hutchinson, 1980.
MacDonald, James Ramsay. *Margaret Ethel MacDonald*. London: Hodder and Stoughton, 1912.
McKibbin, Ross. *The Evolution of the Labour Party, 1910–1924*. London: Oxford U.P., 1974.
McLaren, Angus. *Birth Control in Nineteenth Century England*. London: Croom Helm, 1978.

Manton, Jo. *Elizabeth Garrett Anderson*. London: Methuen, 1965.

Mary Carpenter and the Children of the Streets. London: Heinemann, 1976.

Marcus, Jane. 'Transatlantic Sisterhood'. *Signs*, 3 (1978): 744–755.

Marwick, Arthur. *Women at War 1914–1918*. London: Fontana, 1977.

Matthew, H. C. G., McKibbin, R. I. and Kay, J. A. 'The Franchise Factor in the Rise of the Labour Party'. *English Historical Review*, 91 (1976): 723–752.

Mill, John Stuart. *The Subjection of Women* (1869). Reprinted in Alice Rossi (ed.), *Essays on Sex Equality*, pp. 125–242. Chicago: Chicago U.P., 1970.

Millett, Kate. 'The Debate over Women: Ruskin versus Mill'. In Martha Vicinus (ed.), *Suffer and Be Still*, pp. 121–139. Bloomington: Indiana U.P., 1973.

Mitchell, David. *The Fighting Pankhursts*. London: Jonathan Cape, 1967.

Women on the Warpath. London: Jonathan Cape, 1966.

Queen Christabel. London: Macdonald and Jane, 1977.

Morgan, David. *Suffragists and Liberals*. Oxford: Blackwell Publisher, 1975.

Morgan, K. O. *Wales in British Politics, 1869–1922*. Cardiff: University of Wales Press, 1963.

Moses, Claire G. 'Saint Simonian Men/Saint Simonian Women: The Transformation of Feminist Thought in 1930s France'. *Journal of Modern History*, 54 (1982): 240–267.

O'Neill, William. 'Feminism as a Radical Ideology'. In Alfred A. Young (ed.), *Dissent: Explorations in the History of American Radicalism*, pp. 273–300. Dekalb: Northern Illinois U.P., 1968.

Everyone Was Brave. Chicago: Quandrangle Books, 1969.

The Woman Movement. London: Allen and Unwin, 1969.

Pelling, Henry. *A Short History of the Labour Party*. London: Macmillan, 1961.

The Social Geography of British Elections, 1885–1910. London: Macmillan, 1967.

Popular Politics and Society in Late Victorian Britain. London: Macmillan, 1968.

'Politics and Culture in Women's History' (symposium). *Feminist Studies*, 6 (1980): 26–64.

Prochaska, F. K. *Women and Philanthropy in Nineteenth Century England*. Oxford: Oxford U.P. (Clarendon Press), 1980.

Pugh, Martin. 'Politicians and the Women's Vote 1914–18'. *History*, 59 (1974): 358–374.

Electoral Reform in War and Peace, 1906–1918. London: Routledge and Kegan Paul, 1978.

Quataert, Jean H. *Reluctant Feminists in German Social Democracy, 1885–1917*. Princeton: Princeton U.P., 1979.

Raeburn, Anna. *The Suffragette View*. Newton Abbot: David and Charles, 1976.

Rendel, M. 'The Contribution of the Women's Labour League to the Winning of the Franchise'. In Lucy Middleton (ed.), *Women in the Labour Movement*, pp. 57–83. London: Croom Helm, 1977.

Richards, Eric. 'Women in the British Economy since about 1700: An Interpretation'. *History*, 59 (1974): 337–357.

Roe, Jill. 'Modernisation and Sexism: Recent Writings on Victorian Women'. *Victorian Studies*, 20 (1977): 171–192.

Rosen, Andrew. *Rise Up Women*. London: Routledge and Kegan Paul, 1974.

Ross, Ellen. 'Women's Neighbourhood and Sharing in London before the First World War'. *History Workshop Journal*, no. 15 (1983): 4–27.

Rossi, Alice (ed.). *Essays on Sex Equality*. Chicago: Chicago U.P., 1970.

Rover, Constance. *Women's Suffrage and Party Politics in Britain, 1866–1914*. London: Routledge and Kegan Paul, 1967.

Rowbotham, Sheila. *Hidden from History*. London: Pluto Press, 1973.

A New World for Women: Stella Browne – Socialist Feminist. London: Pluto Press, 1977.

Rowbotham, Sheila and Weeks, Jeffrey. *Socialism and the New Life: The Personal and Sexual Politics of Edward Carpenter and Havelock Ellis*. London: Pluto Press, 1977.

Ryan, Mary P. 'The Power of Women's Networks: A Case Study of Female Moral Reform in Antebellum America'. *Feminist Studies*, 5 (1979): 66–85.

Scott, Joan Wallach. 'Survey Articles. Women in History II: The Modern Period'. *Past and Present*, no. 101 (1983): 141–157.

Sklar, Kathyrn Kish. *Catherine Beecher: A Study of American Domesticity*. New Haven: Yale U.P., 1973.

'The Debate between Florence Kelley and Alice Paul over ERA, 1921–1923'. Paper delivered to the Sixth Berkshire Conference on the History of Women, Smith College, Northampton, Mass., 1984.

Smith Rosenberg, Carroll. 'The New Woman and the New History'. *Feminist Studies*, 3 (1975): 185–198.

'The Female World of Love and Ritual: Relations between Women in Nineteenth Century America'. *Signs*, 1 (1975): 1–29.

'Beauty, the Beast and the Militant Woman: A Case Study in Sex Roles and Social Stress in Jacksonian America'. *American Quarterly*, 24 (1971): 562–584.

Stocks, Mary. *Eleanor Rathbone*. London: Gollancz, 1949.

Strachey, Ray. *Women's Suffrage and Women's Service*. London: London and National Society for Women's Suffrage, 1927.

The Cause (1928). Reprint. London: Virago, 1978.

Millicent Garrett Fawcett. London: Murray, 1933.

Swartz, Marvin. *The Union for Democratic Control in British Politics during the First World War*. Oxford: Oxford U.P. (Clarendon Press), 1971.

Tax, Meredith. *The Rising of the Women*. New York: Monthly Review Press, 1980.

Taylor, Barbara. 'The Woman-Power: Religious Heresy and Feminism in Early English Socialism'. In Susan Lipshitz (ed.), *Tearing the Veil*, pp. 117–144. London: Croom Helm, 1978.

Eve and the New Jerusalem. London: Virago, 1983.

Thompson, E. P. *The Making of the English Working Class*. London: Gollancz, 1963.

Thompson, Laurence. *The Enthusiasts*. London: Gollancz, 1971.

Thompson, William. *Appeal on Behalf of One Half the Human Race . . .* (1825). Reprint. New York: Source Book Press, 1970.

Thönnessen, Werner. *The Emancipation of Women: The Rise and Decline of the Women's Movement in German Social Democracy 1863–1933*. London: Pluto Press, 1973.

Tilly, Louise A. and Scott, Joan W. *Women, Work and Family*. New York: Holt, Rinehart and Winston, 1978.

Trevelyan, Janet Penrose. *The Life of Mrs. Humphry Ward*. London: Constable, 1923.

Vellacott Newberry, Jo. 'Anti-War Suffragists'. *History*, 62 (1977): 411–425.

Vernon, Betty D. *Ellen Wilkinson 1891–1947*. London: Croom Helm, 1982.

Vicinus, Martha. 'Male Space and Women's Bodies: The Suffragette Movement'. In her *Independent Women: Work and Community for Single Women, 1850–1920*, pp. 247–280. Chicago: Chicago U.P., 1985.

Walkowitz, Judith. 'The Politics of Prostitution'. *Signs*, 6 (1980): 123–135.

Ward, Margaret. ' "Suffrage First – Above All Else!": An Account of the Irish Suffrage Movement'. *Feminist Review*, 10 (1982): 21–36.

Webb, Catherine. *The Woman with the Basket*. Manchester: Women's Cooperative Guild, 1927.

Wollstonecraft, Mary. *Vindication of the Rights of Woman* (1795). Reprint. Harmondsworth: Penguin Books, 1975.

Unpublished theses and essays

Cahalan, Peter. 'The Treatment of Belgian Refugees in England during the Great War'. Ph.D dissertation, McMaster University, 1977.

Holton, R. J. 'Syndicalism and Its Impact in Britain, with Particular Reference to Merseyside 1900–1914'. D.Phil. dissertation, University of Sussex, 1973.

Holton, Sandra. 'Feminism and Democracy: The Women's Suffrage Movement in Britain with Particular Reference to the National Union of Women's Suffrage Societies, 1897–1920'. Ph.D. dissertation, University of Stirling, 1980.

Logan, James. 'The East of Scotland Suffragist/Suffragette Movement 1900–1914'. Open University essay, 1977.

Scott, Gillian. 'The Politics of the Women's Cooperative Guild: Working Women and Feminism during the First World War'. M.A. dissertation, University of Sussex, 1980.

Taylor, Barbara. 'The Feminist Theory and Practice of the Owenite Socialist Movement in Britain 1820–45'. D.Phil. dissertation, University of Sussex, 1980.

INDEX